MONETARY ECON

P. CHECKLEY
B.A.(Econ.) Hons., M.Sc., M.A.B

PETER ANDREW PUBLISHING COMPANY

Also available for Stage 2 banking students:

Finance of International Trade

P. Brear, ACIB

Investment

P. Checkley, B.A.(Econ)Hons, M.Sc., MABE, ACIB

Available from any bookshop or direct from the publishers:

PETER ANDREW PUBLISHING COMPANY
4, Charlecot Road,
Droitwich,
Worcestershire,
WR9 7RP
England
Telephone Number 0905 778543

First edition 1980
Second edition 1981
Third edition 1982
Fourth edition 1986
Fifth edition 1987

Published by
PETER ANDREW PUBLISHING COMPANY

ISBN 0 946796 00 9

Typeset in Great Britain by
Steven Graphics,
Droitwich, Worcestershire.

To my wife Joan and children, Steven, Andrew and Peter

in thanks for their patience and consideration

PREFACE

This text has been written specifically for the student who is preparing to take the examination in 'Monetary Economics' set by The Chartered Institute of Bankers and The Institute of Bankers in Scotland.

The banking student will find that the book fully covers the syllabus requirements for the examination. To assist the banking student in developing a technique for answering examination questions I have included, at the end of each chapter, more recent Chartered Institute of Bankers' examination questions. Guidance on how to tackle some of them (those marked *) is given in Appendix A.

The structure of this book makes it ideal for the student attending college as well as for the student who is not able to do so.

Grateful acknowledgement is due to The Chartered Institute of Bankers for kindly granting permission to use past examination questions and to the Bank of England for allowing me to use information contained in their Quarterly Bulletin. Other sources of information are gratefully acknowledged.

P. Checkley
July, 1989

CONTENTS

Chapter

CHAPTER 1

The Concept of Money

1.1.1 The Nature of Money

Money can be defined as anything that is accepted by virtually everyone in exchange for goods and services. In other words, it is anything which serves as a medium of exchange. If anything is to serve as money, people must have confidence in it as a medium of exchange. For example, after the Second World War the Germans lost confidence in their official money and so it became worthless but cigarettes were readily acceptable in payment for goods and services so that an unofficial cigarette currency came into existence.

Money is important because it facilitates the working of an economy in the following ways:

1. The existence of money allows for division of labour and specialisation which pre-supposes the payment of wages and salaries in money.
2. Money facilitates the implementation of modern productive processes which break down production into more elaborate stages.
3. Money facilitates the development of a sophisticated financial system which allows the store of value function of money to make us better off. It does this by allowing financial institutions to channel funds from lenders to borrowers so that capital investment in plant, machinery and buildings can take place and this, of course, provides us with a higher standard of living than we would have had in a barter economy.
4. The existence of money allows governments to use monetary policy to help achieve their economic goals.

Money has a number of functions and the efficiency of different kinds of money can be judged by the way that they satisfy these functions.

1. A Medium of Exchange

Money facilitates the exchange of goods and so assists the development of trade. If there was no money goods would have to be exchanged by barter, one good being directly swapped for another. Every transaction in a barter system entails a double coincidence of wants. For example, if I have a pig to trade, I must find a person who not only wants a pig but that person must also have something that I want in exchange. In addition, a swap rate must be determined, for example, one pig equals two goats. However, if my trading partner has only one goat to trade, I cannot give him half of my pig, so that there is the additional problem of giving change.

The use of money removes these problems provided that money is readily acceptable. For example, if I wish to sell my pig then I need merely find someone who wants it, I can then exchange my pig for money and use it to purchase some other good. Under the barter system of exchange people are forced to become self-sufficient but with the use of money, people are able to specialise in producing those goods at which they are best.

If money is to serve as an efficient medium of exchange, it must have a number of characteristics:

(a) It must be readily acceptable.

(b) It must be portable i.e. a high value for its weight.

(c) It must be divisible.

(d) It must not be readily counterfeitable.

(e) It must be durable.

(f) It must be homogeneous.

(g) It must have a degree of scarcity, for example, gold has a natural scarcity but paper money requires official control.

2. A Measure of Value and a Unit of Account

Money prices are assigned to goods and this enables us to compare values. The unit of account function relates to accounting or calculation. For example, the U.S. dollar can be used to compare the national income statistics of several countries each one having its own currency.

3. A Store of Value

Both individuals and firms put aside amounts of money to meet future needs but in order that money may be a satisfactory store of value it must have a stable value, i.e., prices must be stable. The value of money is determined by what can be exchanged for it - its purchasing power. If prices rise, then the value of money falls whilst a fall in prices means that the value of money has risen. Thus, the value of money changes inversely with changes in the price level. It is obvious that rapid increases in the price level seriously curtail the usefulness of money as a store of value because of the uncertainty as to money's purchasing power in the future.

4. A Standard of Deferred Payments

If the value of money is stable then contracts can be undertaken where payment is deferred to some future date. Both individuals and firms enter into such contracts, for example, firms often purchase raw materials for immediate delivery but for settlement at a future date whilst most households order milk from their milkman and pay at the end of the week. However, it is important that money has a stable value otherwise traders will be loath to give credit if the value of the money they receive in the future has fallen.

1.1.2 Types of Money

1. Commodity Money

The first type of money used by man consisted of some generally accepted commodity such as, for example, cattle, shells, precious metals and stones. The main advantage of commodity money is that it has an *intrinsic value* and in the past, this attribute made commodity money more acceptable. An intrinsic value means that a commodity has some value other than its value-in-exchange. For example, commodities such as foodstuffs can satisfy physical wants, commodities such as tools can satisfy physical wants by enabling people to produce more goods, whilst precious metals and stones can satisfy psychological wants by satisfying a person's desire for ornament or decoration. During inflationary times, having an intrinsic value makes money a better store of value.

People soon discovered that precious metals produced the most satisfactory forms of money. They found that precious metals had a high and stable price because both the supply and demand for those metals was stable. The supply of precious metals increased very slowly but their durability ensured a continuous supply whilst the demand for them was permanent because of their intrinsic value. On the other hand, agricultural products were found to be unsatisfactory because of the volatility of their supply so that, for example, after a poor harvest when the supply was short their prices would rise sharply.

Precious metals also have the important characteristic of durability and this facilitates the store of value function because if the commodity used as money deteriorates over time no one would wish to hold it. Thus, a perishable foodstuff would not be a satisfactory money because its value falls each day.

Precious metals are homogeneous that is, one unit of precious metal is the same as every other unit. If money is not homogeneous then the measure of value function would break down, for example, ten pigs might be worth one fat cow or two thin cows and so on. It would be almost impossible to assign money prices to goods under these circumstances. However, precious metals can be subject to debasement by being mixed, in alloy form, with base metals and coins may be clipped to reduce the metallic content. In these cases, people tend to hoard the good coins and metals and use the clipped coins and debased metals. This process is characterised by *Gresham's Law* which states that 'bad money drives out the good'.

The characteristics of divisibility is satisfactorily fulfilled by precious metals, whereas the use of other forms of commodity money, such as livestock, means that transactions have to be large because change cannot be given. Although precious metals are divisible their use was impractical where transactions were small because the requisite amount of metal had to be weighed out carefully on a scale. For this reason, those societies which used precious metals as money often used inferior metals to effect small transactions.

Finally, precious metals meet the requirement of portability fairly well especially where they are converted into coins. Precious metals such as gold have a high value for their weight.

2. Money in a Modern Economy

Commodity money suffers from a number of disadvantages which affects its ability to function as a medium of exchange and a store of value. Its creation entails costs of production, its use entails costs of transport and storage. The development of a sophisticated financial system reduces the economy's dependence on commodity money. In a modern economy the money stock largely consists of bank deposits which are assets, i.e., financial claims on banks.

In a modern economy money can be classified as follows:

(a) *Representative Money*

This classification includes bank notes and coins. They are representative because the nominal value of the notes or coin exceeds the value of their constituent paper or metal.

(b) *Token Money*

This classification includes bank deposits. Whilst bank notes are legal tender, bank deposits are not, the reason being that if a bank wished to repay a depositor it could merely credit another account at the same bank so as to discharge the debt. However, this distinction is of little practical importance because so long as people have confidence that a bank will be able to repay depositors in the form of legal tender, bank deposits will be readily accepted in settlement of debts. In addition, bank deposits have the advantages of greater convenience and security and they may often be more acceptable than legal tender for a wide range of transactions.

3. Quasi-money

Quasi-money consists of financial assets which do not function directly as a medium of exchange but they can be quickly and easily turned into cash or sight deposits so that debts may be settled. In other words, they function more as a store of value than a medium of exchange. Examples of these financial assets includes time deposits with banks, building society deposits and finance house deposits. Whilst bank current accounts (sight deposits) are used directly as a medium of exchange, they do not earn interest. Bank deposit accounts (time deposits) on the other hand earn interest which is paid net of tax. The tax treatment of bank deposits and building society deposits is similar in that they both have the privilege of being able to pay interest net of basic rate tax. In addition, in recent years, both banks and building societies have begun to offer a wide range of higher yielding term deposit accounts.

The payment of interest is particularly important to depositors during inflationary periods. Thus, the purchasing power of a bank current account balance will be falling if the general price level is rising. However, the application of interest will protect the purchasing power of quasi-money so long as the rate of interest is not less than the rate of inflation. If the rate of interest is less than the rate of inflation then the 'real' rate of interest is negative. If, on the other hand, the rate of interest is higher than the rate of inflation the 'real' rate of interest is positive. For many years during the 1970s and early 1980s, the real rates of return on bank deposit accounts and building society deposits were negative but from about 1982 the rate of inflation fell below the rates of interest offered on these deposits which provided depositors with the opportunity of earning positive real (pre-tax) rates of return. Real rates of interest are discussed more fully in Chapter 5.

1.2 The Concept of Liquidity

A liquid asset is an asset that can be fairly easily converted into a means of payment at or near to its full monetary value. The more liquid the asset, the more easily it can be converted. Thus, a building society share account is highly liquid because the investor can withdraw his money quickly without capital loss. Ordinary shares (equities), on the other hand, are less liquid because of the time it takes to realise them and the risk of capital loss if the price of the shares falls.

We can, therefore, think in terms of a spectrum of liquidity with cash and very liquid assets at one end of the spectrum and physical assets (such as plant and machinery) at the opposite end. A simple liquidity spectrum is shown Diagram 1.1.

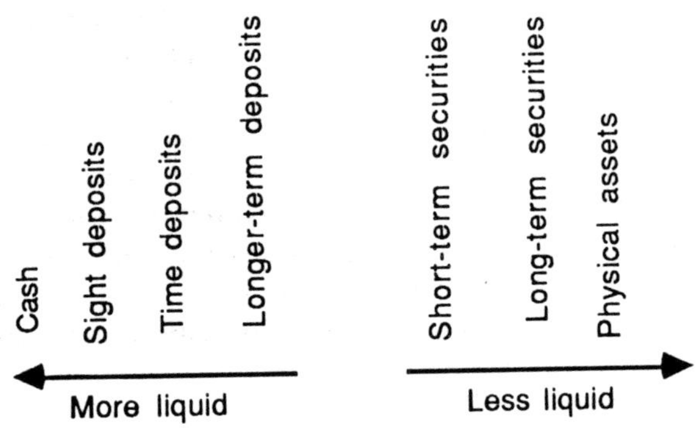

Diagram 1.1

1.3.1 Measuring the Value of Money

We saw earlier that the value of money is determined by its purchasing power. If prices rise then the value of money falls. The value of money can be measured by reference to a suitable index. The Retail Price Index, the Tax and Price Index, the Index of Wholesale Prices and the GDP deflator are considered in the next sections.

1.3.2 The Retail Price Index

The value of money can be measured by reference to the price of a basket of goods and services and index numbers can be used to show changes in prices. Not all prices are included in the calculation because there are so many goods so that only prices of those goods and services are included which are representative of the 'average' budget. An example of such an index is the UK General Index of Retail Prices (RPI) which is published monthly. The RPI measures the price of a basket of goods and services which are grouped as follows - housing, food, fuel and light, transport and vehicles, durable household goods, services, and meals outside the home. Each group is divided into a number of separate items. Each item is weighted according to its relative importance in the 'average' budget. An index is calculated covering all the items and it is related to a base date. The index has a value of 100 at the base date so that changes in the index over time reflect the movement in prices and the value of money. For example, if the index rises in the second year to 110, it means that prices have risen by 10%. Table 1.2 shows the RPI and percentage changes on the year earlier together with the purchasing power of the pound based on movements in the RPI. It can be seen that since 1979 the value of the pound has fallen each year. In the mid-1980s prices rose at a much slower rate (see Figure 1.3), although the inflation rate has once again risen to higher levels during 1989 (over 8%).

The RPI will not reflect the value of money of those individuals and families whose expenditure patterns do not fit in with the 'average' budget. For example, an increase in tobacco duty will affect the value of money of smokers but not non-smokers. Similarly, a fall in the mortgage rate affects the value of money of those with mortgages but not others. It is for this reason that it is difficult to make a precise calculation of the changes in the value of money. Other problems involved in the calculation of changes in the value of money include changes in expenditure patterns over time. Expenditure patterns change as a result of increases in income, different goods coming on the market and differences in the quality of goods. However, to get over this problem the weightings for the RPI are revised regularly (every January) in line with changes in the Family Expenditure Survey of the previous year.

Table 1.2 RPI and Purchasing Power of the Pound

Year	*RPI*	*% increase on year earlier*	*Purchasing power of the pound (Average 1980 = 100)*
1979	84.8	13.4	118
1980	100.0	18.0	100
1981	119.9	11.9	88
1982	121.5	8.6	82
1983	127.1	4.6	79
1984	133.4	5.0	75
1985	141.5	6.1	71
1986	146.3	3.4	68
1987	152.4	4.2	66
1988	159.9	4.9	63

(Source: Central Statistical Office)

Finally, there may be technical problems in choosing an appropriate base year and also in the collection of data which is used in the calculation of the index. Because of the problems involved in calculating accurately changes in the value of money, the RPI can at best give an approximation of the changes in the value of money. However, despite its limitations the RPI is extremely useful as an indicator of changes in the cost of living.

Figure 1.3 Annual % increase in RPI

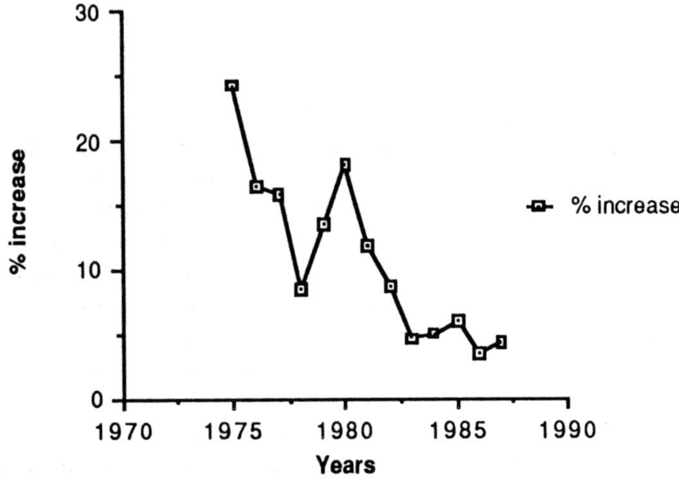

1.3.3 The Tax and Prices Index

In the UK another index has been constructed to take into account the effect of direct taxes and national insurance contributions on take-home pay. It is called the Tax and Price Index (TPI) and its publication commenced in August 1979. The TPI takes into account changes in prices, direct taxes and national insurance contributions. The change in prices is measured by the RPI and accounts for a weighting of approximately 75% of the TPI with the remaining 25% accounted for by changes in direct taxes and national insurance contributions.

1.3.4 Other Measures of Inflation

The usual measure of inflation is the RPI. However, there are other measures apart from the TPI and these include the Index of Wholesale Prices and the 'GDP deflator'. The Index of Wholesale Prices consists of two parts - the prices of raw materials and fuel entering the factory and secondly, the 'factory gate prices' as they leave the factory. These indicate the future trend in the RPI. The GDP deflator is based on the movement in prices of all goods and services produced in the UK.

1.3.5 Theories of the Value of Money

Until the 1960s, there were two extreme theories of the value of money - the classical quantity theory of money and the Keynesian theory of money. However, the 1960s saw the emergence of a 'monetarist' or 'Chicago' school led by Professor Milton Friedman whose theory is a development of the quantity theory.

1.3.6 Keynesian Theory of Money

Keynesian theory states that a difference between the demand for and supply of money alters the demand for and supply of securities (i.e. stocks and bonds) because they are close substitutes for each other. This is because Keynesian theory sees cash as being wanted for itself and not merely as a medium of exchange. For example, if the demand for cash exceeds its supply, the public will sell bonds and increase their cash balances. If the supply of money exceeds its demand, then the public will purchase bonds to eliminate their surplus cash balances. Thus, a difference between the demand for and supply of money will not directly affect the demand for goods and services. However, there is an indirect effect in that purchases or sales of bonds in large numbers will alter the rate of interest. Demand may be affected because investment decisions are influenced by changes in the rate of interest. Changes in the money supply will only have a weak and indirect effect on expenditure and only on that part which comprises investment expenditure.

The effect of increased expenditure on the price level depends on whether the economy is at full employment. Below full employment, an increase in expenditure will cause an increase in output and employment leaving prices unchanged but at full employment, an increase in expenditure will cause prices to rise because output cannot be increased.

Because Keynesian theory sees changes in the money supply as only having a weak and indirect effect on expenditure, then monetary policy is considered to be a fairly impotent tool for controlling the economy.

To illustrate the theory we can see what happens when the public have excess cash. Under these circumstances, the public will try to buy bonds to reduce their cash balances. This causes the price of bonds to rise because the demand for bonds has increased. An increase in bond prices means that the rate of interest has fallen.

When the rate of interest falls the public are prepared to hold higher cash balances because the opportunity cost of doing so is reduced and because bonds will be unattractive to hold so the public will maintain large speculative cash balances. Thus, an increase in the money supply will not increase demand directly but there may be an indirect increase via changes in interest rates which may increase investment expenditure. The changes in income and investment are magnified by the multiplier and accelerator.

Because Keynesian economists believe that monetary policy is a weak policy weapon, they have tended to place greater reliance on the use of other weapons, particularly fiscal policy.

1.3.7 Monetarist Theory of Money

We noted earlier that until the 1960s, there were two extreme theories of money - the classical Quantity Theory of Money and the Keynesian Theory of Money.

The quantity theory asserts that changes in the demand for or supply of money, causes changes in the demand for currently produced goods and services. For example, if the public have more money than they wish to hold, they will spend their surplus requirements of money on currently produced goods and services. If money balances are lower than they would like, they will try to increase their balances by reducing their expenditure on goods and services. Because changes in the demand for and supply of money has such a direct effect on expenditure, the quantity theorists believe that monetary policy is a very potent weapon.

The quantity theory was presented in the form of an equation by an American economist, Irving Fisher, in 1911. This equation has become known as the Fisher equation, the quantity theory equation or the Equation of Exchange and it states that:

$MV = PT$ where -

M is the quantity of money.

V is the velocity of circulation which is the average number of times each unit of money changes hands to finance transactions over a given period of time.

T is the number of transactions over a given period of time.

P is the average price of these transactions.

MV represents the total value of expenditure in a given period whilst PT also represents the total value of expenditure in a given period; so that MV is by definition equal to PT. In other words, the equation is a tautology - it says the same thing but in a different way. However, although it does little to explain what is happening in the economy, it does have certain predictive powers.

The theory assumes that in the short-term V and T are constant. V is constant because money is demanded merely to effect transactions so that if income and expenditure are at a given level, then the amount of money demanded would depend on institutional factors in making payments and receipts - these factors, the theory assumes are constant in the short-term. T is assumed to be constant because it represents the value of the economy's output of goods and services. The theory assumes full employment, therefore, T is dependent on the state of technology which is assumed to be constant in the short-term. Finally, the theory assumes that prices are flexible so that a change in the money supply leads to an equi-proportional change in prices.

Fisher's presentation of the quantity theory can be criticised on a number of grounds:

1. As we have already seen, the quantity theory equation is a truism - the net value of sales over a given period will equal the number of transactions, multiplied by the average price of each transaction. It states the obvious and does little to explain what actually happens in the economy.
2. Fisher's equation does not show how the value of money is first determined, it merely explains changes in the value of money.
3. The use of the term 'the general price level' has been criticised because all prices do not move together in the same direction - some prices will be rising whilst at the same time some will be falling.
4. The theory does not take account of interest rates.

In the long-term there is considerable evidence linking changes in the price level to changes in the quantity of money. For example, between the First and Second World Wars, many governments were unable to finance fully their committed spending by taxation and so borrowed money from the central bank, which in turn printed more money. These rapid increases in the supply of money were quickly followed by increases in the price level.

However, in the short-term, the quantity theory is of little use as an aid to practical policy making because of the breakdown in the real world of the various assumptions noted above. In particular, observation has shown that V varies considerably over short periods of time so that the relationship between changes in M and P cannot be predicted.

The quantity theory has been developed by monetarist economists. Monetarist theory is similar to the old quantity theory in two ways - monetarists believe that the economy gravitates naturally towards full employment and the velocity of circulation is predictable. Thus in the long-run a change in the stock of money will manifest itself in a change in the price level. However, in the short-run, most monetarists argue that a change in the stock of money will manifest itself in a change in real income.

Monetarists see money as being unique in that it is not wanted for itself but as a form of wealth waiting to be spent, i.e., 'a temporary abode of purchasing power'. Money is not considered to be a close substitute for other short-term financial assets as is the case in Keynesian theory so that if the public have excess cash balances they are just as likely to buy goods and services as financial securities. Expenditure on goods and services will raise national income.

The monetarists rely greatly on the empirical evidence that changes in national income appear to be closely linked to changes in the stock of money. However, they believe that changes in the money stock will only affect the level of national income after a time lag which can sometimes be as much twelve months or more.

For this reason, they argue that monetary policy should not be used to even out the trade cycle but that the money stock should be steadily expanded in line with the rate of growth of the economy. For example, if the U.K. economy grows at 2% per annum, then the supply of money should be allowed to grow at 2% per annum and if this is done, there will be no inflation. Monetarists contend that inflation never occurs without an expansion in the supply of money so that the only cure is to reduce the money supply which will reduce prices and perhaps also real output.

Monetarists argue that inflation cannot arise from increased costs, i.e. cost inflation. This is because if workers press for higher wages than are consistent with stable prices they are pricing themselves out of a job and if the government spends to create jobs it will only lead to inflation.

The assumption that the velocity of circulation is stable has been criticised by other economists on the grounds that it has been observed that it is neither stable in the short-run nor long-run.

1.3.8 The Effect of Inflation on Money

We have already seen that if money is to function efficiently, people must have confidence in it. One instance in which people may lose confidence is during periods of inflation. A loss of confidence can lead to a breakdown in the ability of money to fulfil its functions, but this depends on the rate of inflation. Money can function efficiently during periods of 'creeping inflation' but as the rate of inflation increases, it seriously affects the use of money as a store of value. Further increases in the rate of inflation will begin to affect money's unit of account function which will lead to the need to adjust business accounts through inflation accounting. Money's ability to function as a standard of deferred payments would be seriously curtailed by this time and finally money will no longer be able to function as a medium of exchange when the rate of inflation rises to extremely high levels.

1.3.9 Index-linking of Financial Assets

Index-linking of financial assets attempts to overcome the inability of money to fulfil its functions during periods of inflation. As the name suggests, index-linking links the prices of financial assets to an index of prices, so that if the price level rises then the capital values of these assets also rises.

There are two index-linked financial assets available in the U.K. at present:

1. *Index-linked National Savings Certificates (4th Issue)*
   These are available to everyone of any age. There is a maximum holding of £5,000 per person. If the certificates are held for more than one year, they are re-valued in line with the Retail Price Index (RPI) and in addition, the investor receives an extra rate of interest. Repayments of certificates are free of U.K. income tax and capital gains tax. The main disadvantages are twofold. Firstly, the extra interest represents a fairly low real return and secondly, these certificates are less attractive when the rate of inflation is falling because a higher return can be often obtained from other fixed-interest investments.

2. *Index-linked Gilt-Edged Stock*
   The issue of this stock was announced in the 1981 Budget. Initially, its availability was restricted to pension funds and to life insurance companies and friendly societies in respect of their U.K. pension business but this restriction was removed in 1982. Both principal and interest are related to the RPI.

Other varieties of index-linking includes the index-linked civil service pensions and current cost inflation accounting which revalues assets at current cost to give an inflation-adjusted profit or loss figure.

1.4.1 The Composition of the Money Stock

Although we are able to define money in terms of the functions listed earlier, in practice it is difficult to decide which assets should be included in a definition of money. This is because some assets fulfil some of the functions but not all. However, the following definitions have been suggested.

1. **The Conventional Approach**
   This definition is restricted to those financial assets which serve directly as a medium of exchange and are generally acceptable in the settlement of transactions. The assets would include notes and coin together with bank demand deposits. This is a narrow definition of money.

2. **The Chicago Approach**
   The Chicago or monetarist approach to the definition of money is wider than the conventional approach and it includes notes and coin, bank demand deposits and time deposits. According to the Chicago School, time deposits are included because the holder views them as a 'temporary abode of purchasing power' - in other words, they are held for the monetary function of filling the period between receipts and payments of income rather than for the investment function of increasing purchasing power in the future.

3. **The Gurley and Shaw Approach**
   These two economists argue for a wider definition of money which includes not only notes and coin, bank demand and time deposits but also quasi-money assets because they are very good substitutes for each other. Gurley suggests that quasi-money assets should be weighted according to their substitutability. Thus, notes and coin and demand deposits would be given a weight of unity, whilst building society deposits, for example, would be given a smaller weighting and so on.

1.4.2 The Official Definitions of Money in the U.K.

In the U.K., the monetary authorities use six definitions of the money stock - M1, M2, M3, M3c, M4 and M5. These are sometimes classified according to whether they are *narrow* or *broad* definitions of money. M1 and M2 are narrow definitions whilst M3, M3c, M4 and M5 are all broad definitions. These definitions are all sterling-denominated except for M3c (the suffix c reflecting the inclusion of currencies).

M1 consists of notes and coin in circulation with the public, plus sterling sight deposits held by the U.K. private sector with U.K. banks.

M2 comprises notes and coin in circulation with the public plus sterling retail deposits held by the U.K. private sector with U.K. banks, with building societies and in the National Savings Bank ordinary account.

M3 includes M1 plus UK private sector sterling time deposits (including certificates of deposit) with U.K. banks.

M3c comprises M3 plus all U.K. private sector deposits in other currencies (including foreign currency certificates of deposit) with U.K. banks.

M4 equals M3 plus holdings of building society shares, deposits and sterling certificates of deposit held by the U.K. private sector less building society holdings of M3 (bank deposits and certificates of deposit and notes and coin).

M5 equals M4 plus U.K. private sector (excluding building societies) holdings of certain money-market instruments (bank bills, Treasury bills, local authority deposits), certificates of tax deposit and national savings instruments (excluding certificates, SAYE and other long-term deposits).

In these definitions, 60% of the net (debit) value of sterling transit items is deducted from non-interest-bearing deposits.

Table 1.4 shows a tabulated analysis of M1, M3 and M3c definitions.

Table 1.4 Analysis of M1, M3 and M3c Definitions

Number		M1	M3	M3c
1	Notes and coin in circulation with the public	x	x	x
	UK private sector deposits with U.K. banks			
2	Sterling sight deposits	x	x	x
3	Sterling time deposits		x	x
4	Non-sterling deposits			x
	....			
5	Less 60% of transit items	x	x	x

M1 = 1 + 2 - 5
M3 = M1 + 3
M3c = M3 + 4

M2 was introduced by the Bank of England during 1982. The monetary aggregate is designed to measure those deposits which are used for transactions purposes. Thus, M2 is a measure of money which focuses on 'transactions balances' or 'retail deposits' of the private sector. The construction of this aggregate was announced by the Bank of England in November 1980. (This monetary aggregate should not be confused with the old M2 definition which fell into official disuse in 1971).

The aim of M2 is to provide more information about the narrower measures of money. Thus, it is constructed in such a way as to be less sensitive to changes in interest rates than M1 and to take a greater account of transactions balances than M3. The bulk of M1 consists of private sector sterling sight deposits held with U.K. banks. However, seven-day deposits are excluded and a part of these are likely to be used as transactions balances because they are effectively withdrawable on demand (the seven-day notice period in practice is usually waived). In addition, because much of M1 is non-interest bearing an increase in interest rates will result in holders tending to move some of their balances into interest-bearing deposit accounts on which money transmission services are available but which may be outside the scope of M1. On the other hand, M3 may include balances which are held for investment purposes and would not be considered as transactions balances. Thus, M2 is an intermediate aggregate. Table 1.5 gives a breakdown of M2 at end-December, 1987.

Table 1.5 M2: Amounts Outstanding at end-December, 1987 (£m) - not seasonally adjusted

Notes and coin in circulation with the public	14,149
UK private sector sterling non-interest-bearing sight bank deposits	31,642
= Non-interest-bearing M1	45,791
UK private sector sterling retail interest-bearing bank deposits	47,233
UK private sector retail shares and deposits with building societies	93,164
National Savings Bank ordinary account	1,655
M2	187,843

(Source - Bank of England Quarterly Bulletin - February 1988)

Table 1.6 shows amounts outstanding for M1, M3 and M3c, whilst Table 1.7 gives a breakdown of M3 into its constituent parts at end-December, 1987.

Table 1.6 Money Stock: Amounts Outstanding
Components of M1, M3 and M3c (not seasonally adjusted)

		Year-end (£ millions)		
		1983	*1985*	*1987*
Notes and coin in circulation with public	(1)	11,848	12,717	14,149
U.K. Private sector sterling sight deposits:				
Non-interest bearing	(2)	21,624	24,339	31,642
Interest bearing	(3)	11,700	24,550	46,504
Money stock M1	(4)	45,172	61,606	92,295
U.K. Private sector sterling time deposits	(5)	57,119	66,016	93,816
Money stock M3	(6)	102,291	127,622	186,111
U.K. Private sector deposits in other currencies	(7)	16,376	20,128	30,256
Money stock M3c	(8)	118,667	147,750	216,367

Notes

M1 = 1 + 2 + 3
M3 = M1 + 5
M3c = M3 + 7

(Source: Bank of England Quarterly Bulletin - February 1988)

Table 1.7 Breakdown of M3 at end-December 1987 (not seasonally adjusted)

	£ millions	*%*
Notes and Coin	14,149	7.6
U.K. Private Sector Sterling Sight Deposits	78,146	42.0
U.K. Private Sector Sterling Time Deposits	93,816	50.4
	186,111	100.0

(Source: Bank of England Quarterly Bulletin - February 1988)

It can be gleaned from the information in Tables 1.6 and 1.7 that notes and coin in circulation with the public forms only a small part of the money stock. Figure 1.8 shows that M3 consists largely of bank deposits.

Figure 1.8 Constituents of M3 at end-December 1987
(based on figures in Table 1.7)

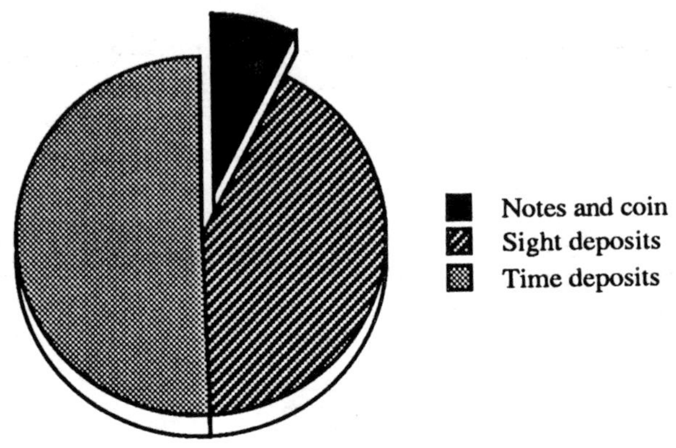

Table 1.7 shows that at end-December, 1987, notes and coin represented approximately 7.6% of M3. Indeed, in their evidence to the Radcliffe Committee, the authorities stated 'that Government's function in issuing notes is simply the passive one of ensuring that sufficient notes are available for the practical convenience of the public'. This feature is seen in all more developed countries having sophisticated financial systems. Thus, if the monetary authorities in more developed countries wish to control the supply of money, control can be directed at bank deposits, leaving the note issue to find its own level.

In more developed countries there is the problem of whether or not to include all money market financial instruments. In the U.K., certificates of deposit are included in the M3 definition whereas certain money-market instruments (bank bills, Treasury bills and local authority deposits) are only included in the broadest definition of M5. In addition, more developed countries have the problem of whether to include quasi-money assets in a wider definition of money. For example, in the U.K., retail building society deposits and National Savings Bank ordinary accounts are included in the M2 definition of money but other building society deposits and other quasi-money assets have been included in the wider measures, M4 and M5, because these assets are often considered by the public as being equivalent to bank deposits when making expenditure/savings decisions.

In less developed countries, the proportion of notes and coin in the money stock is much higher because they have only a rudimentary financial system. The problem as to whether or not to include money market financial instruments or quasi-money assets does not usually exist.

Table 1.9 gives information on M4 and M5.

Table 1.9 Components of M4 and M5 - Amounts Outstanding December 1987 (£ millions)

M3	1	186,111
UK private sector holdings of building society shares and deposits	2	133,241
Building society holdings of M3	3	15,005
M4 (1 + 2 - 3)	4	304,347
Holdings of money market instruments by UK private sector excluding building societies	5	4,595
National savings deposits and certain securities	6	10,643
M5 (4 + 5 + 6)		319,585

(Source: Bank of England Quarterly Bulletin - February 1988)

1.4.3 M0

M0 is a monetary aggregate measuring the monetary base. The term monetary base is frequently referred to when changes in monetary control are being discussed. Indeed, the Treasury and the Bank of England conducted a review of the methods of monetary control (see Chapter 4) which considered the possibility of a move towards a system of monetary base control. Although there is no widely accepted single definition of monetary base, it is generally accepted that it would include a part or all of the monetary authorities' liabilities. In the U.K. the bulk of these consist of the liabilities of the Bank of England. The remaining liabilities consist of coin issued by the Royal Mint which is a Government Trading Fund.

The Bank of England provides statistics on a broader definition of monetary base. The wide monetary base measure includes notes and coin together with those bankers' deposits which are operational. Notes and coin consists of two parts - notes and coin in circulation with the public and notes and coin held by the banks in their tills. Only operational deposits are included in the wide monetary base calculation because they can be easily turned into till money whilst cash ratio deposits are fixed and are not therefore liquid in the same way as operational balances. Similar considerations apply to special deposits so that they too are excluded. However, there has been no special deposits since August 1980. Finally, other liabilities of the Banking Department such as deposits of overseas central banks are excluded because changes in these have less effect on U.K. economic and monetary conditions than do similar changes in bankers' deposits. Table 1.10 shows M0, the wide monetary base in December, 1987.

M0 has over recent years replaced M1 as an indicator of narrow money because of the unpredictable growth of M1 which has been due in part to the unstable nature of the interest-bearing component of M1. Monetary base control is considered further in Chapter 4.

Table 1.10 M0, the Wide Monetary Base (not seasonally adjusted)

	(£millions) *Average amount outstanding in calender month December, 1987*
Notes and coin in circulation outside the Bank of England	16,447
Bankers operational deposits with the Banking Department	186
M0, wide monetary base	16,633

(Source: Bank of England Quarterly Bulletin - February 1988)

1.4.4 Recent Changes in the Measures of Broad Money

In 1987, the Bank of England made a number of changes in the information provided on the wider definitions of money such as changes in title (sterling M3 to M3 and M3 to M3c); the provision of information on levels, changes, growth rates and counterparts to M4 and M5; and the phasing out of information on a measure of private sector liquidity titled PSL1.

These changes in the measures of broad money reflect a number of factors. The continuing importance of broad money growth in assessing monetary conditions together with the difficulties of targeting growth of broad money particularly as a result of deregulation of financial markets and innovation within them. In recent years there has been intense competition between banks and building societies with its consequent effect on broad money. This competition will intensify as a result of the passing of the Building Societies Act 1986, and indeed, some building societies may decide to become banks. Over recent years, building society deposits have increasingly been used for transactions purposes and this development has been given impetus by the building societies offering cheque accounts and cash dispenser facilities. In addition, in the 1980s, building societies began to offer a wide range of accounts (other than the traditional share and deposit account). The increased competition between banks and building societies led to building society interest rates becoming more flexible and the banks offering a wider range of interest bearing retail accounts. The substitutability between financial assets influences the relative growth of different measures of broad money. For example, if building society term shares are withdrawn, and a proportion is placed in M3 assets, then M3 will grow faster relative to the growth of M4 and M5.

The broad definitions of M4 and M5 reflect the blurring of the distinction between banks and building societies. Both institutions' liabilities are included in these definitions.

The advantage of M4 over M5 is that it is institutionally based and is therefore more simple and comprehensible. However, M4 suffers from the same disadvantage as M3, namely that of switching (i.e. switching of assets within the definition to those assets outside the definition). M5 suffers a similar disadvantage.

These changes in measuring broad money reflect the fact that there is no single definition of broad money and that the authorities find a number of broader aggregates to be more useful in assessing monetary conditions than relying just on one aggregate such as M3.

1.4.5 Domestic Credit Expansion (DCE)

DCE was introduced in the late 1960s to monitor the effects of the balance of payments on the money stock. The DCE in a given period is equivalent to the increase in the domestic money stock after taking into account changes in money balances caused by a balance of payments surplus or deficit. When the non-bank private sector is in balance of payments deficit, then DCE shows the importance of external finance as a source of credit, for the banking and public sectors. When the private sector is in balance of payments surplus then the banking and public sectors will use external finance to accumulate assets or repay debt. Thus, when the private sector is in balance of payments deficit, then DCE will be larger than the increase in M3, and usually smaller, when it is in surplus.

Whilst M3 is measured from the liabilities side of banks' balance sheets, DCE is measured from the assets side. DCE includes bank and overseas lending to the public sector plus bank lending in sterling to the private and overseas sectors plus changes in the publics holdings of notes and coins. In broad terms, the total of external and foreign currency finance is equivalent to external transactions of the UK non-bank private sector on the current and capital account of the balance of payments.

The importance of DCE is that it shows the the current spending power in the economy which is financed from overseas and this is not reflected in the M3 figure. For example, a large increase in DCE arising from a large increase in bank lending to the non-bank private sector which is financed from overseas means that M3 has not risen. Thus, M3 has not indicated that potential spending in the economy has increased whereas DCE has.

1.5 Summary

1. Money can be defined as anything that is accepted by virtually everyone in exchange for goods and services.
2. The functions of money are:
   (a) Medium of exchange
   (b) Measure of value and unit of account
   (c) Store of value
   (d) Standard of deferred payments.
3. Types of money include:
   (a) Commodity money
   (b) Representative money
   (c) Token money
   (d) Quasi-money
4. A liquid asset is an asset that can be fairly easily converted into a means of payment at or near to its full monetary value.
5. The value of money is determined by its purchasing power and can be measured by reference to a suitable index such as the Retail Price Index.
6. The two main theories of the value of money are the Keynesian and Monetarist Theory of Money.
7. High levels of inflation seriously curtail the efficient functioning of money.
8. Index-linking links the price of financial assets to an index of prices. Index-linking attempts to overcome the inability of money to fulfil its functions during periods of inflation.
9. It is difficult to decide which assets should be included in a definition of money.
10. The U.K. monetary authorities use the following definitions of the money stock; Narrow (M1 and M2), Broad (M3, M3c, M4 and M5).
11. M0 is a monetary aggregate measuring the monetary base.
12. The M4 and M5 definitions reflect the blurring of the distinction between banks and building societies.

13. DCE monitors the effects of the balance of payments on the money stock.

Questions

1.* 'Official control of the money supply should be aimed at the level of bank deposits, leaving the note issue to find its own level'. Discuss, with reference to communities in different stages of development.

2.* (a) What attributes must an asset possess if it is to be considered as money?

(b) By international agreement the maximum liability for damage to persons and to property, caused by a yacht, is expressed in terms of pre-war gold French francs. What advantages and disadvantages are there is using such a little-known monetary standard for this purpose?

(c) Most British electricity undertakings now sell vouchers and gift tokens to be used to pay electricity bills. To what extent, if any, do such vouchers and tokens fulfil the functions of money?

3.* Discuss the problems which arise in identifying the 'quantity of money' both in general terms and in the context of:-

either (a) An advanced country such as the United Kingdom
or (b) A developing country.

4.* Analyse how changes in the value of money affect its ability to fulfil its functions.

5.* Discuss the qualities which anything should possess if it is to be used as money.

6.* In what ways does the existence of money facilitate the working of an economy?

7.* (a) What are the functions of money and in what circumstances does it fail to fulfil them?

(b) Explain in non-technical terms, what is understood by 'index-linking of financial assets'.

8.* 'The value of money does not depend upon whether it has any intrinsic value'. Discuss.

9.* Compare and contrast the principal liabilities of the commercial banks and building societies with particular reference to the following:-

(a) money as a medium of exchange;
(b) money as a store of value;
(c) the control of the money supply.

10.*(a) What is meant by the statement that money is the measuring rod of value? With what precision can changes in the value of money itself be measured?

(b) How well has money performed its function as a store of value in the United Kingdom during the last three years?

11. Some of the functions of money are performed by other liquid assets. What are these assets? Why are they often held in preference to bank notes and bank deposits in the performance of these functions?

12. Why is it difficult to provide an unambiguous definition of the money stock in a modern economy? Illustrate your answer by reference to any country with which you are familiar.

13. (a) Distinguish between 'narrow' and 'broad' measures of a country's money stock;
(b) With reference to any country with which you are familiar, discuss the problems of defining 'narrow' and 'broad' money.

14. Discuss the statement that it is only commercial banks' liabilities which rank as money in modern economies. Illustrate your answer by reference to any country with which you are familiar.

15. (a) Distinguish between narrow and broad concepts of the money stock, briefly illustrating your answer with reference to the definitions used in any country with which you are familiar. (13)

(b) Indicate, giving reasons, whether the following are included in measures of money and in each case state whether it is the broad or narrow measure:

(i) certificates of deposit issued by banks;
(ii) building society term shares;
(iii) bank current accounts;
(iv) equity shares in a public company. (12)

16. The broad money aggregates in the UK were reclassified in May 1987.

 (a) Why was this considered necessary? (7)

 (b) Outline briefly the broad measures of money currently used in the UK. (10)

 (c) Why do the authorities consider it important to monitor the money supply? (8)

17. (a) Distinguish between 'narrow' and 'broad' measures of money.(8)

 (b) Tabulate the relevant liabilities of the central bank, commercial banks, and building societies according to whether they feature in narrow or broad money definitions. Indicate in this table the money supply definitions in which these liabilities appear. (13)

 (c) Apart from the liabilities considered in (b), what other items are included in the money supply? (4)

CHAPTER 2

U.K. Financial Institutions

2.1.1 The Nature of Financial Intermediation

Financial intermediaries channel funds from lenders to borrowers. They operate by issuing their own liabilities which are acceptable as assets to depositors. Thus, a person depositing his money with a bank will have a financial claim on it and when the bank lends money to a customer a financial claim on the borrower comes into existence. Financial intermediaries essentially channel funds from those economic units and sectors (groupings of economic units) which have a *financial surplus* to those economic units and sectors with a *financial deficit*. If an economic unit has a financial surplus, it means that its total receipts are greater than its total expenditure over a given period. On the other hand, if it has a financial deficit then its total expenditure is greater than its total receipts over a given period.

Financial intermediation usually entails the transformation of risk and maturity characteristics. For example, the depositor in a building society will have a reduced risk of loss because the building society accepts many deposits and lends to many house buyers and so spreads the risk. If the depositor lent his money directly to a house buyer his risk of loss would be much greater. Financial intermediaries are usually involved in *maturity transformation* which means that their deposits are for a shorter term than their loans. Thus, a large proportion of a building society's deposits are withdrawable on demand or at short notice whilst its mortgages may be for terms of up to 25 years. In addition, there is often an element of *aggregation* which refers to the acceptance of relatively small deposits which are then aggregated to meet the demand for large loans.

Financial intermediation is an important process because of the different requirements of lenders and borrowers. Lenders seek a high return and low risk. They do not want to spend a long time searching for someone suitable to lend to and they require their loan to be liquid so that they can obtain repayment of the loan quickly if they need their money back. Borrowers seek to borrow money for a long period of time (in the case of house purchase, for example) and they want to find funds quickly. Financial intermediaries seek to match the differing requirements of lenders and borrowers.

Financial intermediaries seek to make a profit by paying a lower rate of interest on the funds they receive and charging a higher rate of interest on the funds they lend. The difference between the two rates is called a *margin* and it is used to cover operating expenses and to provide a profit.

Financial intermediaries compete on both sides of their balance sheet. They compete for deposits and advances through the price and quality of their services.

Financial intermediaries usually compete with those of the same type, for example, deposit banks with deposit banks, but they also compete with other types of financial intermediaries. For example, deposit banks compete with building societies for both deposits and loans. Such competition has increased in recent years as a result of the diversification of financial services by many financial intermediaries. However, competition between them can be distorted by a number of factors including the application of a regulatory framework which affects some financial intermediaries but not others, the unequal application of privileged circuits and the application of monetary controls on some but not others.

The way in which funds flow from savers to borrowers through the intermediation of financial institutions can be illustrated by an analysis of financial transactions. Table 2.1 shows the financial surplus/deficit of the various sectors of the economy.

Table 2.1 Financial surplus/deficit by sector 1987: 3rd quarter (Seasonally adjusted)

(£ millions)

	Financial surplus + *Financial deficit -*
Public sector	-925
Monetary sector and other financial institutions	+2,027
Industrial and commercial companies	+2,183
Personal sector	-2,375
Overseas sector	+1,146
Residual error	-2,056

(Source: Bank of England Quarterly Bulletin - February 1988)

We have already seen that a financial surplus means that an economic unit's or sector's total receipts are greater than its total expenditure over a given period of time. A financial surplus or deficit of a sector is calculated by first ascertaining the level of saving, (i.e. total income less consumption expenditure). A financial surplus or deficit is then calculated by taking away from saving all capital expenditure which includes gross fixed-capital formation, any increase in the value of stocks and work in progress and taxes on capital and capital transfers. Put simply, a financial surplus shows the amount that a sector's saving exceeds its own investment. Thus, if a sector has a financial surplus, it is contributing to the financing of another sector's financial deficit. Table 2.1 shows that the largest financial surplus is accounted for by industrial and commercial companies. There were also surpluses in the monetary sector and other financial institutions and in the overseas sector. These surpluses contributed to the financing of the deficits in the public sector and the personal sector.

Having ascertained each sector's financial surplus or deficit we can go on to analyse the various transactions, which in value, must add up to the amount of the surplus or deficit. If an economic unit has a financial surplus it could pursue a number of courses including:

1. paying off any debts which it may have (liabilities +) or
2. buying financial assets (assets +) or
3. a combination of (1) and (2) or
4. buying financial assets (assets +) to a value greater than the surplus resulting in an increase in borrowing (liabilities-).

If an economic unit has a financial deficit then it could:

1. increase its borrowing (liabilities -) or
2. sell financial assets (assets -) or
3. a combination of (1) and (2) or
4. buy financial assets (assets+) and increase its borrowing (liabilities-).

Thus, there are many courses of action but the changes in assets and liabilities must equal the financial surplus or deficit.

We can now go on to analyse the financial transactions of the personal sector and these are shown in Table 2.2. It can be seen from Table 2.2 that many of the financial assets acquired by the personal sector were highly liquid and included notes and coin, national savings, bank deposits, and deposits with building societies. The remaining financial assets acquired consisted of longer-term instruments such as life assurance and pension funds, UK company and overseas securities and unit trusts. Table 2.2 also shows an increase in borrowing by the personal sector much of which was for house purchase.

An analysis of financial transactions between the other sectors can similarly be made. This would show that during the 1970s industrial and commercial companies relied more heavily on banks as a source of external finance rather than the capital market but in the 1980s their reliance on bank finance was reduced. In addition, their holdings of liquid assets grew rapidly and these in the main consisted of bank deposits. The financing of the public sector is considered in Chapter 4.

Table 2.2 Financial Transactions:Personal Sector 3rd quarter 1987 (Seasonally adjusted)

(£ millions)

Financial deficit -	-2,375
Assets: increase +/decrease -	
Liabilities: increase -/decrease +	
Borrowing	
For house purchase	-7,845
Bank borrowing (other than for house purchase)	-1,725
Credit extended by retailers	-115
Other	-180
	-9,865
Financial assets	
Notes and coin	+214
British government securities	-1,222
National savings	+360
Certificates of tax deposit	-1
Local authority debt:	
Temporary	+178
Long-term	-385
Bank deposits	
Sterling sight	+1,729
Sterling time	+477
Foreign currency	-8
Deposits with building societies	+2,581
Deposits with other financial institutions	-
Unit trusts units	+2,212
U.K. company securities	+3,736
Overseas securities	+923
Life assurance and pension funds	+5,797
Other	-110
	+16,481
Total financial transactions	**+6,616**
Balancing item	-8,991

(Source: Bank of England Quarterly Bulletin - February 1988)

The non-bank financial intermediaries depend primarily on the personal sector for their funds and these are lent to the public sector and to the personal sector (mainly by building societies for house purchase). They also invest in U.K. company and overseas securities. The sources and uses of funds for the banking sector are considered later in this chapter.

2.1.2 Financial Intermediaries

Financial intermediaries can be classified into two groups in accordance with the way in which they operate - deposit-taking institutions and other institutions which are involved in the attraction of longer-term savings.

1. Deposit-Taking Institutions

These institutions operate by taking short-term deposits and use these to lend for longer terms or to buy other long-term assets. These institutions include commercial banks, the National Savings Bank, building societies and finance houses. The operations of the commercial banks are varied but their activities can be split into retail banking business and wholesale banking business. A bank's retail operations are concerned with cash handling and money transmission and this entails having an extensive branch network. Wholesale banking business is concerned with deposits and loans which are for large amounts.

Table 2.3 shows the liabilities and assets of the monetary sector.

Table 2.3 U.K. Monetary Sector: 1986 (1st Quarter)

(£ million)

Liabilities		*Assets*	
Public sector deposits	3,764	Lending to public sector	16,971
Private sector deposits:		Lending to private sector:	
Personal sector	67,067	Personal sector	63,453
Industrial & commercial companies	40,918	Industrial & commercial companies	66,051
Other financial institutions	33,526	Other financial institutions	45,914
Overseas sector deposits	424,493	Lending to overseas sector	410,895
Non-deposit liabilities (net)	33,516		
	603,284		603,284

(Source: Financial Statistics)

Table 2.3 shows that the main source of domestic funds for the banks is the personal sector and the banks predominantly channel funds from the personal sector to industrial and commercial companies and to the public sector. The banks are involved in intermediation between sectors and across sectors. Financial institutions other than banks provide a part of the bank's deposits and receive more bank finance. The overseas sector deposits have been channelled by the banks to the overseas and other sectors.

The banks are very important financial intermediaries, not only because of the size of their balance sheets but also because their liabilities form part of the official money supply calculation and the other intermediaries maintain accounts with them.

Table 2.4 and Figure 2.5 shows that at the end of February, 1986 manufacturing and other production accounted for about 23% of total advances made to U.K. residents by the banks.

Table 2.4 Analysis of Loans, Advances and Acceptance to UK Residents by the Banks

Amounts outstanding : February 1986

	£ million	%
Manufacturing	21,845	13.8
Other production	15,668	9.9
Financial	30,021	18.9
Services	49,695	31.3
Persons	41,885	26.1
	159,114	100.0

(Source: Financial Statistics)

Figure 2.5 Sector Analysis of Loans, Advances and Acceptances to UK Residents by the Banks: February 1986

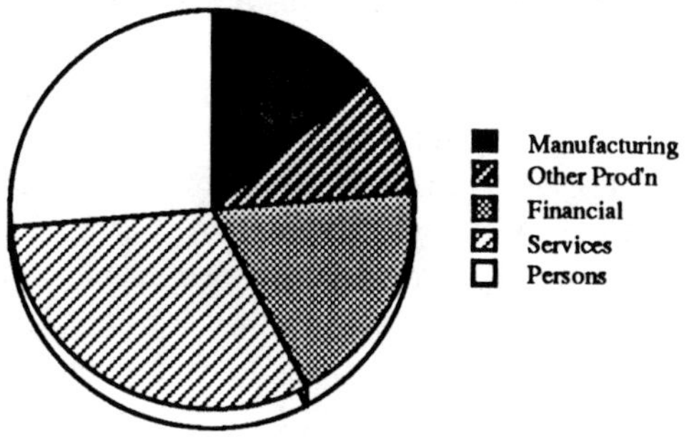

Based on figures taken from Financial Statistics

A further 31% was accounted for by services which includes for example, transport, communication, distribution and professional services. The personal sector accounted for about 26% of the total. From about the beginning of 1979 the retail banks aggressively competed in the home loan market. At the end of February, 1986 advances made by banks for house purchase totalled £21,136 million (£1,931 million on 19th November 1980).

Bank lending takes a number of forms ranging from the flexible and relatively low cost overdraft facility, to term loans over two to seven years or more. Where a loan is too large for one bank to handle it can be syndicated. As far as the clearing banks are concerned the overdraft still accounts for approximately half of their total lending although in recent years the term loan has increased in relative importance. The clearing banks also provide asset finance to industry through the provision of instalment credit (via the banks' subsidiaries) and leasing operations. Industrial companies need finance for investment in working capital, to finance trade credit, to buy new plant and equipment and for new investment. The banks provide finance for the first three but they have not generally lent money for long-term investment for industry. Consideration of whether bank finance has been sufficient for industry's needs involves looking at the availability of other sources of finance such as new issues of shares and loan capital; retained profit; trade credit; and funds provided by the government. In addition, there is the question of whether industry's demand for finance has been met and whether they are being crowded out of the bank finance which is available by the public sector.

The building societies and the National Savings Bank are involved in retail operations. The building societies obtain virtually all their funds from the personal sector and they lend to persons for house purchase. The National Savings Bank is geared mainly to providing banking services for the individual.

The finance houses obtain most of their funds from the wholesale markets although some also accept retail deposits.

Deposit-taking institutions other than banks generally lend in specific areas. Thus, building societies lend primarily for house purchase and the finance houses specialise in the provision of instalment credit.The National Savings Bank does not make loans.

2. Other Financial Intermediaries

This grouping includes life insurance companies, pension funds, unit trusts and investment trust companies. These institutions essentially attract long-term funds enabling them to provide long-term finance. The funds attracted by both life assurance and pension funds are of a contractual nature so they provide a steady and predictable flow. These funds are then invested in a portfolio of assets so that maturing life and pension policies can be paid in the future. However, provided these institutions attract new business sufficient to cover any claims and payments, their assets can be held undisturbed and even added to. They can, therefore, hold assets which are long-term. The main assets held by life insurance companies and pension funds are company securities, government stocks and property and these account for about 90% of their total assets. The remaining assets consist of mortgages and loans, cash and other short-term assets.

Life insurance companies perform two main functions, - they insure a person's life and provide facilities for saving. Pension funds attract savings which are used to provide income in old age. Both life insurance companies and pension funds receive tax advantages.

Unit trusts and investment trust companies both operate by attracting funds and investing them in a portfolio of assets. Their chief advantages to investors are the spread of risk and professional investment management. These advantages are of particular importance to the investor of moderate means. Both unit trusts and investment trust companies invest the bulk of their funds in company securities (about 90% of total assets). The remaining assets consist of government stocks, cash and other short-term assets.

2.2.1 The Structure, Functions, Operations and Profitability of Commercial banks

The commercial banks in the U.K. consist of two types of bank —retail (primary or deposit) banks and wholesale (or secondary) banks. The retail banks are those banks with extensive branch networks in the UK or have a direct participation in the UK clearing system and they include the London and Scottish clearing banks and the Northern Ireland banks. The wholesale banks can be broken down into the following groupings:

1. Accepting houses
2. Other British banks
3. American banks
4. Japanese banks
5. Other overseas banks
6. Consortium banks

2.2.2 Retail Banks

Retail banks are those banks which operate the payments mechanism and in order to fulfil this function, the large retail banks have extensive branch networks which cover the whole of the U.K. The London clearing banks have branches covering the whole of England and Wales whilst the Scottish clearing banks and Northern Ireland banks provide a separate branch network in their own countries.

2.2.3 Operation of Retail Banks

Because retail banks are involved in the payments mechanism it is essential that their deposits should be widely accepted in settlement of debts and this entails the need for retail banks to operate extremely prudently. The retail banks have a large number of fairly small accounts, many of them withdrawable on demand, so that they are able to treat their deposits as a revolving fund. This is because that at any one time, some customers will be making withdrawals whilst other customers will be making deposits so that for an individual retail bank movements in total deposits will generally be small. However, to meet the movements in total deposits, banks will hold liquid assets which can be realised to cover withdrawals. To show that they are acting prudently, they will also hold liquid assets above the minimum required. This is because if the authorities lay down a fixed ratio of liquid assets to deposits, those assets will no longer be able to perform their original function. Retail banks get over this problem by holding a proportion of liquid assets which do not form part of the formal liquidity calculation. We can see how the retail banks satisfy their need for liquidity by listing the assets which appear in a retail banks balance sheet.

Cash	- Notes and coin
	- Working balances with other banks
Other liquid assets	- Money at call and short notice
	- Bills discounted
Other market loans	
Investments	
Advances	

The assets are listed in descending order of liquidity and ascending order of yield. The retail banks hold two forms of cash —notes and coin to meet their customers' withdrawals and a working balance to settle inter-bank indebtedness. These working balances are normally held with a bank outside their own group. The London clearing banks have accounts at the Bank of England whilst the other banks usually have an account with a London clearing bank.

The other liquid assets consist of money at call and short notice which is lent to the discount houses and bills discounted which are held to maturity. The former asset is held to meet unpredictable fluctuations in the bank's need for cash whilst the latter is held to meet predictable fluctuations. Other market loans, consist of secondary money market assets and include funds lent on the inter-bank market, local authority market and inter-company market.

The investments are predominantly gilt-edged stocks and they provide a cushion between liquid assets and advances. Being marketable, banks can sell them either to top up their liquid assets or to satisfy their customers' demands for advances. A full analysis of liquidity is given in Chapter 4.

Banks require liquidity to meet withdrawals of cash by customers, to settle inter-bank debts, to satisfy unforeseen demand for advances, to cover unforeseen reductions in cash flow.

Profitability is important because profit is required to pay dividends to shareholders, to top up reserves, to enhance capital adequacy and to finance expansion.

2.2.4 The Liabilities and Assets of the Retail Banks

Table 2.6 shows the liabilities and assets of the retail banks and we shall now examine the main items appearing in the table.

Liabilities

1. Notes Issued

Notes issued comprise sterling notes issued by the Scottish clearing banks and the Northern Ireland banks. The Scottish clearing banks and the Northern Ireland banks conduct their business in a similar way to the London clearing banks. There are, however, two main differences - both groups of bank can issue their own notes and they both keep working balances with the London clearing banks. Each bank has an 'authorized' circulation of notes (about £2.7 million for the Scottish clearing banks and about £2 million for the Northern Ireland banks) and the remaining notes are covered by the holding of an equivalent amount of Bank of England notes. However, this cover is not required until the notes actually pass over the counter into circulation.

2. Deposits

There a number of factors which influence the level of bank deposits including the general economic climate, competition between banks themselves and other financial institutions, the government's monetary policy and the preferences of depositors. There are two main ways of analysing the types of deposit. Firstly, they can be analysed according to whether they are retail deposits (i.e. current and deposit accounts) or wholesale deposits and secondly, according to whether they are sight deposits (current accounts and wholesale overnight and call deposits) and time deposits. A further distinction can be made in each case between sterling and foreign currency. We shall adopt the former approach.

Table 2.6 Balance Sheet of the Retail Banks as at May 21, 1986

	£ million		%
Liabilities			
Notes Issued		998	0.5
Sterling deposits:			
Sight deposits	54,097		
Time deposits	59,864		
CDs	8,083		
Total sterling deposits		122,044	61.0
Other currency deposits:			
Sight and time deposits	40,434		
CDs	5,852		
Total other currency deposits		46,286	23.1
Other liabilities		30,754	15.4
Total Liabilities		200,082	100.0
Assets			
Sterling assets:			
Notes and coin		2,228	1.1
Balances with the Bank of England		670	0.3
Market loans		30,294	15.1
Bills:			
Treasury bills	368		
Eligible local authority bills	395		
Eligible bank bills	3,594		
Other	76		
		4,433	2.3
Advances		83,489	41.7
Investments		8,851	4.5
		129,965	65.0
Other currency assets:			
Market loans		33,033	16.5
Advances, bills and investments		21,628	10.8
Sterling and other currency miscellaneous assets		15,459	7.7
Total Assets		200,082	100.0

Acceptances £3,732 million

(Source: Bank of England Quarterly Bulletin - June 1986)

Current accounts are those accounts which enable customers to withdraw cash on demand, issue cheques and use the bank's money transmission services. They may be non-interest-bearing and because of the costs involved in operating these accounts, banks levy an extra charge (although there may be no charge if the account stays in credit during the charging period). In 1989, banks began offering interest-bearing current accounts.

Other retail deposits consisting chiefly of 7-day deposits are technically subject to seven day's notice of withdrawal but in practice this requirement is normally waived. They are interest-bearing and so provide a liquid form of saving which competes with other forms of savings such as building society and National Savings Bank accounts. Some banks provide savings accounts which enable depositors to draw limited amounts at the bank's branches, but these form only a very small proportion of total deposits and are normally amalgamated, for statistical purposes, with 7-day deposits.

Throughout the 1970s and early 1980s the rate of growth of balances on deposit account was higher than on current accounts. Prior to the introduction of the Competition and Credit Control measures in 1971, the rate of interest paid on 7-day deposits was agreed between the clearing banks and for some years it had been pegged at 2% below Bank Rate. After Competition and Credit Control, the banks were free to formulate their own rate but because of their increased competitiveness the authorities reserved the right to protect savings banks and building societies by limiting the rate which banks could offer for savings deposits. Although each bank is free to determine its own rate, there has tended to be a uniformity in the terms offered because of competitive pressures.

In the early 1980s, the retail banks introduced various new deposit accounts such as regular savings accounts and higher interest deposit accounts as a result of the intense competition from building societies in the retail savings market.

Sterling wholesale deposits consist of large deposits received through the branch network, together with deposits raised in the wholesale markets such as inter-bank and other money market deposits and certificates of deposit.

The bulk of the retail banks' sterling deposits are short-term in nature with a large proportion being repayable in less than eight days. However, we have already seen that a retail bank's deposit base remains fairly stable but the confidence of depositors is essential so that deposit banks have to maintain adequate levels of liquidity and capital. On the other side of the retail bank's balance sheet, the advances are longer term. The transformation of short-term deposits into longer-term loans is known as 'maturity transformation' and this enables banks to lend more cheaply.

So far we have dealt only with sterling deposits. Table 2.6 shows that foreign currency deposits accounted for about 23% of the retail banks' total deposits. The bulk of foreign currency deposits is attributable to overseas residents which include overseas central banks and commercial banks, financial institutions, industrial and commercial corporations and a few wealthy individuals. Further foreign currency deposits are provided by the U.K. banking sector and issues of dollar certificates of deposit. These eurocurrency deposits are wholesale deposits.

3. Other liabilities

The other liabilities in Table 2.6 consists of the retail banks' own capital funds and items in suspense and transmission.

Assets

1. Notes and coin

We have already seen that deposit banks must hold notes and coin in their branches and head offices to meet withdrawals. Until the introduction of Competition and Credit Control in 1971, the clearing banks were required to maintain a minimum ratio of cash to deposits of 8% with cash consisting of notes and coin and balances at the Bank of England. However, after the 1971 measures, notes and coin was excluded from the calculation of the reserve asset ratio so that banks now only hold sufficient notes and coin to meet withdrawals (usually about 1.5% of total assets).

2. Balances with the Bank of England

Special and cash ratio deposits

Special deposits are deposits called for by the Bank of England in furtherance of its monetary policy. Only those institutions with average eligible liabilities of £10 million or more are liable for calls to lodge special deposits. The interest paid on special deposits is linked to the average rate for Treasury bills issued at the latest Treasury bill weekly tender. The cash ratio deposits are required under the monetary control arrangements introduced on August 20th, 1981. Those banks with average eligible liabilities of £10 million or more are required to lodge with the Bank of England non-operational, non-interest-bearing deposits of 0.45% of their eligible liabilities.

Other balances with the Bank of England

These consist of all balances with the Bank of England other than special deposits and cash ratio deposits. These balances are operational balances for clearing purposes. Under the Competition and Credit Control measures the London clearing banks were required to maintain these balances at an average of 1.5% of their eligible liabilities. However, since August 20th 1981 the banks themselves have determined the level of these balances. They are used to settle any indebtedness arising from the cheque clearing and any other inter-bank indebtedness.

3. Market loans

Table 2 .6 shows that these assets accounted for about 15% of total assets on May 21, 1986. They may be further sub-divided as follows:

	£ millions
Market loans:	
Secured money with LDMA	3,721
Other UK monetary sector (including unsecured money with LDMA	19,893
UK monetary sector CDs	3,352
U.K. local authorities	1,658
Overseas	1,670
	30,294

Secured money with LDMA

This asset consists of funds lent to, or placed with, members of the London Discount Market Association. These loans are secured and immediately callable. They are important because they enable the banks to adjust their day-to-day liquidity needs.

Other UK monetary sector

This asset includes all balances with, and funds lent to, other members of the monetary sector (excluding certificates of deposit).

Certificates of deposit (CDs)

A certificate of deposit is issued by a bank certifying that it has received a deposit for a fixed term at a fixed rate of interest. The advantage of certificates of deposit to both banks and to depositors are considered fully in Chapter 3.

U.K. local authorities

In 1955 local authorities were forced to borrow from the market because they were no longer allowed to borrow from the Public Works Loans Board at will. After the introduction of Competition and Credit Control in 1971, the retail banks became active in the provision of temporary loans to the local authorities. This asset includes only funds lent through brokers or in special financial markets, such as the local authority money market.

Overseas

Market loans made to overseas include all balances with, and funds lent to, banks overseas; discounted bills of exchange drawn by overseas banks including overseas offices of the reporting bank; and certificates of deposit, promissory notes and other negotiable paper issued by banks overseas and owned by the bank.

4. Bills

Treasury bills

The mechanics of the Treasury bill market will be examined later in this chapter. The retail banks usually buy their Treasury bills in the secondary market and purchases are arranged so as to ensure a steady flow of maturities thereby aiding balance sheet management.

Eligible local authority bills

These bills comprise U.K. local authority bills eligible for rediscount at the Bank of England.

Eligible bank bills

These comprise all commercial bills which are payable in sterling and have been accepted by a bank whose bills are eligible for rediscount at the Bank of England.

Other bills

These bills include local authority and bank bills which are ineligible, and promissory notes and other negotiable paper owned by the bank.

5. Advances

Advances are the most profitable and least liquid of a bank's assets. In 1959, the Radcliffe Committee found that the sterling advances of the clearing banks were 40% of their total sterling deposits, by the mid-1970s they had risen to over 70%.

6. Investments

The investments include gilt-edged stocks (i.e. stocks issued by the Government and stocks of nationalised industries guaranteed by the Government), local authority stocks and bonds, and investments in subsidiaries and associates.

7. Other currency assets

Until the introduction of the Competition and Credit Control measures in 1971, most foreign currency business was conducted through the London clearing banks' secondary banking subsidiaries. Since then, the London clearing banks have been able to undertake such business in their own names. Table 2.6 shows that other currency assets accounted for about 27% of total assets on May 21, 1986.

The market loans consist of secondary money market assets such as funds lent on the inter-bank market and eurocurrency markets.

8. Miscellaneous assets

These assets, in both sterling and currency, include items in suspense (e.g. debit balances awaiting transfer to customers' accounts), collections (i.e. cheques drawn on and in course of collection on banks and other institutions in the U.K. and debit items in transit between U.K. offices), assets leased (i.e. all plant and equipment beneficially owned by a bank which has been leased out), and other assets (e.g. gold bullion, gold coin, other commodities such as silver, land, premises, plant and equipment owned by the bank).

2.2.5 The Operation of Secondary Banks

Before examining the various banks that make up the secondary (wholesale) banking system, we can initially look at the main features of secondary banking. Secondary banks are involved primarily in wholesale banking in which deposits and loans are for large amounts. Most of the loans and deposits are fixed for definite periods (term loans and term deposits) and much of their business is conducted in foreign currency. The secondary banking system is highly competitive and because secondary banks are not involved in the payments mechanism, they do not have extensive branch networks. Much of their liquidity is provided by the secondary money markets rather than the discount market.

We have already mentioned that the bulk of their advances take the form of term loans which can range from a few months to 5 or 7 years. There were a number of reasons for the increased popularity of term loans since the 1960s. Term loans have the attraction of being secure during credit squeezes (particularly important during the 1960s when lending ceilings applied) unlike overdraft limits which may be reduced. With the greater use of investment appraisal techniques such as discounted cash flow, term loans tie in with these techniques and they also facilitate budgeting. The overdraft is more suitable for working capital. The overdraft is a generalised form of finance whilst the term loan is tied to the cash flow of a particular project so that the latter extends the credit-worthiness of companies.

We have already noted that secondary banks are involved in wholesale banking so that their balance sheets will show a relatively small number of large accounts which are fixed for definite terms. In addition, much of their business is conducted in foreign currency, so that if the secondary banker is to conduct his business prudently he must consider matching his assets and liabilities according to maturity and currency. A completely matched position is where a loan, in a particular currency, matures at the same time as a deposit for the same amount and in the same currency. However, a secondary banker does not usually completely match his assets and liabilities because he takes a view on the future level of interest rates. If he expects interest rates to fall in the future, he will keep his assets as long as possible and his liabilities as short as possible.

Inter-bank deposits and certificates of deposit are important to secondary banks from the point of view of matching assets and liabilities on both sides of their balance sheets. If a secondary banker is offered business, whether deposit or loan, on acceptable terms, he can accept it knowing that he can match it by going to the inter-bank or certificate of deposit market.

Secondary banking business is highly competitive and they generally work on lower margins than the retail banks. Their customers are first class companies, their business is conducted in large amounts and they are not involved in the costs of operating the payments mechanism. Although they pay more for their deposits than the retail banks, their lower margins mean that they are extremely competitive on the terms of their loans.

The type of business undertaken by secondary banks can be illustrated by analysing the services offered by the accepting houses. The accepting houses are members of the Accepting Houses Committee and any bank can become a member provided; that a large part of its business consists of accepting bills for the purposes of financing trade; that the accepted bills can be sold in the discount market at the finest rates; and that the Bank of England takes the accepted bills from the market.

Accepting houses provide a number of services - acceptance business, commercial banking, corporate finance, portfolio management and miscellaneous services.

1. Acceptance business

Acceptance of bills of exchange is the accepting houses' traditional business. Many of the present-day houses began business as commodity merchants using bills of exchange to finance their own transactions. As their standing and reputation grew, they found that they could 'lend their names' to lesser-known merchants by accepting bills of exchange. An accepting house 'accepts' a bill drawn on it by endorsing the bill with its name and for this service it receives a commission. The bill can then be discounted at the finest rates in the discount market because it bears a first-class name. Acceptance credits can not only be used to finance international and domestic trade but they can also be used in what is termed 'soft arbitrage'. Soft arbitrage is the use of acceptance credits to repay clearing bank overdrafts when the former is a cheaper source of finance.

2. Commercial banking

Accepting houses provide term loans and overdrafts and accept term deposits. They also provide current and deposit accounts for their customers.

3. Corporate finance

This service includes assisting their customers in the raising of new capital. Accepting houses not only organise the raising of new capital or the flotation of a company but they also provide general financial advice to companies. Such advice covers rights issues, mergers and take-overs. The accepting houses assist their customers in the raising of funds on the international bond market and syndicated loans market.

4. Portfolio management

Accepting houses are involved in the management of portfolios on behalf of pension funds, insurance companies, larger charities and private individuals. Since the late 1920s and early 1930s they have been involved in the management of investment trusts but more recently they have become involved in the management of unit trusts.

5. Miscellaneous

The accepting houses' new issue services often results in them taking a stake in a small company showing promise with a view to flotation in the future. More recently, many houses have taken stakes in companies involved in factoring, leasing, hire purchase and insurance broking. A small number of houses are involved in bullion dealing and commodity dealing. The accepting houses together own ARIEL (Automated Real-time Investment Exchange Limited) which is a computerised share dealing system set up in 1974. Finally, a number of houses act as company registrars.

Table 2.7 shows the accepting houses' assets and liabilities. A number of the features of secondary banking can be gleaned from the Table. The importance of foreign currency business, certificates of deposit and time deposits. Over half of their assets consist of market loans giving them a high degree of liquidity.

We are also able to see how important acceptance business still is for the accepting houses. However, under the new system of monetary control introduced on August 20th 1981, the Bank of England has increased its list of eligible banks (i.e., banks whose bills it is prepared to buy) and this has resulted in greater competition for the accepting houses which have suffered a sharp decline in their share of acceptance credit business whilst American, Japanese and other foreign banks have raised their share of the market.

The total liabilities/assets of the American banks are similar to the equivalent figures for the London clearing banks. Their deposits are dominated by other currency deposits whilst their assets are dominated by other currency market loans and advances. Virtually all their business is wholesale.

Table 2.7 Balance Sheet of the Accepting Houses as at May 21, 1986

	£ million		%
Liabilities			
Sterling deposits:			
Sight deposits	3,238		
Time deposits	8,664		
CDs	1,538		
Total sterling deposits		13,440	46.7
Other currency deposits:			
Sight and time deposits	11,188		
CDs	434		
Total other currency deposits		11,622	40.4
Other liabilities		3,701	12.9
Total liabilities		28,763	100.0
Assets			
Sterling assets:			
Notes and coin	4		
Balances with Bank of England	31		
Market loans	7,659		
Bills	389		
Advances	5,142		
Investments	1,561		
Total sterling assets		14,786	51.4
Other currency assets:			
Market loans and advances	10,601		
Bills and investments	1,469		
		12,070	42.0
Sterling and currency miscellaneous assets		1,908	6.6
Total assets		28,763	100.0

Acceptances £4,085 million

(Source: Bank of England Quarterly Bulletin - June 1986)

These figures are impressive considering the relatively small number of American banks in London. These banks are attracted to London because it is the centre of the eurodollar market. In the 1960s and 1970s, the American banks aggressively participated in the eurodollar market to enable them to lend to their head offices because of the tight monetary scene which periodically obtained in the U.S.A. and they are still very active in the market today. The American banks have also extended their activities to the U.K. market and in recent years they have accounted for about 15-20% of total bank advances to U.K. manufacturing industry.

In the 1970s and 1980s a number of American banks opened branches outside London, but their retail operations are so small that they have not challenged the dominant position of the U.K. clearing banks.

The main reasons for the influx of Japanese and other foreign banks into London is essentially the same as for the American banks - the ability to tap the eurodollar market. Japanese banks have been particularly active in the market in the late 1970s and 1980s. These foreign banks now account for about 10% of total bank advances to U.K. manufacturing industry.

Consortium banks are banks which are owned by other banks but in which no one bank has a direct shareholding of more than 50%, and in which at least one shareholder is an overseas bank. Many of these banks were formed to service the medium-term borrowing requirements of multi-national companies. Because the borrowing needs of these companies are so large, consortium banks often syndicate their loans. They also provide term loans in foreign currencies to public borrowers overseas. Much of their business is conducted in foreign currency and because many of them have loan capital in addition to share capital, their other liabilities are higher than for foreign banks in London.

They provide trade finance through acceptance credits. Their sterling deposits represent about 10% of liabilities of which about 60% consists of inter-bank deposits and certificates of deposit. About 50% of their sterling assets and over 50% of their other currency assets are held as market loans.

2.3.1 Non-Bank Financial Intermediaries

The non-bank financial intermediaries can be divided into finance houses, the National Savings Bank and building societies.

2.3.2 Finance houses

Finance houses have traditionally specialised in providing hire purchase and other instalment credit both to individuals and business. However, over the years the finance houses have diversified so that they also provide personal loans, leasing, factoring and some provide current and deposit accounts. Usually, these services are provided by subsidiaries or associated companies. Finance houses obtain their funds from two main sources. Firstly, they accept deposits from companies and the general public and secondly, they borrow from the banks and other financial institutions. A number of the larger houses have obtained recognition as banks, and although this means that they are subject to the same monetary controls as those applied to banks they do have the benefit of being able to borrow on the inter-bank market and issue their own certificates of deposit. Many finance houses have been taken over by banks and other financial institutions but they still retain their separate identity.

The amount of credit granted by finance houses can be controlled by the authorities by the use of terms controls. These controls are used to specify the minimum down payment and the maximum repayment period. They have not been used in the 1980s.

2.3.3 National Savings Bank

The National Savings Bank is operated by the Post Office but it is under the control of the Department for National Savings. The main feature of the National Savings Bank is that it has a vast number of small accounts. The National Savings Bank offers two types of account: the ordinary account and the investment account. A tax concession applies to the ordinary account which stipulates that the first £70 of interest earned each year is tax free. Interest is paid gross of tax. At the end of 1985 ordinary account balances totalled £1,715 million and there were over 18 million active ordinary accounts.

Investment accounts were introduced in 1966. Investment accounts offer a higher rate of interest than on ordinary accounts but there is no tax concession. Interest is paid gross of tax. At the end of 1985 investment account balances amounted to £5,505 million and there were around 2 million investment accounts.

The investment of funds deposited with the National Savings Bank is controlled by statute. The National Investment and Loans Office invests the deposits in the Ordinary Account Fund (in which ordinary account deposits are invested). Investments in the Ordinary Account Fund comprise of government and government guaranteed securities and the income from these investments is used to cover interest payments and expenses (including depreciation in the value of investments) and any surplus is paid into the Consolidated Fund. National Savings Bank investment deposits are paid into the National Loans Fund. Should the National Savings Bank's deposit liabilities exceed the funds available to meet them, the Treasury guarantees to cover any deficiency.

2.3.4 Building societies

Building societies are specialised savings banks. They accept deposits which are short-term in nature and their assets consist primarily of mortgages (see Table 2.8). The other main assets consist of cash, investments and premises. Their investments consist primarily of British government securities and local authority debt securities. They work to a liquidity ratio consisting of cash and investments as a percentage of assets. Building societies are non-profit institutions so that they set their rates of interest to provide enough income to cover all their expenses and to make a contribution to their reserves. In the early days of the building society movement, depositors and borrowers were often the same people, but today they are more separate although a society often gives preference to a person seeking a mortgage if he has an account with that society.

In recent years the number of societies has been falling due largely to the transfer of engagements. Since the 1960s, total deposits have been growing rapidly. Today, their total deposits exceed those of the London clearing banks. The societies attract deposits by offering a number of different accounts such as share accounts, deposit accounts, regular savings accounts, term share accounts and Save-As-You-Earn. The rate of interest on share accounts is slightly higher than on deposit accounts, the reason being that in the event of liquidation deposit account holders will be paid before ordinary share account holders, because the former is a creditor and the latter is a shareholder. One of the main attractions of building societies to a saver is that interest is paid net of income tax. Under an arrangement that the societies have with the Inland Revenue, they are able to deduct a composite (average) rate of tax from interest payments which is less than the standard rate of tax.

During 1982 the building societies established an investor's protection scheme. The scheme covers up to 90% of an investor's funds should a building society get into financial difficulties. When the scheme was set up not all societies decided to participate but those that did accounted for the bulk of building society assets. Under the scheme, each building society would be called upon to make a contribution to a protection fund should the need arise. However, this voluntary scheme was made a statutory one under the Building Societies Act 1986 (see below).

During 1979 the Anglia, Hastings and Thanet Building Society raised £20 millions of mortgage funds in the money markets to supplement its mortgage lending programme. Since then a small number of other building societies have also raised funds in the money markets. In 1980, Alliance Building Society issued an unlisted bond which was followed in 1981 by the issue of a listed bond by Nationwide Building Society. These bonds are similar to local authority yearling bonds. Building societies have in recent years issued certificates of deposit and more recently floating rate notes.These moves reflect the search for alternative sources of finance to meet the tremendous demand for society mortgages.

Table 2.8 Building Societies' Assets and Liabilities (end-1986)

Liabilities	*(£m)*	*Assets*	*(£m)*
Shares and Deposits	117,554	Mortgages	116,938
Interest accrued but not credited	1,965	Short-term assets and investments	21,783
Time deposits	3,470	Other assets (land, buildings and equipment)	2,019
Certificates of deposits	1,521		
Bank borrowing	2,137		
Bonds	5,439		
Reserves, official loans and other liabilities	8,654		
	140,740		140,740

(Source: Financial Statistics)

However, since 1980 the London clearing banks have been aggressively competing in the house mortgage market which has traditionally been dominated by the building societies. The increased competition between the clearing banks and building societies over the last few years has resulted in the building societies offering a wide range of banking and financial services. For example, during 1982 the Leicester Building Society teamed up with Citibank Savings to provide a cheque book account on which interest is paid on credit balances, personal loans and travellers' cheques. Similar services are now offered by other building societies. Building societies have in recent years installed cash dispenser machines which can be used to withdraw cash both during and outside normal opening hours. The building societies' ability to offer a wide range of services has been enhanced by the passing of the Building Societies Act 1986. Most of the provisions of the Act came into effect on 1st January 1987. This new Act replaces the Building Societies Act 1962.

The main provisions of the 1986 Act are as follows.

1. There is no change in the principal purpose of building societies i.e., that of the provision of savings and mortgage lending services.
2. Building societies are required to adopt a Memorandum (like companies) which notes their principal purpose and other purposes and powers.
3. The assets of the building societies are to be divided into two types - commercial assets and other assets. Commercial assets comprise: -

   (a) Class 1 - fully secured residential first mortgages on land to individuals.

   (b) Class 2 - other first or second mortgages wholly or partly secured on land.

(c) Class 3 - other permitted assets such as personal loans, land held by the building society for permitted commercial purposes (such as housing developments) and investment in subsidiaries.

Other assets comprise:-

(a) fixed assets

(b) investments (including liquid funds)

(c) cash.

A minimum of 90% of the commercial assets must comprise of Class 1 mortgages. Societies must not hold Class 3 assets in excess of 5% of the total commercial assets.

4. Supervision of the building societies is to be undertaken by a new body known as the Building Societies Commission (instead of the Registry of Friendly Societies).
5. The present voluntary scheme of investor protection will be made statutory.
6. Any complaints against a building society will be investigated by an independent adjudicator or ombudsman.
7. From 1988, building societies will be able to form themselves into limited companies. This will be achieved by calling a General Meeting and there will be special voting and publicity requirements.
8. With regard to such matters as commercial assets, unsecured lending and Directors' shareholdings, the Act provides for maximum or minimum financial limits. The bulk of these limits may be changed by statutory order.

In future building societies will be able to:

1. Make unsecured loans or allow overdrafts of up to £5,000 to individuals.
2. Undertake residential development of land for sale and renting.
3. Acquire shares in certain other corporate bodies, and to provide them with loans. The Act requires building societies to offer personal equity plans, unit trust schemes for pensions and estate agency services through subsidiaries.
4. Offer some services which are similar to those offered by banks such as cheque accounts, and a cheque guarantee card scheme (i.e. offer money transmission services).
5. Offer foreign exchange services to an individual up to £5,000.
6. Arrange for the buying and selling of shares and other securities for individuals.
7. Arrange for the provision of credit to individuals by third parties and to manage such services.

8. To act as an insurance broker.
9. Offer conveyancing services.

A joint Treasury/Building Societies Commission review announced in early 1988 that the building societies would be given a wide-ranging extension of powers. Whilst stressing that the building societies' mainstream business must continue to be the attraction of funds from the public for lending on house purchase, the review stated that they should be allowed to offer a wider range of financial services. These services would either complement their main business or allow them to compete more effectively. Thus building societies will be allowed to:

1. have an equity participation in both life and general insurance companies;
2. be involved in fund management including management of unit trusts;
3. have an equity participation in stockbrokers;
4. offer a wider range of banking services.

In addition, the limit on unsecured lending to individuals will increase to £10,000 and asset limits will be gradually changed in the future. Class 2 and 3 limits will be increased to 17½% and 7½% respectively in January 1990, to 20% and 10% respectively in January 1991 and to 25% and 15% respectively in January 1993.

2.3.5 Competition between Retail Banks and Building Societies

The traditional area of operation of the building societies has been the provision of mortgages for private individuals funded by retail savings. They have built up a dominant position in the retail savings market and the mortgage market. However, since about 1980, when the retail banks began to compete aggressively in the home loans market, the building societies have had to face increasing levels of competition in both markets. This increased competition has led to a rise in the price of retail deposits and a greater volatility in their level. Thus, the structure of interest rates on both sides of the building societies' balance sheet have risen relative to the rates in the wholesale money markets. The result of this has been to make mortgage business more attractive to the retail banks because they can fund such lending in the wholesale money markets. A problem for building societies is that they are restricted as to the amount that they can raise in the money market.

Since about 1980, there have been changes in the sphere of operation of both building societies and banks.

(a) *Building societies*

As noted earlier, up to about 1980 the traditional business of building societies was the provision of mortgages funded totally by retail deposits. During the 1980s, the building societies have raised funds in the wholesale money markets, have moved into the provision of money transmission services and the Building Societies Act 1986 allows them to offer personal loans and other types of business such as foreign exchange.

(b) *Retail banks*

Up to about 1980 the traditional business of the retail banks was the provision of both personal and business loans funded by the wholesale money markets and their retail deposits. Since 1980, the retail banks have aggressively competed in the mortgage market and retail savings market.

Thus, there has been a movement towards each of them offering similar services in the areas of cash handling, money transmission and financial intermediation. However, there are still substantial differences in the structure of their balance sheets. The balance sheet of the retail banks show a more diversified structure on both sides of the balance sheet (assets and liabilities, reflecting the retail banks' heavy usage of the wholesale money markets) and a comparison of assets reveals that the retail banks hold a larger number of different types of asset with differing yields. The building societies do not have the benefit of current account balances (on which the retail banks do not pay interest). All of their deposits are interest-bearing with most paying interest rates which are higher than those found in retail banks' balance sheets. The building societies' balance sheets show a narrower range of assets. Thus, the structure of the buildings societies' balance sheets are less diversified. When interest rates rise, the profits of retail banks are enhanced by the endowment element in retail bank profits.

Further differences arise in the regulation of building societies and their ability to compete with the retail banks.

The passing of the Building Societies Act 1986 has limited the extent to which building societies can compete with retail banks. This is because although the Act allows building societies to extend their range of services, the provision of these is severely curtailed. For example, building societies can offer non-mortgage loans (Class 3 loans) but these are restricted under the Act to no more than 5% of total commercial assets, (although as noted earlier, the limit is to be raised in the future).

In addition, there are other onerous restrictions which distort competition between building societies and retail banks which will hinder the building societies' attempts to reduce risk by diversification. This is particularly so in the area of funding.

The Building Societies Commission restricts the amount of wholesale deposits in the building societies' balance sheets to less than 20% of total (retail and wholesale) deposits. The Building Societies Act 1986 allows for 40% so that the Commission can raise the amount of wholesale deposits in the future up to this maximum . The retail banks, on the other hand, have not had such limits imposed upon them so that there is unequal competition between the two types of financial institution.

The following conclusions can be made:

1. Current regulation is not neutral as between retail banks and building societies.
2. The ability of building societies to diversify has been limited.
3. Building societies have not been allowed to make unlimited use of wholesale money markets.

2.4 The Relationship of Commercial Banks to Other Financial Institutions

We have already noted that the commercial banks are important because their balance sheet totals are very large and their liabilities form part of the official money supply calculation. The retail banks carry out the important functions of cash handling and money transmission as well as financial intermediation. It is for this reason that the other financial institutions maintain accounts with them. The commercial banks compete with other financial institutions on the terms and quality of their services.

2.5.1 The Nature of Central Banking

A central bank is an organ of government. It is responsible for the major financial operations of the government and the way in which it carries out these operations and by other means, it is able to control the activities of financial institutions so as to support the government's economic policy. Historically, many of the institutions which developed into central banks were essentially commercial banks. However, central banks differ from commercial banks in three very important ways:

1. Because central banks are organs of government, they are governed by individuals who are often closely connected with other government departments. In the 1930s many held the view that central banks should be independent but since then, this view has

largely disappeared. The argument for allowing central banks a large degree of independence is that it can provide a safeguard - by preventing a government from financing its excessive expenditure by the printing of money.

It is for this reason that the Federal Reserve Bank in the United States and the German Bundesbank still enjoy a large measure of independence. However, it is difficult to ascertain how much independence the Bank of England enjoys but general opinion considers that the government should have the final authority for policies implemented by the Bank because it is ultimately answerable to the electorate. Montague Norman, the Governor of the Bank of England during the period 1922-44, said that the Bank of England has 'the unique right to offer advice and to press such advice even to the point of nagging; but always, of course, subject to the supreme authority of the Government'. (Committee on Finance and Industry, 1931).

2. Central banks do not exist to maximise profits. They do not compete with commercial banks for private business although the Bank of France is an exception, and central bank staff are more involved with the work of government departments rather than with the business of banking.
3. They must have a special relationship with the commercial banks so that they are able to influence them in furtherance of the government's economic policy.

The role of central banks can be summarised as follows:

1. To implement and advise the government on monetary policy.
2. To act as a banker to the government and the commercial banks.
3. To act as lender of last resort.
4. To be responsible for the note issue.
5. To intervene in the foreign exchange market to even out excessive exchange rate movements.
6. To be responsible for the prudential regulation of commercial banks.
7. To be responsible for a number of miscellaneous duties such as running the clearing system (applicable to a number of countries), acting as registrar for government stocks (applicable to the U.K.), and for exchange control.

Because the work of central banks is so important and because most countries have a central bank, it is doubtful whether the functions listed above could be performed by other agencies effectively. Nearly all countries today have a central bank. If countries do not have a central bank they often have close links with other countries having a central bank. For example, Hong Kong and Luxembourg do not have central banks but the former is a Crown Colony and the latter has an economic union with Belgium resulting in some inter-dependence in monetary matters.

2.5.2 The Functions of Bank of England

The functions of the Bank of England can be ascertained through an analysis of its balance sheet. The balance sheet of the Bank of England is shown in Table 2.9. The balance sheet is divided for accounting purposes, into two departments - the Issue Department and the Banking Department, in accordance with the Bank Charter Act 1844. In national income statistics, the Issue Department is generally included in the central government sector, while the Banking Department is part of the banking sector. The Exchange Equalisation Account is not included in the balance sheet because it is a Treasury account.

Turning first of all to the balance sheet of the Issue Department, its liabilities consist solely of Bank of England notes, including those held by the Banking Department. On the assets side of the balance sheet, there is the £11 million of 'government debt' which represents loans made to the government in 1694 by the Bank's founders together with some later loans. The government securities include British government and government guaranteed securities, Treasury bills, ways and means advances to the National Loans Fund and any special Treasury liability. Ways and means advances are sums that are borrowed by the government overnight. Special liability arises when the market value of the Bank's assets is less than the note issue. Other securities include commercial bills, local authority bills and occasionally local authority deposits and bonds acquired in the course of market operations together with other miscellaneous securities.

The function of the Bank, as a banker, is brought out by certain items on the liabilities side of the balance sheet of the Banking Department. The Bank acts as a banker to the Government, to the banks, to overseas central banks and international organisations and to a small number of private sector customers and its staff.

The liabilities of the Banking Department includes:

1. Capital (£14.6 million held by the Treasury).
2. Public deposits - these consist of balances held by the central government and include the accounts of the Exchequer, the National Loans Fund, the National Debt Commissioners and the Paymaster General together with dividend accounts, accounts connected with tax collection and various other government funds.

3. Special deposits - these deposits are made by banks when required to do so by the Bank of England.
4. Bankers' deposits - these are the current accounts of banks and discount houses.
5. Reserves and other accounts - these include deposits made by overseas central banks, local authority and public corporation accounts and some private sector accounts.

Table 2.9 Balance Sheet of the Bank of England December 30, 1987

(£ million)

Liabilities		Assets	
Issue Department			
Notes in circulation	14,548	Government debt	11
Notes in Banking Department	12	Government securities	9,150
		Other securities	5,399
	14,560		14,560
Banking Department			
Capital	15	Government securities	637
Public deposits	109	Advances and other accounts	815
Special deposits	-		
Bankers deposits	1,086	Premises, equipment and other securities	1,664
		Notes and Coin	12
Reserves and other accounts	1,919		
	3,129		3,129

(Source: Bank of England Quarterly Bulletin - February 1988)

The assets of the Banking Department include:

1. Government securities, including government and government guaranteed stocks together with Treasury bills.
2. Advances and other accounts includes market advances made to the discount market, loans to customers and support loans to deposit-taking institutions. These items bring out one of the Bank's important functions, that of lender of last resort.
3. Premises, equipment and other securities - the other securities includes ordinary shares, local authority bills and bonds, and commercial bills.

Having analysed the Bank of England's balance sheet we can now go on to consider the functions of the Bank of England in greater depth.

1. The Bank of England as a Banker

(a) Banker to the Government

We have already seen that the Government's main accounts are held at the Bank of England. The Bank is responsible for ensuring that finance is always available to cover a deficit. Residual requirements will be met by ways and means advances, otherwise deficits will be covered by the issue of government securities (Treasury bills or stocks) whilst a surplus will be used to purchase securities. The Government can settle its debts with the private sector by issuing cheques on its account at the Bank. If funds are not available on the account to meet cheques on presentation, the Bank will, as a matter of course, make a loan to the Exchequer.

(b) Banker to the Banks and Other Financial Institutions

The Bank of England acts as a banker to a large number of banks ranging from clearing banks and accepting houses to overseas banks operating in London and to the discount houses. Under the 1971 Competition and Credit Control measures, not all banks and other financial institutions were required to have an account at the Bank of England but the London clearing banks were required to hold an average of 1.5% of their eligible liabilities in the form of deposits at the Bank of England, whilst discount houses were required to have accounts to enable them to borrow from the Bank. However, under the Bank of England's monetary control arrangements of August 20th, 1981, the 1.5% requirement on the London clearing banks was lapsed and now all institutions authorised under the Banking Act 1987 are required to lodge non-interest-bearing deposits with the Bank equal to 0.45% of their eligible liabilities. In addition, the London clearing banks are required to hold at the Bank whatever operational balances they think necessary to settle any indebtedness arising from the cheque clearing and any other inter-bank indebtedness.

(c) Banker to Overseas Central Banks and International Organisations

The services it offers to overseas central banks and monetary institutions range from the holding of working balances which are used to settle indebtedness arising from the Bank's operations in the foreign exchange markets and the provision of advice on investment in the gilt-edged market to the investment of short-term funds on their behalf. The international organisations holding accounts at the Bank include the International Monetary Fund, the World Bank and the Bank for International Settlements.

(d) Banker to Private Sector Customers and its Staff

The Bank of England does not compete with the banks for private business although it does have a small number of private customers. The Bank continues to hold these accounts because they provide the Bank with practical commercial banking experience

2. The Regulation of the Note Issue

The Issue Department is restricted as to the amount of notes that it can issue. Under the Currency and Bank Notes Act 1954, the Issue Department is restricted in two main ways. Firstly, the Issue Department can issue notes to the value of gold it holds and secondly, the Bank is allowed to issue notes without being backed by gold to the tune of £1,575 millions or any sum agreed upon by the Treasury. The former restriction is ineffective since the Bank holds little gold. Treasury permission to increase the fiduciary issue has to be notified to Parliament but authorization is more or less automatic so that fluctuations in the public's demand for notes can be met.

The book-keeping involved in the issue of notes is straightforward. If the Banking Department wish to increase their stock of notes, which appear as assets in their balance sheet, they will buy notes from the Issue Department, payment being made in the form of securities. If the Banking Department wish to reduce their stock of notes, they will be sold to the Issue Department. When notes are paid out to or paid in by the banks, the transactions involve the exchange of bankers' deposits at the Bank for notes.

3. Lender of Last Resort

This function is essential since if the Bank (or other central bank) wishes to have effective control over the banks it must not only have the sole note-issuing authority but it must also be able to create more cash when the public demand more liquidity and this demand threatens to bring about a financial crisis. Because banks know that the Bank will always provide assistance when required, they will be willing to work to a stable cash ratio and this results in a stable financial system. The position of the Bank of England as a lender of last resort is unique because when assistance is required it does not usually give it directly to banks but indirectly via the discount houses. This feature of the U.K. banking system is discussed further in Chapter 3.

In October 1987, the Chancellor of the Exchequer made the decision that the Bank of England should make arrangements to buy back newly issued partly paid BP shares over a limited period at a price below that which they were initially sold. The aim was to set a floor under the BP share price which had fallen greatly as prices of shares generally fell on the Stock Exchange.

This decision had the effect of extending the Bank of England's role as lender of last resort to both U.K. and international investment institutions and securities firms (because they had been involved in underwriting the issue).

Underwriting a new issue means that institutions (underwriters) agree to take up any unsold shares for a commission. As stock market prices fell worldwide, there were few takers of the BP shares so the vast bulk were left in the hands of the underwriters. Payment for these would have imposed severe liquidity problems so that the ability to resell to the Bank of England would have helped investment and securities firms over the worst of their liquidity problems.

4. Registrar of Government Stocks

This role was adopted by the Bank of England in 1715. The Bank acts as registrar not only for Treasury bills and British government stocks but also for stocks issued by the nationalised industries, some local authorities, public boards and Commonwealth governments. The Bank's duties are similar to any other registrar in that it makes a record of all transfers of stock, pays dividends and interest and repays stock on maturity.

5. Management of the Exchange Equalisation Account

The Exchange Equalisation Account is discussed fully in Chapter 8.

6. Monetary Policy

The Bank of England not only implements monetary policy but also advises the government on all aspects of monetary policy. The role of the Bank in monetary policy can be split into three parts:

(a) ***Market Intervention***

The Bank intervenes in three markets: the bill market, the gilt-edged market and the foreign exchange market. In all three markets, the Bank operates directly. As far as the foreign exchange market is concerned the Bank acts as an agent for the Exchange Equalisation Account and it deals directly in that market.

(b) ***Moral Suasion***

Moral suasion is the use a central bank makes of its special position in the financial community to influence the banks in certain ways. The Bank has in the past used quantitative directives which place a ceiling on bank lending but it has also issued qualitative directives which request banks to give priority in their lending to certain sectors of the economy. Further examples of moral suasion include the implementation, on a voluntary basis, of the Competition and Credit Control measures which were introduced in September 1971 and the monetary control arrangements which took effect on August 20th, 1981. It is difficult to assess how much agreement is genuinely voluntary because in their evidence to the Radcliffe Committee the clearing banks said - "We listen with great care to what the Governor says to us at any time. He might give us a hint and we should not be likely to ignore it".

(c) ***Adviser to the Government***

The Bank collects and analyses a wide range of statistics. It also uses economic models so as to provide a greater understanding of the workings of the economy.

7. Supervision of the Financial System

The Bank's supervisory role can be broken into three separate parts. Firstly, the Bank represents the views of not only the bankers but of all the City institutions. Secondly, the Bank concerns itself on an informal basis with ensuring that the principles of conduct in the City continue to be observed. Thirdly, the Bank has a direct responsibility for the efficient working of the banking system.

Prior to the passing of the Banking Act 1979, the supervision of the banks was conducted by the Bank on an informal basis, with the potential backing of the powers given to it under the Bank of England Act, 1946. However, the secondary banking crisis of 1973/74 led to the acceptance of a need for a formal system of bank regulation. A number of factors contributed to the secondary banking crisis.

In the 1960s, the credit control measures distorted competition so that many sound borrowers went to the secondary markets for finance. After the introduction of the Competition and Credit Control measures in September 1971, clearing banks were able to compete more effectively with the secondary banks so that they were able to win back many of these customers. The collapse of London and County Securities led to a loss of confidence in many secondary or 'fringe' banks. A number of these were faced with a sudden withdrawal of deposits but their liquidity resources were insufficient to meet these withdrawals. The gravity of the situation led the Bank of England and the London and Scottish clearing banks to organise assistance which became known as the 'life-boat operation'. In all twenty-six institutions received assistance which amounted to approximately £1,200 million at one stage.

The Banking Act 1979

The Banking Act 1979, arose from the requirement to harmonize banking regulation in the U.K. with the rest of the European Community. The main provisions of the Act were as follows:

(a) the recognition or licencing of deposit-taking institutions;
(b) control over the use of banking names and descriptions;
(c) the setting up of a Deposit Protection Scheme.

The Act provided that no bank or other financial institution could accept deposits without first obtaining authority to do so from the Bank of England. The authorisation took one of two forms, that of a recognized bank or licensed deposit-taker. In either case authorisation would only be granted to those applicants who could satisfy the Bank as to their solvency and competence of their management. To obtain recognised status applicants had also to demonstrate that they commanded the highest standing and reputation in the financial community and that they provided a wide range of services.

The Banking Act 1987

The Government published a White Paper on Banking Supervision in December 1985. The Paper stated the Government's intention of reforming the Banking Act 1979. Its recommendations were as follows.

1. The setting up, within the Bank of England, of a Board of Banking Supervision to help the Governor supervise the banking system.
2. The classification of recognised banks and licensed deposit-taking institutions will be abolished. All institutions will be similarly classified and each must have a paid-up capital of at least £5 million to enable it to be called a bank.

3. There will be a requirement on authorised institutions to maintain appropriate records, books and internal control systems and banks' auditors are to take a more active role in the supervision of banks. The Bank of England will be obliged to monitor each bank more closely. The misreporting of information by banks to the Bank of England is to be a criminal offence.
4. Banks will be legally required to advise the Bank of England of any large exposure (over 10% of its capital) to a single customer (this requirement resulted from the Johnson Matthey Bank collapse in 1984 when the Bank of England had to take it over).

The provisions of the Banking Act 1987 are based on the proposals embodied in the White Paper on Banking Supervision and they are as follows:

1. Deposit-taking institutions must seek authorization from the Bank of England under the Banking Act 1987.
2. As noted in the White Paper, all institutions will be similarly classified and each must have a paid-up capital of at least £5 million to enable it to be called a bank.
3. The setting up, within the Bank of England, of a Board of Banking Supervision.
4. As noted in the White Paper, all authorised institutions must maintain appropriate records, books and internal control systems and banks' auditors are to take a more active role in the supervision of banks. The Bank of England will be obliged to monitor each bank more closely.
5. The misreporting of information by banks to the Bank of England is to be a criminal offence.
6. Banks will be legally required to advise the Bank of England of any large exposure (over 10% of its capital) to a single customer and also to advise the Bank of England in advance of any proposed loan that would be greater than 25% of its capital.
7. Notification must be given in advance to the Bank of England of the intention of any person or company to take control of an authorised institution which has been incorporated in the U.K. This gives the Bank of England the power to veto any take over which it does not consider desirable.

Before granting authorisation, the Bank of England will consider the following matters. The Bank of England will ensure that the institution conducts its business prudently and with integrity; it has adequate levels of capital and liquidity; it maintains proper accounting records, books and internal control systems; its directors and other important personnel are fit and proper persons.

The Bank of England concerns itself with an institution's capital adequacy. As an aid in assessing capital adequacy the Bank uses two measures - the free capital to deposits ratio and the risk assets ratio. The Bank does not work to any particular level for each ratio but it uses them as a yardstick because variations in the ratios of various institutions reflect the differing nature of their business. The free capital ratio is calculated as follows:

$$\frac{\text{Shareholders' funds less fixed assets}}{\text{Total deposit liabilities}}$$

In the past, whenever the banks were concerned that their free capital ratios had fallen to uncomfortable levels, they raised additional capital.

The risk assets ratio specifies the extent to which individual risk assets need to be covered by a bank's capital and is calculated as follows:

$$\frac{\text{Individual risk assets}}{\text{Capital}}$$

Some assets such as Treasury bills and some other money market assets require little or no capital cover because the risk that the debtor will default is virtually non-existent so that these assets can be financed solely by deposits. At the other extreme, infrastructure assets require a high degree of capital cover because they may not only fall in value but a large proportion of them are purpose-built so that they would be unlikely to realise their book value on the open market.

A bank needs adequate capital to reduce the risk of insolvency arising from bad debts or investment losses for example; to facilitate expansion of the bank's business; to enhance the confidence of depositors, shareholders and the general public.

The Deposit Protection Scheme

The Deposit Protection Scheme was first introduced under the provisions of the Banking Act 1979. It came into operation during 1982 and it continues under the provisions of the Banking Act 1987. The scheme is aimed at protecting small deposits in a failed institution. All authorised institutions pay into the fund which is available to repay 75% of 'protected deposits'. These protected deposits are limited to £20,000 so that no depositor receives more than £15,000. Contributions into the fund are dependent on the size of each institution's deposit base. In addition, further calls may be made if the need arises.

When initially introduced, the scheme came under criticism from the clearing banks because they felt that they were underwriting the activities of their less sound competitors.

2.6 The Bank of England and National Debt Management

The government borrows from two main markets - the gilt-edged market and the Treasury bill market.

1. The Gilt-Edged Market

Issues of new stocks are in large tranches and are usually sold 'through the tap'. The Bank of England and official agencies take up most of the issue. The Bank of England then determines a 'tap' price which is usually slightly higher than market levels so that when there is a demand for the stock, the Bank of England will be prepared to sell at that price.

Because of considerable fluctuations in demand for stocks in the gilt-edged market, due to changing expectations as to future levels of interest rates, the Bank of England has since 1979, issued a number of new stocks by tender rather than by fixed price issue. Under this method of issue, the Bank of England fixes a minimum price at which offers will be accepted and tenders are invited at or above that price. Any stock not sold will be taken up by the Bank and it will be sold when the conditions are right.

A recent development in the market has been the introduction of 'gilt auctions' on a limited basis whereby new issues of gilts are auctioned off to the highest bidders.

The Bank intervenes in the market through the Government Broker and the authorities buy and sell stock according to their needs at that time. Because government stocks are an important part of the portfolios of financial institutions and other holders the whole structure of interest rates is affected by movements in the yields on government stocks.

The Bank considers three main objectives in its management of the gilt-edged market:

(a) To influence the level of interest rates and the money supply.

(b) To ensure that the market is healthy and active so that firm holders can be found for as much government debt as possible.

(c) To minimise the cost of servicing the debt.

An important problem for the Bank is the conflict between the first two objectives. If there is too much interference by the Bank in the gilt-edged market for the purposes of monetary control, investors may be loath to purchase gilts if they feel that the market is being manipulated for monetary control purposes.

Funding policy is conducted by the Bank of England and is essentially the substitution of long-dated debt for short-dated debt. Because the accumulated national debt is so large, with a number of issues maturing each year and others moving towards maturity, it is important that the public continues to hold debt so that little or no cash is paid out at maturity. If those stocks which have matured are not covered by new issues, the money supply would be inflated.

The Bank offers for sale comparatively long-dated stocks to the public. The proceeds are used to purchase stock which is nearing maturity so that little or no cash is paid out on maturity. The Bank always has at hand a small number of stocks, of differing maturity, to sell whenever market conditions permit. In practice, sales of stocks are not continual and the Bank may sometimes have to buy stocks to support a falling market.

Prior to 1971, the conduct of debt management was dominated by the support function. The authorities believed that institutions and other holders of debt would be loath to hold large quantities of stock if they felt the authorities were manipulating the market for monetary policy reasons. Thus, the Bank would intervene in the market to moderate fluctuations in price and yield. However, the Bank's conduct of debt management changed when the Competition and Credit Control arrangements were introduced in May 1971. The Bank declared that it would not, as a matter of course, support a falling market, although it reserved the right to do so. The effect of funding operations on banks is the same as open market operations.

Sales of gilts are more attractive to the public when interest rates are high (and prices are low). To finance government borrowing, interest rates are raised and then lowered. When new debt has to be sold, interest rates will be raised once again. This process has been nicknamed 'The Grand Old Duke of York' because interest rates are marched up and then down again.

2. The Treasury Bill Market

The residual borrowing needs of the government are met by sales of Treasury bills. Treasury bills mature 91 days after issue and are sold at a discount. They are issued in two ways - by weekly tender and by direct issue to government departments. The former are known as tender bills and the latter as tap bills.

Only banks, discount houses and money brokers are allowed to tender for Treasury bills and the minimum tender is £50,000. Every Friday, the amount of Treasury bills to be offered for tender on the next Friday is announced by the Bank of England. Tenders are submitted and tenderers are able to choose the day in the following week on which they will take up the bills. All tenders must be submitted to the Bank by 1 p.m. on Friday and at 3 p.m. the Bank announces the total amount of tenders, the amount allotted, the average rate of discount and the amount to be offered on the following Friday. Bills are allotted in descending order of price until the allotment has been exhausted.

Because the anticipated financial needs of the Exchequer are uncertain, there may be either a surplus or a shortage of bills. To overcome this problem the Bank creates tap bills which it sells to foreign central banks. In addition, when the Bank calls for special deposits from the banks, the funds will be used to take up these bills.

A recent development has been the introduction of 63 day bills with the aim of overcoming liquidity shortages which normally obtain during January.

The most active participants in the Treasury bill market are the discount houses and they undertake to cover the tender on a collective basis. Most of the bills are retained by the discount houses although some are sold to the banks. The Bank of England is a marginal provider of funds to the market when there is a shortage so that the Bank is in a monopoly position under such conditions. Thus, the Bank can control the market but because it is a monopolist it cannot control both price and quantity so that the Bank has to decide whether it wishes to control the supply of cash to the banking system or the general level of short-term interest rates. Bank of England intervention in the market will be considered further in Chapter 3.

2.7 The Financial Services Act 1986

This Act provides a new legal structure to regulate the carrying on of investment business. Its objective is to ensure that no investment business occurs unless authorised by regulatory authorities. The Securities and Investments Board (SIB) acts as the regulatory authority at the head of the system. There are also self-regulating organisations (SRO) and investment businesses may seek authorisation by being granted membership of a recognised SRO. The banks (and building societies) are affected by the so-called 'polarization' requirements. Under the Act, banks have had to decide whether to sell a wide range of financial services or alternatively to sell their own products only.

The passing of both the Financial Services Act 1986 and the Banking Act 1987 has resulted in some overlap between the responsibilities of the Bank of England and the SROs.

2.8 Summary

1. Financial intermediaries channel funds from lenders to borrowers. Financial intermediation usually entails the transformation of risk and maturity characteristics.
2. Deposit-taking institutions operate by taking short-term deposits which are used to lend for longer terms or to buy other long-term assets. Life insurance companies, pension funds, unit trusts and investment trust companies attract long-term funds which enables them to provide long-term finance.
3. Commercial banks can be classified according to whether they are retail or wholesale banks.
4. Retail banks are involved in cash handling, money transmission and financial intermediation.
5. Wholesale banks deal in deposits and loans which are for large amounts and which are often fixed for definite periods (term deposits and term loans) and much of their business is conducted in foreign currencies.
6. The non-bank financial intermediaries can be divided into finance houses, the National Savings Bank and building societies.
7. Building societies are specialised savings banks. The Building Societies Act 1986 enables the building societies to offer a wide range of financial services.
8. The Bank of England performs a number of functions:
   (a) Banker to the Government; the banks and other financial institutions; overseas central banks and international organisations; and to private sector customers and its staff.
   (b) The regulation of the note issue.
   (c) Lender of last resort.
   (d) Registrar of government stocks.
   (e) Management of the Exchange Equalisation Account.
   (f) Implementation of monetary policy.
   (g) Supervision of the financial system.
9. The Bank of England borrows from two main markets - the gilt-edged market and the Treasury bill market.

Questions

1.* What is meant by the term 'financial intermediary'? To what extent are banks the principal financial intermediaries? Illustrate your answer by reference to one particular country.

2. (a) Using the figures shown below as a guide, assess the role of the UK banks in channelling finance for trade and industry. [18]
(b) What other figures are needed in order to prepare a complete assessment of the adequacy of bank finance for trade and industry?[7]

UK Banking Sector (Sterling) 31 March 1979

	Deposits from UK residents	*Lending to UK residents (including holdings of securities issued by public and private sectors)*
	£m	£m
Public Sector		
Central government	518	6,128
Local authorities	241	4,881
Public corporations	383	600
Private Sector		
Industrial and commercial companies	11,133	24,169
Personal sector	24,901	11,259
Other financial institutions	5,357	3,534
	42,533	50,571

NOTE: the discrepancy between the two columns is due to the omission of non-deposit liabilities, such as capital and reserves, and to the omission of data relating to overseas residents.

3.* What is meant by liquidity and why does a commercial bank need it? How and to what extent does a commercial bank provide for liquidity in the use of the deposits lodged with it?

4. (a) Explain the basic role of financial intermediaries. (10)

(b) Classify the main types of financial intermediary in the United Kingdom according to whether their liabilities are included in official measures of the money supply. (15)

5. Explain why and how the existence of financial intermediaries benefits both borrowers and lenders. Illustrate your answer by reference to the main activities of commercial banks and building societies.

6. (a) What changes have occurred since 1970 in the functions and operations of the Bank of England? (15)

   (b) Has the bank lost some of its independence during this period? Give reasons for your answer. (10)

7. Is it essential for a country to have a central bank?

8. (a) What do you understand by the terms 'retail' and 'wholesale' as applied to financial transactions? (7)

   (b) Compare and contrast the activities of the clearing banks and the building societies in:
   (i) the retail market;
   (ii) the wholesale market. (18)

9. 'Recent developments have led to a convergence between the activities of the clearing banks and the building societies, to the point where they are now identical as financial institutions.' Discuss.

10. (a) Explain why each of the following is important to a commercial bank:
    (i) capital adequacy;
    (ii) liquidity;
    (iii) profitability.

    (b) With reference to the structure and components of a bank's balance sheet, discuss how a bank provides for capital adequacy, liquidity and profitability.

CHAPTER 3

U.K. Financial Markets

3.1 The Nature and Functions of the Money Market

In every banking system, there must be a money market to enable banks to adjust their day-to-day liquidity positions. Until about 1955, there was only one money market in London, the discount market. However, since then, a *parallel* or *secondary* money market has emerged alongside the secondary banking system, with the discount market catering for the needs of retail banks and the parallel market for the secondary banks. For some time these two markets were quite separate although the secondary banks were occasionally active in the discount markets and the discount houses widened their activities to the parallel markets. After the introduction of the Competition and Credit Control measures in 1971, these two markets were brought closer together. However, there are still important differences between the two markets. The discount market has a lender of last resort whilst the parallel money market does not and lending in the discount market is normally secured, whilst lending on the parallel market is unsecured.

3.2.1 The Discount Market

The participants in the discount market are the members of the London Discount Market Association. The origins of the market can be traced back to the early nineteenth century. At that time the country banks would normally discount their customer's bills but if they were short of funds they would send the bills to London, so that the bill brokers could place the bills with those banks which were more liquid. Thus, the country banks were able to adjust their liquidity position by the purchase and sale of these bills. During the 1820s, the bill brokers began to deal as principals financing their book of bills by using their own funds and by borrowing from the banks against security. In the latter half of the nineteenth century, the bill of exchange became important in foreign trade and the discounting of these bills became an important part of the discount houses' business. The 'bill on London' became less important after the First World War but about the same time the government began to make greater use of the Treasury bill to cover its short-term financing and the discount houses supplemented their business by organising a secondary market for these bills. In the 1960s and the 1970s the bill of exchange once again became important in both domestic and international trade and the discounting of these bills has assumed some of its old importance to the discount houses. In addition, they have widened their activities to the parallel money market, acting as dealers in the sterling and dollar certificates of deposit markets and in local authority negotiable bonds ('yearlings'). They are also active in the inter-bank market.

3.2.2 Liabilities and Assets of the Discount Market

Table 3.1 shows the liabilities and assets of the discount market as at 31st December 1987 which comprises the eight discount houses that are members of the London Discount Market Association.

The liabilities of the discount market consist of borrowed funds, most of which is call and overnight money which is the cheapest source of funds for the discount houses. This money, as the name suggests, can be withdrawn by the banks either on demand or at very short notice, so enabling the banks to adjust their day-to-day liquidity needs. The banks protect themselves by requesting security which not only covers the amount of the loan but also provides a margin of security in excess of the discount houses' borrowing. The reason for the margin is twofold; in the first place the banks are protected against a reduction in the capital value of the security and in the second, it ensures that the discount houses conduct their business with caution because the margin has to be provided out of their own resources.

The main assets of the discount market are other sterling bills (mainly commercial bills), certificates of deposit, Treasury bills, local authority securities and British government stocks. In 1959, the Radcliffe Report referred to the 'vestigial' commercial bill business of the discount houses but since then their holdings of these bills has risen fairly rapidly and they now account for about half of their total sterling assets. The discount houses hold sterling certificates of deposits in which they make a market. The discount houses also hold a large amount of British government stocks. They act as market makers in the short-end of the gilt-edged market (up to five years). Their market making business helps to even out fluctuations in the gilt-edged market by buying when prices are falling and selling when prices are rising. Their opportunity for making dealing profits in the market was increased after the introduction of Competition and Credit Control in 1971 when the authorities announced that they would not support the market although they reserved the right to do so.

Table 3.1 Discount Market as at December 31, 1987

	£ million		%
Liabilities: borrowed funds			
Sterling:			
Money at call and overnight	9,950		
Other borrowed funds	1,178		
		11,128	95.9
Other currency liabilities		184	1.6
Capital and other liabilities		297	2.5
Total Liabilities		11,609	100.0
Sterling assets			
Cash ratio deposits with the Bank of England	10		
Treasury bills	261		
Local authority and other public sector bills	132		
Other bills	5,219		
Loans to U.K. monetary sector	525		
UK monetary sector CDs	3,705		
Building society CDs and time deposits	747		
UK local authorities	43		
Funds lent to other U.K.	260		
Funds lent overseas	32		
British government stocks	33		
Local authorities	2		
Other investments	400		
Other sterling assets	58		
Total Sterling Assets		11,427	98.4
Other currency assets:			
CDs	38		
Bills	25		
Other	119		
		182	1.6
Total assets		11,609	100.0

(Source: Bank of England Quarterly Bulletin - February 1988)

The local authority securities consist of yearling bonds, local authority stocks and local authority bills. Their sterling assets also include building society CDs and time deposits. These amounted to £747 million at 31 December 1987 and represented about 6.5% of their total assets.

Their holdings of Treasury bills account for approximately 2% of their total assets and this reflects the decline in the importance of Treasury bills although more recently their holdings have risen. Under the monetary control arrangements which took effect on August 20th 1981, those discount houses which have eligible liabilities which average £10 million or more are required to hold cash deposits equivalent to 0.45% of their eligible liabilities with the Bank of England.

The discount houses maintain a small portfolio of assets and liabilities in currencies other than sterling. Their other currency assets consist in the main of dollar certificates of deposit in which the discount houses make a market.

3.2.3 Bank of England Intervention

The Bank of England is necessarily involved in the day-to-day operations in the London discount market because as we have already noted, the Bank acts as a banker to both the Government and the banks. Each day the banks make their final cash settlements in respect of transactions within the banking system (such as cheque clearance) and transactions between the Bank and the banking system. These are settled by the accounts that the banks maintain at the Bank of England and most of the flows of funds are accounted for by the London clearing banks. The clearing banks have to ensure that they always have sufficient funds at the Bank to cover these settlements.

The Bank is involved in the flow of funds between the Government and the clearing banks because it is a banker to both of them. Because of the size of Government transactions with the non-bank private sector, the daily net flow of funds between the Bank and the banks may be substantial. Without Bank of England intervention a net flow of funds from the banks to the Government would result in a fall in bankers' deposits at the Bank, whilst a net flow from the Government to the banks would result in a rise in bankers' deposits. The Bank can act to smooth out these flows by operating in the discount market. These operations are conducted in the main through the intermediation of the discount houses and the rates of interest at which the Bank deals in the market will influence the general level of interest rates.

Since 1980, the Bank's money market operations have changed and in order that we can assess these changes we must first of all see how the Bank operated prior to that date. The Bank operated on the basis that the banks had portfolios of government debt sufficiently large to enable it to alleviate any cash shortages in the money market by the purchase of Treasury bills and local authority bills. If the shortage of cash in the market was so great that the banks' holdings of Treasury and local authority bills were reduced substantially, the Bank would buy eligible bank bills. Purchases of bills were made through the Bank's bill broker in the market, the discount house of Seccombe, Marshall and Campion, known as the 'special buyer', the 'hidden hand' or the 'back door'. The bill broker could be instructed to purchase bills from the discount houses (called 'direct help') or from the banks (called 'indirect help').

Under this system, if the banks were short of cash, they could withdraw their money at call and short notice from the discount houses or they could sell liquid assets such as Treasury and local authority bills, commercial bills and certificates of deposit to the discount houses. The discount houses, if short of cash, could sell bills to the Bank to provide them with the required amount of cash. Sometimes assistance was provided by the Bank granting a loan. This method was first used in June 1966. These loans were granted on an overnight basis, although longer periods have been used. Such loans were granted against the security of Treasury bills, local authority bills, eligible bank bills or short-dated British government securities. Prior to the introduction of the new monetary control arrangements in 1981, eligible bank bills were bills which were accepted by a major British or Commonwealth bank, however, the list has now been widened to include some foreign-owned banks. Eligible bills are those bills which are acceptable to the Bank either for purchase or as security for a loan.

If the banks had surplus cash, they would deposit it with the discount houses. If the Bank wished to remove this surplus cash it would sell Treasury bills to the discount houses and sometimes to the banks themselves.

The Bank's operations in the money market were at rates which were based on the previous week's Treasury bill tender. On the other hand, any lending by the Bank was in the main at minimum lending rate (Bank rate prior to 1972), which was a penal rate of interest to the discount houses.

The Bank of England's aim in the money market was to maintain a slight shortage of cash and this enabled it to influence interest rates. It could do so because the Bank would be a monopolist in this situation and could therefore control either price or quantity but not both. The amount of Treasury bills on offer each week was set at a level which ensured that there was a slight cash shortage. All bills were taken up because of the discount houses' agreement to underwrite the tender (this agreement is still operative). However, the Bank was not always able to ensure that there were cash shortages because successful bidders for Treasury bills could choose the days in the following week in which the bills would be taken up. Even though the market need not have required assistance each day the bank was still able to exert control over the structure of short-term interest rates.

During the period to October 1980, other instruments were used to reinforce MLR as a long-term instrument of monetary control and these included the special deposits scheme (first introduced in 1960), the reserve asset ratio (introduced in 1971 and lapsed in 1981) and the supplementary special deposits scheme (used periodically between 1973-80). Thus, a call for special or supplementary special deposits took cash out of the banking system whilst the reserve asset ratio effectively tied up certain short-term assets so that they could not be used to meet cash shortages.

During the 1970s, interest rates became more volatile and increased attention was directed at controlling the money supply. Thus, greater flexibility was required in the management of short-term interest rates.

In addition, there were continual shortages of cash in the market which resulted from the authorities giving greater attention to the control of the money supply at the same time that bank lending to the private sector was growing rapidly. To reduce monetary growth the Bank sold large amounts of government debt to the non-bank private sector which created cash shortages in the market. To overcome this problem the Bank initially reduced the amount of Treasury bills on offer at the weekly tender. However, the shortages of cash were so great that it meant that at times the Bank was buying Treasury bills at a faster rate than they were being issued which meant that the amount of Treasury bills held by the banks fell. This forced the Bank to deal increasingly in eligible bank bills and to increase its lending. During 1980, these activities were supplemented by providing the banks with sale and repurchase arrangements in gilts.

Because of these problems the authorities reviewed the methods of controlling the money supply and they issued the consultative paper 'Monetary control' in March 1980 followed by 'Monetary control - next steps' in March 1981 and 'Monetary control - provisions' which took effect on 20th August 1981 (considered in Chapter 4).

Under the 1981 monetary control arrangements the Bank's dealing practices in the money market have changed. The Bank no longer posts a minimum lending rate although the authorities reserve the right to announce in advance the minimum rate that would apply to any future lending by the Bank. In addition, the Bank relies mainly on open market operations rather than on direct lending with a view to keeping interest rates at the very short end of the market within an undisclosed band. This band is moved from time to time. The Bank no longer quotes its dealing rates in advance but it makes public the rate at which it has dealt in the market.

The Bank may under exceptional circumstances be willing to lend to the discount houses. Such circumstances include an extremely large and unexpected cash shortage or when the Bank wishes to raise interest rates and it feels that its dealings in the market will not lead to a rise in interest rates quickly enough. In the latter case, the Bank may force the discount houses to borrow when they have a cash shortage by stopping or reducing its dealings in bills. The rate at which it lends will be set so as to achieve the higher level of rates required.

Table 3.2 shows the Bank's dealings in the money markets on December 22, 1987.

It can be seen from Table 3.2 that outright purchases are shown according to maturity bands. Band 1 equals up to 14 days; band 2 equals 15 to 33 days; band 3 equals 34 to 63 days; and band 4 equals 64 to 91 days. On a few occasions the Bank sells Treasury bills to the market in order to mop up surplus funds. Since August 1983, the Bank of England has given details of late assistance which relate to late transactions in bills and/or market lending. For example, on 22 December 1987, late assistance amounted to £365 million. Occasionally the Bank enters into purchase and resale agreements and these usually involve a combination of Treasury bills, local authority bills or eligible bank bills. The Bank of England also occasionally lends directly. For example, on 4 November 1987, the Bank lent £625 million at a rate of interest of 9% for repayment on November 5-9th.

Table 3.2 Official Operations in the Money Markets

(Amounts in £ millions: rates per cent)

Outright purchases December 22, 1987:

	Treasury bills		Local authority bills		Bank bills	
Band	Amount	Rates	Amount	Rates	Amount	Rates
1	2	$8^3/_8$			329	$8^3/_8$
2						
3					28	$8^3/_8$
4			2	$8^3/_8$	51	$8^3/_8$

(Source: Bank of England Quarterly Bulletin - February 1988)

Although the Bank of England deals mainly with the discount houses, more recently the Bank has also increasingly dealt with other institutions. Indeed purchase and resale agreements between the Bank and the commercial banks have become a fairly common occurrence particularly at those times when large tax payments are made to the Government. The Bank also provides borrowing facilities for the clearing banks when conditions in the money market warrant it.

Because the Bank of England can control interest rates at the very short end of the market, it is able to influence the structure of interest rates in both the discount market and the parallel money market. The rates in the inter-bank market play an important role in the setting of bank base rates and in particular the three-month London Inter-bank Offered Rate (LIBOR) has since the 1970s represented the marginal cost of funds to the banks. Changes in LIBOR exert a strong influence on the level of bank base rates. In addition, banks will also alter their base rates if their customers engage in arbitrage or 'roundtripping' (see Chapter 5).

The Bank of England provides information relating to the cash position of the money market. The factors which affect the markets' cash position includes the CGBR, net sales of central government debt (which includes gilt-edged stocks, national savings and certificates of tax deposit), changes in the currency circulation and reserves. The Bank of England undertakes official offsetting operations in commercial bills, Treasury bills and purchase and resale agreements in securities. Table 3.3 below shows the factors which influenced the cash position of the money market for the period January-December 1987.

Table 3.3 Factors Affecting the Market's Cash Position, January - December 1987 (Calender months) £billions; not seasonally adjusted

(Increase in the market's cash +)

Factors affecting the market's cash position	
CGBR (+)	+4.0
Net sales (-) of central government debt (a)	-6.5
Currency circulation (increase -)	-1.1
Reserves	+12.4
Other	-1.0
TOTAL (A)	+7.8
Official offsetting operations	
Net increase (+) in Bank's commercial bills (b)	-5.6
Net increase (-) in Treasury bills in market	-2.2
Securities (c) acquired (+) under sale and repurchase agreements with banks	-
Other	-0.1
TOTAL (B)	-7.9
Changes in bankers' operational balances at the Bank (= A + B)	-0.1

(a) Other than Treasury bills.

(b) By the Issue and Banking Departments of the Bank of England.

(c) Gilt-edged stocks and promissory notes related to guaranteed export credit and shipbuilding paper.

(Source: Bank of England Quarterly Bulletin - February 1988)

The figures above show that official assistance was provided in the main by purchases of commercial bills and a net increase in Treasury bills in the market.

During 1985, the Bank of England announced that it proposed to transfer the conduct of its money market operations to a dealing room located inside the Bank of England. This was the result of a bid being made by Citicorp International Bank Ltd for the shares of Seccombe, Marshall & Campion plc. The transfer was made with effect from the beginning of 1986 so that the Bank of England now intervenes directly in the money market.

3.2.4 Control of the Discount Market

When the Competition and Credit Control measures were introduced in September 1971, the Bank of England stated that it would be prepared to continue to act as a lender of last resort to the discount market provided that the market continued to cover the weekly Treasury bill tender. In addition, the Bank of England sought agreement from the discount market that they would hold a minimum of 50% of their funds in public sector debt but this requirement was removed in July, 1973. Until 7th May 1981, credit control was applied through a limit on each house's aggregate holdings of 'undefined assets' to a maximum of twenty times its capital and reserves. The maximum was raised with effect from that date to twenty-fives times capital and reserves. Undefined assets consisted of assets other than:

1. balances at the Bank of England;
2. U.K. and Northern Ireland Treasury bills;
3. government stocks with not more than 5 years to final maturity;
4. local authority stocks with not more than 5 years to final maturity;
5. local authority and other public boards' bills eligible at the Bank;
6. local authority negotiable bonds;
7. bank bills drawn by nationalised industries under specific government guarantee.

New arrangements for the prudential supervision of the discount market were set out by the Bank of England in June 1982. The Bank introduced a multiplier limiting the 'adjusted total book' to 40 times a house's capital base.

The discount houses now comply with the monetary control arrangements set out in 'Monetary control-provisions' introduced on August 20th, 1981 (see Chapter 4).

3.2.5 The Role of the Discount Houses

Discount houses are important for the following reasons:

1. They act as a buffer between the commercial banks and the Bank of England and aid the authorities in influencing interest rates.
2. They undertake to cover the weekly Treasury bill issue.
3. They channel finance to the public sector by using their short-term funds to invest in public sector debt.
4. They enable banks to adjust their liquidity needs and to obtain a satisfactory return on their surplus cash which might otherwise have been lying idle.
5. They provide short-term finance to the private sector by discounting bills of exchange.
6. They make a secondary market in certificates of deposit and local authority yearling bonds.

3.3.1 The Parallel Money Market

The various markets which make up the parallel or secondary money market are local authority, inter-bank, certificate of deposit, finance house, inter-company and eurocurrency.

Transactions in the parallel money market are unsecured with lenders relying on the good name of the borrower. However, lenders get some measure of protection by placing a limit on the amount that they lend to each 'name'. There are a number of deposit brokers operating in the various markets and they are willing to quote rates on various maturities, earning commission on completed deals. The distinction can be made between sterling and eurocurrency markets.

3.3.2 Sterling Markets

1. Local Authority Money Market

This market is the oldest of the parallel money markets. It originated in 1955 because local authorities were stopped by the government from borrowing at will from the Public Works Loans Board, thereby forcing them to go to the market to cover their short-term finance requirements. It was not long before some secondary banks paid market rates of interest for deposits and then lent them to local authorities seeking finance. The market is divided into a number of sub-markets. Local authority deposits range from two days up to three hundred and sixty-four days but deposits with maturities of up to one week predominate. The other main sub-markets include local authority yearling bonds in which the discount houses make a secondary market and local authority bills. The latter may only be issued by large local authorities that have the necessary legal powers to do so. Local authorities issue three-month and six-month bills and discount houses deal in them because most are eligible for re-discount at the Bank of England.

2. Inter-bank

The inter-bank market is the largest of the sterling secondary money markets. The main participants in the inter-bank market are banks but outsiders may place deposits in the market through deposit brokers. Dealings on this market are usually for large amounts ranging from a minimum of £250,000 up to £1 million or more. Maturities range from call or overnight up to one year, although most dealing is for overnight and very short-term funds. Most deals are negotiated directly between the banks. Since the introduction of the Competition and Credit Control measures in 1971, the clearing banks have become very active in this market.

The key rates in the parallel market are those on the inter-bank market, which since the 1970s have represented the cost of money in London because they are freely determined by market forces. Interest rates charged on overdraft lending to selected company customers have increasingly been linked to the three months LIBOR (London Inter-Bank Offered Rate) and rollover terms on loans have also been related to this rate. LIBOR is also used in the same way in the euromarkets in respect of rollover credits and floating rate bonds.

3. Certificate of Deposit

A certificate of deposit (CD) is issued by a bank certifying that it has received a deposit for a fixed term at a fixed or floating rate of interest. Sterling CDs were first issued in 1968 and are issued in multiples of £10,000 from a minimum of £50,000 up to a maximum of £500,000 and very occasionally £1 million. They are issued for terms ranging from three months up to five years. Unlike Treasury, local authority and commercial bills which are issued at a discount, CDs are issued at par value and interest is paid until maturity. The bulk of sterling CDs are held by the banks and discount houses but other financial institutions such as building societies and non-financial companies also hold them. The advantage of CDs over ordinary bank deposits is that they are negotiable. Because CDs are issued in bearer form, it is essential that there should be a secondary market in which depositors are able to sell their certificates if they need their deposit before maturity. The secondary market is provided by the discount houses for sterling CDs. However, other dealers in the market include a small number of accepting houses.

There are two main attractions to issuing banks. Firstly, depositors are more likely to enter into longer-term deposits if they know that they can sell their CDs in the secondary market. Secondly, CDs can be used by issuing banks to match their term loans. The main disadvantage to the holder of a CD is the risk of capital loss resulting from an increase in interest rates.

4. Finance House

This is a small market in which banks are the main lenders, although insurance companies, pension funds, non-financial companies and individuals also provide funds for the finance houses. Deposits are placed overnight or for terms of three months and six months. Since the recognition of some of the larger finance houses as banks, the finance house market has contracted greatly because these houses are able to borrow on the inter-bank market.

5. Inter-company

This market developed in the late 1960s as a result of the tight credit conditions imposed by the authorities from about 1965 onwards. A market developed where those companies with surplus funds could lend directly to those companies which were short of funds. Thus, the market developed to circumvent the lending ceilings imposed on the banks. The term 'inter-company' is rather a misnomer because the main lenders are banks, although companies and other financial institutions also provide funds. It is generally thought that in the last few years deposits outstanding have been fairly small.

3.3.3 Eurocurrency Market

The eurocurrency market consists of a number of markets - deposits from outside the market, inter-bank deposits, dollar CDs, euroacceptances (i.e. acceptance credits denominated in U.S. dollars) and eurodollar commercial paper. Although much eurocurrency business is transacted in London, the eurocurrency market is essentially an international market. The market is highly competitive and it is not subject to any controls from monetary authorities (see Chapter 10).

The inter-bank market in both sterling and other currencies has grown rapidly since its beginnings in the early 1960s. At the end of 1980 net foreign currency lending to the inter-bank market by banks in the U.K. reached $60.8 billions. In the inter-bank eurocurrency market, banks borrow unsecured large sums for periods ranging from overnight up to five years although most deals are for periods of up to six months.

Dollar CDs were first issued in New York in 1961 and were introduced into London by the First National City Bank in 1966. The secondary market is provided by the discount houses for dollar CDs. However, other dealers in the dollar CD market include a small number of branches of U.S. and Canadian security houses. The bulk of dollar CDs are held by banks overseas and other overseas holders.

3.4 The Capital Market

The capital market in London comprises the Stock Exchange and the New Issue Market (the international capital market is considered in Chapter 10). When an individual purchases a good or service, he can either use his savings or borrow money from relatives, friends, a bank, or a finance house for example. Similarly, smaller businesses may be able to buy equipment by using their retained profits or by borrowing from a bank or finance house. However, the capital expenditure of large companies is often greater than the cash generated by their operations or that raised from private sources. These companies will raise money from the general public. The general public are asked to lend money or to take a share in the business in exchange for the right to participate in the future profits of the company. The company does this by offering loan capital or shares through the Stock Exchange.

Similarly, the amount spent by government, both central and local on the provision of services such as transport, education and health may be greater than revenue obtained from taxation or rates income. The central government, local authorities and nationalised industries can borrow from the general public through the Stock Exchange. Thus, the government and industry both use the Stock Exchange to tap the nation's savings.

The Stock Exchange is important to the investor because it is also a market for the buying and selling of existing shares and loan stocks. If an investor requires the repayment of his loan or recover the cash invested in shares, the money has probably been tied up in plant and equipment or a factory so that the company will not be able to repay him. However, the investor can sell his loan stocks and shares on the Stock Exchange to another investor. Without the Stock Exchange, loan stocks and shares would not be marketable and investors would be loath to provide companies with their savings.

The largest component of Stock Exchange trading is accounted for by the gilt-edged market which comprises British government and government guaranteed stocks, local authority stocks, stocks issued by public boards and Commonwealth governments. All gilt-edged stocks are issued in sterling. The gilt-edged market can be sub-divided into *shorts*, *mediums*, *longs*, and *undated*. Short-dated stocks are those with up to five years to redemption, medium-dated stocks have maturities of between 5 and 15 years, long-dated stocks have lives of over 15 years and undated stocks are irredeemable. The Bank of England is responsible for the issue of new government stock and these are offered to the public. Issues of British government stocks are not underwritten. If all the stock on offer has not been taken up then the unsold stock is taken up by the Issue Department of the Bank of England. This stock is then sold through the *tap*, that is, it is sold by the Government Broker who responds to bids from the gilt-edged market makers. More recently gilts have been sold by way of gilt auctions.

Banks are involved in new issues, they give advice to companies on such matters as rights issues, mergers, takeovers, and the raising of funds on the international money and capital markets. In recent years they have been allowed to take a stake in stockbroking and stockjobbing which will allow them to provide their customers with a comprehensive package of financial and investment services.

Since mid-1983 radical reforms on the Stock Exchange gathered pace. These reforms resulted from a decision to abolish minimum scales of commission on transactions in securities. This decision was taken in exchange for the abandonment by the Government of a Restrictive Trade Practices Court case brought by the Office of Fair Trading against the Stock Exchange.

The decision to introduce negotiated commissions by end-1986, commonly known as the 'Big Bang', resulted in the setting up of alliances between Stock Exchange firms and outside institutions. This was because the increase in competitive pressures meant that Stock Exchange firms required more capital. Buyers were initially limited to a stake of 29.9% but the rules were subsequently relaxed to enable institutions to take full control. Such alliances have proved attractive for commercial banks because it enables them to offer an even wider range of financial and investment services.

Other changes introduced in 1986 included the adoption of a radical new system for share dealings. This system removes the traditional boundaries between stockbrokers and market makers, so that firms are now dual capacity broker-dealers (as distinct from the single-capacity system where stockbrokers and market makers were completely separate). However, firms may, if they wish, continue to act either as brokers or as market makers.

The reform of the Stock Exchange has also led to changes in the operation of the gilt-edged market. The Bank of England has responsibility for supervising the market and acting for the government. Gilt-edged stocks are issued by the Bank of England on behalf of the Government. The link between the Bank of England and the Stock Exchange is the Government Broker who is employed by the Bank of England. The Government Broker supervises the Bank of England's own dealing room which deals with firms nominated as Gilt-Edged Market Makers (GEMMS). GEMMS make continuous and effective bid and ask prices on demand, in all trading conditions to other members of the Stock Exchange and to their outside clients. Because the market is based on 'cash' settlement, then next day delivery is facilitated by the existence of Stock Exchange Money Brokers (SEMBS) who 'lend' stock to GEMMS to satisfy their immediate requirements for repayment at a later date. In addition, there are inter-dealer brokers (IDBs) which enable GEMMS to unwind large amounts of stock without the need to expose their book. The gilts market continues to form part of the Stock Exchange.

3.5 Summary

1. Money markets enable banks to adjust their day-to-day liquidity positions.
2. The London money market comprises the discount market and the parallel or secondary money market.
3. The discount market has a lender of last resort and lending is normally secured.
4. The parallel money market does not have a lender of last resort and lending is unsecured.
5. The liabilities of the discount market consist of borrowed funds, the bulk of which is call and overnight money.
6. Their assets include; sterling bills; CDs; local authority securities, Treasury bills; and British government stocks.
7. The Bank of England is involved in the day-to-day operations in the London discount market.
8. Under the 1981 monetary control arrangements the Bank of England changed its dealing practices in the money market.
9. The parallel money market comprises the following markets; local authority; inter-bank; CD; finance house; inter-company; and

eurocurrency.

10. The capital market in London comprises the Stock Exchange and the New Issue Market.
11. The capital market provides long-term funds for companies and government.

Questions

1. Describe the present role and assess the significance of the following in the U.K. banking system;
   (a) the discount market;
   (b) the interbank market.

2.* Describe the so-called 'parallel' sterling money markets in London.

3.* What assets are held by London discount houses today and why?

4. Outline the ways in which the Bank of England carries out its role as;
   (a) banker to the government;
   (b) banker to the banks;
   (c) lender of last resort to the banking system.

5. (a) Describe in detail the way in which the Bank of England currently seeks to influence interest rates in the money markets.

   (b) To what extent do the Bank's operations influence changes in commercial banks' base rates?

6. (a) What attributes must an asset possess in order to be considered liquid?

   (b) To what extent do the following possess the attributes referred to in (a) necessary for them to be considered liquid:
   1. Treasury bills;
   2. gilt-edged stock;
   3. banknotes;
   4. building society term shares;
   5. certificates of deposit issued by a commercial bank?

   (c) Classify the assets set out in (b) above according to whether they are included in measures of the money stock in the U.K.

7. To what extent is it now valid or useful to distinguish between the discount and parallel money markets in London.

8. (a) How does a commercial bank provide for liquidity? (13)

   (b) Explain in detail how the Bank of England ensures that there is always adequate liquidity in the banking system. (12)

9. (a) What are the basic benefits arising from financial intermediation? (10)

   (b) What do you understand by the term 'disintermediation'?(5)

   (c) Outline the clearing banks' response to:
   (i) challenges from the building societies in the area of financial intermediation;
   (ii) challenges from developments in the UK capital markets in the area of disintermediation. (10)

10. (a) Discuss the role of the parallel sterling money markets in London. (15)

    (b) Is it still valid to distinguish the parallel markets from the discount market? (10)

11. Discuss the significance of the following in the UK financial system:
    (a) the inter-bank market; (9)
    (b) commercial (eligible) bank bills; (8)
    (c) the Stock Exchange, including reference to the changes introduced by 'Big Bang'. (8)

CHAPTER 4

The Money Supply and Demand for Money

4.1.1 Money as an Economic Indicator

Money is important, not only because of the functions that it fulfils but also because of its effect on both output and prices. However, as we shall see in the following sections, there is considerable disagreement among economists as to the mechanism by which money affects output and prices. Despite this disagreement money is an important indicator of what is happening in the economy and in the financial system.

The use of money as an indicator has its limitations. The importance of being able to define money lies in the fact that the different definitions may all be used as indicators of what is happening in the financial system and in the economy. However, once the monetary authorities place a target rate of growth on a definition of money then its use as an indicator ceases.This is because its growth will be determined by supply which the government attempts to control rather than by demand. This observation was made by Goodhart, an economic adviser at the Bank of England, and it has become known as 'Goodhart's Law' which states that 'any observed statistical regularity will tend to collapse once pressure is placed upon it for control purposes'.

4.1.2 The Process of Credit Creation

Money in a modern economy takes the form of cash and bank deposits so that we can consider the creation of money by looking at each of these in turn.

4.1.3 Cash

One of the important functions of a central bank is to regulate the amount of cash in the economy. It is the central bank which normally produces cash and it is brought into circulation by the banks who purchase it from the central bank. The banks pay for the cash with their deposits at the central bank. The cash goes into circulation with the general public when the customers of the banks demand repayment of their deposits in the form of cash. Central banks generally do not directly control the volume of cash in circulation with the public as part of their monetary policy. We saw in Chapter 1 that the monetary policy implication of this is that if the monetary authorities in more developed countries wish to control the supply of money, control can be directed at bank deposits leaving the note issue to find its own level. Thus, as far as monetary policy is concerned, the process by which bank deposits are created is very important.

4.1.4 Bank Deposits

For the purposes of the following analysis we will assume that the bank deposits created are money, i.e. they would be included in the monetary authorities' definition of money. Before we enquire into the process of bank deposit creation it is important to note that not all customers of a bank require to be paid in cash so that they in turn can settle in cash. Generally payments are effected by the use of bank deposits so that a bank's balance sheet will not show cash balances equal to the amount of customer deposits. Indeed, the actual amounts of cash held by banks is relatively small compared to total deposits.

Deposits are created in the following ways:

(a) When a bank receives a cash deposit from its customer

Let us suppose bank X receives a cash deposit of £100. The bank will have £100 of cash in its till (an asset) and a customer deposit of £100 (a liability). Banks use their deposits in effect to buy assets so that a bank's total liabilities must always be equal to its total assets. In other words, the general principles of double-entry book-keeping apply - the total of credits (liabilities) must be equal to the total of debits (assets) so that the financial system can be viewed as a system of credits and debits. We can illustrate the effect of the cash deposit on bank X by drawing up a balance sheet which is a statement of assets and liabilities as follows:

Bank X's balance sheet

Liabilities	£	*Assets*	£
Deposit	100	Cash	100

(b) When a bank grants a loan to a customer

In this case the customer's current account will be credited (i.e. the bank's deposits increased) and a loan account debited (i.e. the bank's assets increased). We can illustrate this by the following example. Let us suppose that bank X lends £500 to a customer, bank X's balance sheet (including the transaction in (a) above) would be as follows:

Bank X's balance sheet

Liabilities	£	*Assets*	£
Deposits	600	Cash	100
		Loan	500
	600		600

Thus, bank deposits (i.e. money) have been created to a greater extent than the bank's holdings of cash. In other words the bank has obtained an income-earning asset (the loan) for a book-entry and such book-entries are money. An increase in bank lending, therefore, leads to an increase in deposits.

(c) When the bank purchases an investment

Let us assume that bank X buys an investment from a customer for £100. The customer's account is credited and an investment account is debited so that once again deposits have increased. The balance sheet including previous transactions will be as follows:

Bank X's balance sheet

Liabilities	£	*Assets*	£
Deposits	700	Cash	100
		Investment	100
		Loan	500
	700		700

So far we have considered one bank in isolation but the introduction of other banks will not affect our argument in any material way. For example, let us suppose that there are two banks Y and Z and bank Z buys an investment from a customer of bank Y for £100. Each bank will maintain working balances (i.e. a current account) at the Bank of England so that bank Z will use its working balance at the Bank of England to pay for the investment. Thus, bank Y's customer will receive a cheque for £100 from bank Z and this will be deposited so that bank Y's deposits will increase by £100. Bank Y pays the cheque into its account at the Bank of England so that the balance sheet of bank Y shows an increase in its liabilities (deposits) of £100 and an increase in its assets (balances at the Bank of England) of £100. On the other hand, bank Z's balances at the Bank of England are reduced and its investments increased with no effect on its deposits. However, the combined balance sheets of the two banks show that deposits have risen by £100 and investments have risen by £100.

Bank Y's balance sheet

Liabilities	£	*Assets*	£
Deposits	+100	Balances at the Bank of England	+100

Bank Z's balance sheet

Liabilities	£	*Assets*	£
		Balances at the Bank of England	-100
		Investments	+100

Combined balance sheet of banks Y and Z

Liabilities	£	*Assets*	£
Deposits	+100	Investments	+100

4.1.5 The Credit Creation Multiplier

We saw in the previous section that banks create money by creating liabilities against themselves. We can examine the credit creation multiplier by considering a simplified system. Let us assume that there is only one bank in the economy and the bank has found from experience that it only needs to maintain cash reserves of 10% of deposits to meet demands for withdrawals in cash. Let us further assume that all money lent by the bank is redeposited in the bank.

First stage

Let us assume that the bank receives a deposit for £1,000. The bank will retain £100 as a reserve.

Second stage

The bank lends out £900 – in other words, the bank purchases an asset.

Third stage

On the assumption that the £900 is redeposited, the bank will be able to lend £810, keeping £90 as a reserve, and so on.

The total amount of credit created can be calculated by using the following formula:

$$\text{total deposits created} = \frac{\text{new reserves}}{\text{percentage reserve ratio}}$$

In our example above:

$$\text{total deposits created} = \frac{1000}{\frac{10}{100}} = £10{,}000$$

Thus, from an initial deposit of £1,000, the bank now has total deposits of £10,000 by a multiplier process. Although we have assumed that there is only one bank in the economy, the removal of this assumption does not invalidate our argument in any material way.

From the analysis above we can see that the credit creation multiplier will be the reciprocal of the banks' reserve ratio. However, in practice, the actual amount of credit created by banks is substantially below this figure because there are a number of leakages in the flow of money in the banking system. Three important leakages are noted as follows:

1. Some individuals prefer to receive payment in the form of cash rather than bank deposits. The more the public wish to hold cash, the lower the level of bank deposits.

2. Transactions between the government and the banks or the public (involving the use of bank accounts) result in an equal and opposite change in bankers' deposits at the Bank of England. If the banks or the public purchase stocks from the government then bankers' deposits will be reduced. If the government purchases stocks from the banks or the public, then bankers' deposits will be increased.

   Similarly, payments (such as tax payments) to the government will reduce bankers' deposits. Banks are involved in the payment of taxes because they act as transmission agents. Suppose an individual wishes to pay his tax liability. He can draw a cheque on his account in favour of the Inland Revenue with the result that not only will the individual's account be debited but bankers' deposits at the Bank of England will be debited and the government's account credited. The flow of taxation payments by the banks' customers will reduce their customers' credit balances (which reduces the money supply) or increase their overdrafts and bankers' deposits at the bank of England will be reduced. The banks will have to alter their asset structure to maintain their required liquid assets.

   Payments by the government to the public, on the other hand, will increase bankers' deposits. Government expenditure affects banks because there will be a flow of funds from the government sector to the rest of the economy. When the government spends money the deposits held by the public with banks will rise, bankers' deposits at the Bank of England will rise and the government's account will decrease. Thus, such flows have beneficial effects on both the deposits and assets of the banks.

Any payments made by the banks to the government reduces the value of the multiplier because bankers' deposits are reduced.

3. The third leakage results from payments being made to foreigners not having accounts with banks in the U.K.

4.1.6 The Demand for Bank Loans

The rate at which banks are able to create deposits will depend to an extent on the rate at which they are able to increase their lending. The volume of bank lending is determined by the banks themselves, by the demand for advances in the economy and by competition from other lenders. The actual amounts lent by banks will be influenced by risk, the requirement to honour agreed borrowing facilities and competition from other financial institutions.

4.2 The Concept of Monetary Base Control

Under such a system, each bank has to keep a minimum proportion of its liabilities (deposits) in the form of base money which comprises balances with the Bank of England, although it may also include notes and coin held by banks and notes and coin in circulation. The proponents of such a scheme contend that if the Bank of England controls the amount of base money in existence then it can control the banks' deposits and the money supply because the banks' balance sheets could not exceed a specified multiple of the base.

The problems associated with monetary base control are as follows:

1. Such a system requires a constant relationship between the cash held by the banks and the cash held by the public. If this is not so, the banks could attract the cash from the public and so increase their lending.
2. For monetary base control to be successful, banks must also work to a stable ratio of cash to deposits. However, this is not generally the case since the public's demand for cash varies on a seasonal and geographical basis. Thus, if the public require less cash, the banks can increase their lending.
3. Monetary base control results in interest rates becoming more

volatile. This is because to maintain their cash ratios banks will be constantly rearranging their short-term assets which will be constantly affecting the prices of these assets and their yields.

The Government has taken some steps towards monetary base control although a full system of monetary base control has not been implemented. These steps are considered in the section on UK monetary policy.

4.3.1 The PSBR and Other Counterparts to Changes in the Money Stock

The importance of the PSBR can be demonstrated by considering its effect on the money stock. We can start by focussing on the liabilities and assets of the banking system as shown below.

The Balance Sheet of the Banking System

Liabilities	*Assets*
Sterling deposits:-	Sterling lending to:-
UK residents	UK public sector
Overseas sector	UK private sector
Foreign currency deposits	Overseas sector
Non-deposit liabilities (net)	Foreign currency assets

The balance sheet can be rearranged and with additional information, the accounting identity shown in Table 4.1 can be formulated. Table 4.1 shows the relationship between the PSBR and the other counterparts to changes in M3 for the financial year 1986/87.

Table 4.1 Counterparts to Changes in M3 for the Financial Year 1986/87 (Unadjusted)

(£ millions)	
Public sector borrowing requirement (surplus -)	+3,381
Purchases (-) of public sector net debt by UK private sector (other than banks)	-1,562
External and foreign currency finance of public sector (increase -)	-1,501
Bank's sterling lending to UK private sector	+30,340
External and foreign currency transactions of UK banks	-619
Net non-deposit sterling liabilities (increase -)	-4,654
Change in M3	+25,385

(Source: Bank of England Quarterly Bulletin - February 1988)

The connection between the PSBR and other counterparts to changes in M3 can be shown more simply as:

	PSBR
MINUS	Purchases of public sector debt by non-bank UK private sector
PLUS	Sterling lending to the UK private sector
PLUS	Bank lending in sterling to overseas sector
PLUS/MINUS	External and foreign currency finance
MINUS	Increase in banks' non-deposit liabilities
EQUALS	Change in M3

We will see in the next sections that if the PSBR is matched by sales of public debt to the non-bank private sector then there will be no increase in money stock. However if sales of public debt to the non-bank private sector is less than the PSBR there will be a positive contribution to the growth in M3. An increase in sterling lending to the private sector will increase M3 because an increase in lending by banks, other things being equal, will have the effect of increasing deposits in the banking system. Similarly, external and foreign currency finance may either increase or decrease the growth of M3. Finally, any increase in banks' non-deposit liabilities reduces the growth of M3. For example, the application of bank charges will reduce customers' credit balances (i.e., bank deposits will be reduced) and increase the banks' non-deposit liabilities.

The Bank of England also provides information on the counterparts to changes in M4 and M5. Table 4.2 shows the counterparts to changes in M4.

Table 4.2 Counterparts to Changes in M4; 4th quarter 1987 (£ millions)

Public sector borrowing requirement (surplus -)	-2,408
Purchases (-) of public sector net debt by UK private sector (other than banks and building societies)	-2,480
External and foreign currency finance of public sector (increase -)	+5,076
Bank's sterling lending to UK private sector excluding building societies	+10,982
Building societies sterling lending to UK private sector	+3,683
External and foreign currency transactions of banks and building societies	-1,826
Net non-deposit sterling liabilities (increase -):	
Banks	-1,005
Building societies	-70
Change in M4	+11,952

(Source: Bank of England Quarterly Bulletin - February 1988)

The connection between the PSBR and other counterparts to changes in M4 can be shown more simply as:

	PSBR
MINUS	Purchases of public sector debt by non-bank, non-building society UK private sector
PLUS	Sterling bank and building society lending to UK private sector
PLUS	Bank and building society lending in sterling to overseas sector
PLUS/MINUS	External and foreign currency finance
MINUS	Increase in non-deposit liabilities of banks and building societies
EQUALS	Change in M4

4.3.2 Public Sector Borrowing Requirement (PSBR)

The PSBR measures the amount that the public sector borrows from other sectors of the economy and overseas to finance any deficit that arises in its payments and receipts. The public sector consists of central government together with local authorities and public corporations. The Government can reduce the PSBR by:

1. Reducing public expenditure, that is, the expenditure of central government, local government and the investment expenditure of nationalised industries.
2. Increasing its revenue. This may be done by raising direct and indirect taxes, by raising national insurance contributions and by raising local authority rates.
3. Reducing any losses made by nationalised industries or raising their profits.
4. Selling public sector assets (privatisation). In the U.K. this has the effect of reducing the PSBR, however, in other countries it is considered as a means of financing a deficit.

Table 4.3 breaks down the PSBR into three parts; the central government borrowing requirement (CGBR); the local authorities borrowing requirement (LABR) and the public corporations borrowing requirement (PCBR).

The authorities place much importance on the CGBR because the central government covers its borrowing requirements in different markets from those used by local authorities and public corporations. Thus, the borrowing of the central government has a greater effect on the banking system than does the borrowing of local authorities and public corporations.

Table 4.3 Public Sector Borrowing

(£ million)

	Central Government (own account)	*Local Authorities*	*Public Corporations*	*Total Public Sector*
1978/79	5,966	1,288	1,977	9,231
1979/80	4,279	2,969	2,772	10,020
1980/81	9,080	2,120	1,486	12,686
1981/82	6,380	-225	2,477	8,632
1982/83	7,247	87	1,531	8,865
1983/84	8,188	1,206	334	9,728
1984/85	6,618	2,385	1,169	10,172
1985/86	4,086	1,672	36	5,794
1986/87	4,485	206	-1,358	3,333
1987/88	-3,462	1,449	-1,562	-3,575

(Source: Financial Statistics)

The PSBR is financed in three main ways:

1. By sales of debt to the non-bank private sector (e.g. gilts, national savings, local authority stocks and bonds). The non-bank private sector includes financial institutions other than banks, such as, for example, insurance companies and pension funds, together with industrial and commercial companies and the personal sector.
2. By external transactions (i.e. government borrowing from abroad and changes in the official reserves). If the price of sterling in the foreign exchange market fluctuates, the Bank of England can smooth them out by buying and selling sterling. If the Bank of England supports a weak pound, it will be buying sterling with its foreign exchange. The sterling it has purchased can be used to finance the government deficit so that a fall in reserves provides finance. A fall in reserves means that the reserves of the Exchange Equalisation Account will be added to and these reserves are mainly held in the form of Treasury bills. An increase in reserves means that foreigners are converting their gold and foreign currencies into sterling so that the Exchange Equalisation Account draws on its reserves, so that its holdings of Treasury bills will fall and the Exchequer has to find alternative sources of finance.

   Changes in overseas holdings of British debt are often accompanied by compensating changes in the Exchange Equalisation Account. For example, if foreign currencies are converted into sterling for investment in government debt then Exchequer financing will be unaffected because the Exchange Equalisation Account will hold less government debt and foreigners will hold more.

3. By borrowing from the banking system.

Approximately 70% of the PSBR is financed by the non-bank private sector. Indeed, this sector has provided much of the required finance in recent years.

When the public sector finances its borrowing requirement it incurs liabilities to the above three sectors. These liabilities include:

1. monetary liabilities (notes and coin);
2. debt instruments (gilt-edged stock, Treasury bills and National Savings);
3. direct borrowing.

The financing of the PSBR is important because the way in which it is financed can have a great effect on the economy. Thus, if the PSBR is financed by sales of debt to the non-bank private sector there will be a reduction in liquid assets (bank deposits) and an increase in the holdings of non-liquid public sector debt. However, if the PSBR is financed by borrowing from the banking system through the issue of Treasury bills, the creation of new liquid assets would allow the banks to increase their lending which may add to inflationary pressures. The PSBR is important to the government because it is an indicator of how its policies are affecting the rest of the economy, particularly financial markets and the money supply.

The PSBR is financed in the main by sales of gilts with approximately two-thirds of gilt sales taken up by the non-bank private sector especially insurance companies, pension funds and the personal sector. Indeed, gilts have been the most important means of funding over recent years. However, excessive reliance on gilt sales pushes up long-term interest rates and the large demand for funds from the public sector may have the effect of crowding out the private sector.

Following gilts, the next most important source of funding is National Savings.The Government has recently placed greater emphasis on sales of National Savings and to improve sales, the Government has made them more attractive. The reason for this is that by relying greatly on sales of gilts, interest rates tend to get pushed up. This is because higher interest rates are needed to make gilts more attractive. The Government's aim has been to reduce its reliance on gilt sales so that long-term interest rates can be lower than they would otherwise be. Issues of Treasury bills have been the residual element in funding.

The local authorities borrow mainly from banks and other financial institutions and in the last few years such borrowing has been in the region of £1 to £2 billion per annum. On the other hand, public corporations have moved into surplus.

Since 1988, the public sector has moved into surplus and the government has embarked on a debt repayment programme in which it has bought back gilts —this is the Public Sector Debt Repayment (PSDR) and the Treasury forecast a PSDR of £14bn for 1988/89.

4.3.3 Public Sector Debt Sales

If the government decides not to finance its budget deficit by issuing notes or borrowing from the Bank of England, then it must issue securities. The effects of such issues depends on whether the securities are short-term or long-term and to whom they are sold.

We must consider two streams of payments. Firstly, the stream of payments from the government to the non-government sector and secondly, the stream of payments arising from the issue of government securities. Let us consider the first stream. A budget deficit means that payments made by the government to the non-government sector exceeds its receipts from that sector so that bank deposits will rise. Because all transactions between the government and the private sector (apart from those directly settled by the use of notes and coin) will be reflected in a change in the accounts held by the banks with the Bank of England, a budget deficit results in an increase in bankers' deposits at the Bank of England. Thus, if the government settles its debts with the non-bank private sector by issuing cheques, then not only will the non-bank private sector's deposits with the banks increase but also bankers' deposits at the Bank of England will increase whilst the government's accounts (public deposits) will be reduced.

We can now turn to the second stream of payments. If the government finances its deficit through the issue of gilt-edged stocks they may be taken up either by the non-bank private sector or the banks. If the non-bank private sector takes up the issue they will draw cheques on their bank accounts in favour of the government and bankers' deposits at the Bank of England will be reduced. Thus, the decrease in the deposits of the non-bank private sector will be matched by the increase in deposits resulting from the government's budget deficit so that the money supply will be unchanged. Bankers' deposits at the Bank of England are initially reduced and then restored. If the stocks are taken up by the banks the money supply will increase. This is because the purchase of stocks results in a reduction of banker's deposits at the Bank of England coupled with a increase in their holdings of gilt-edged stocks. (Note that to maintain their holdings of liquid assets, they will have to alter the structure of their assets). The budget deficit will increase deposits held by the non-bank private sector with the banks.

To summarise, if stocks are taken up by the non-bank private sector there will be a stream of payments from the non-bank private sector to the government and when the government spends the money it has borrowed there will be a stream of payments back to the non-bank private sector so that the money supply will be unchanged. However, if the stocks are taken up by the banks the money supply will rise. The effect of issuing National Savings will be the same as for sales of gilt-edged stocks to the non-bank private sector.

If the Bank of England fails to sell gilt-edged stocks then it must sell Treasury bills. The issue of Treasury bills reduces bankers' deposits at the Bank of England because they are used either to buy Treasury bills or to lend to the discount houses to enable them to take the bills up. The government budget deficit will increase the deposits of the non-bank private sector with the banks and bankers' deposits at the Bank of England will increase. Thus, banks will be left with an increase in their deposits together with an increase in their holdings of Treasury bills or call money lent to the discount houses, or both. The liquid assets of the banks will have increased which will enable them to increase their lending.

4.3.4 Bank Lending in Sterling to the UK Private Sector

Bank lending in sterling to the UK private sector will result in a positive contribution to the growth of M3, (together with M4 and M5). This is because as we saw earlier, an increase in bank lending results in an increase in deposits in the banking system.

4.3.5 Bank Lending in Sterling to the Overseas Sector

An increase in sterling bank lending to the overseas sector will increase M3 if the deposits created are held by UK residents. However, if the deposits created are held by non-residents then M3 will be unchanged because only deposits held by UK residents are included in the calculation of M3.

4.3.6 The Balance of Payments

The money supply is affected by official financing of the balance of payments surplus or deficit. In broad terms, a balance of payments surplus means that money is coming into the UK and when this is spent it creates new deposits and increases the money supply. A balance of payments deficit, on the other hand, broadly means that money is leaving the country thereby reducing the money supply.

4.4.1 Distortions in the Money Supply Aggregates

A number of factors will distort the money supply aggregates including disintermediation, bank mortgage lending, overfunding, inflation and high interest rates.

4.4.2 Disintermediation

This is the term used to describe the use of savings and credit facilities outside the banking system. For example, the depositing of money by bank customers with local authorities rather than banks or instead of borrowing from banks, bank customers resort to using bills (arbitrage). Disintermediation occurs either when banks' interest rates move out of line with other interest rates or when they are prevented from providing finance (for example, by official controls such as the supplementary special deposits scheme).

In the 1970s disintermediation took two main forms. Initially it consisted of companies increasing their holdings of Treasury bills but later it mainly took the form of bank accepted commercial bills held outside the banking system (otherwise known as the 'bill leak'). The effect of these activities were to distort the monetary statistics because holdings of Treasury bills and bank acceptances were excluded from the official money supply statistics (they are now included in M5). Re-intermediation results in a large increase in the money supply.

4.4.3 Bank Mortgage Lending

An increase in bank lending for mortgages will increase M3 because bank lending is an asset counterpart to the growth of M3 but building society lending is not.

4.4.4 Overfunding and the Bill Mountain

During the early 1980s the authorities adopted a policy of overfunding to reduce the growth of M3. Overfunding means that the authorities sell more public debt than is needed to finance the PSBR. Thus during this period the contribution of the public sector to the growth of M3 was negative thereby offsetting to some extent the positive contribution of high bank lending. For example, in 1981/82 sales of public sector debt to the non-bank private sector exceeded the PSBR by £2.5 billion. Such overfunding has occurred in the past (for example, in 1977/78) but not to the same extent as in the early 1980s. Overfunding exerts upward pressure on interest rates so that they are higher than they otherwise would have been. The Chancellor stated in October 1985 that the practice of overfunding would be discontinued.

Since 1976, the UK monetary sectors' holdings of Treasury bills has fallen dramatically. This is a consequence of the cash shortages of the monetary sector in recent years, in part due to the heavy sales of public sector debt other than Treasury bills. These cash shortages were traditionally relieved by the Bank purchasing Treasury bills but over the years this has led to a depletion in the monetary sector's Treasury bill holdings. More recently the Bank relied on purchasing commercial bills instead and the policy of overfunding has led to the so-called 'bill mountain'. The 'bill mountain' refers to the large stocks of commercial bills now held by the Bank of England.

4.4.5 The Effect of Inflation and High Interest Rates

M1 should in theory provide a measure of money which is available for spending in the economy. However, M1 has been both an unreliable and unpredictable measure due in the main to the unstable nature of the interest-bearing component of M1. Because of the very close substitutability of these deposits with building society deposits and other time deposits, changes in rates of return result in switching between these deposits. In addition, the non-interest-bearing component of M1 is affected by inflation. If inflationary expectations increase, there will be switching to interest-bearing deposits resulting in some deposits being outside the scope of M1. M0 has, therefore, replaced M1 as an indicator of narrow money in recent years.

M3 has tended to be a more reliable indicator than M1. This is because the switching which is associated with M1 is less significant in the case of M3.

4.5 Changes in the Money Supply and its Effect on the Bank Balance Sheet

Because the money stock consists in the main of bank deposits, an increase in the money stock means that banks can expand their lending. The increase in lending activity will increase the banks' retail profits. The secondary banks may find that they have to reduce the margin between bid and offered interest rates as the money stock rises and this will reduce the profitability of this type of business. (A decrease in the money stock will affect the banks in the opposite way to that described above).

The expansion of the money stock should have a beneficial effect on the growth of the real economy (assuming full employment has not been reached) and buoyant demand should provide banks with increased lending opportunities for consumer spending and imports and to sell their services. The increase in the money stock will reduce interest rates and the endowment element in retail bank profits will fall.

Eventually the increase in the money stock may lead to an increase in the rate of inflation so that banks' operating costs will rise and this will detrimentally affect profits. Interest rates may rise as the authorities seek to control the growth of the money supply. The consequent reduction in the growth of bank lending will adversely affect their profits although the higher interest rates will increase the endowment element in retail banks' profits.

4.6 The Sale of Public Sector Assets

The sale of public sector assets (or privatisation) provides funds for the Government and has represented an important part of Government policy in recent years. Such sales involve a flow of funds from the non-bank private sector to the Government. Larger flotations such as the British Telecom issue in 1984 result in cash shortages in the money market (because of the large amount of funds flowing to the Government) which have to be alleviated by the Bank of England during the course of its money market operations.

4.7.1 The Techniques Used for the Control of Money

In 1976, the IMF imposed a limit on DCE as a precondition for a loan to the UK. Later in that year targets were applied to Sterling M3 (now titled M3). Table 4.4 shows the monetary targets since 1976.

We noted in Chapter 1 that a number of the monetary aggregates shown in Table 4.4 have been retitled and we shall, therefore, use their current title in the following analysis.

The UK Government in 1979 put the control of inflation at the top of its list of economic objectives. It aimed to control inflation by controlling the money supply by the adoption of monetarist policies. The Government set out its strategy in terms of its Medium-Term Financial Strategy (MTFS).

The MTFS was introduced in 1980 and noted the Government's medium-term objectives. The objectives were to reduce the rate of inflation by a steady reduction in the rate of growth of the money supply secured by the requisite fiscal policies. The MTFS showed the possibility of reducing inflation together with a reduction in the income tax burden. This was to be achieved by progressive reductions in public spending. The MTFS is revised annually.

Table 4.4 Monetary Targets 1976-88

Period	*Aggregates*	*Target growth rate %*		*Actual growth rate%*
Year ended April '77	M3	9-13		7.7
" " " '78	£M3	9-13		16.0
" " " '79	£M3	8-12		10.9
" " Oct. '79	£M3	8-12		13.3
June '79 - April '80	£M3	7-11		10.3
June '79 - Oct. '80	£M3	7-11		17.8
Feb. '80 - April '81	£M3	7-11		18.5
Feb. '81 - April '82	£M3	6-10		14.5
Feb. '82 - April '83	M1,£M3,PSL2	8-12	M1	11.8
			£M3	11.4
			PSL2	11.6
Year ended April '84	M1,£M3,PSL2	7-9	M1	11.1
			£M3	9.7
			PSL2	12.6
Year ended April '85	M0	4-8		
	£M3	6-10		13.4
Year ended April '86	M0	3-7		4.25
	£M3	5-9		18.0
Year ended April '87	M0	2-6		4.0
Year ended April '88	M0	2-6		5.0
Year ended April '89	M0	1-5		
Year ended April '90	M0	1-5		

The MTFS committed the Government to monetary targets expressed in terms of M3. However, to control the money supply the Government did not intend to rely excessively on high interest rates. The Government planned to secure control by reducing the PSBR as a percentage of gross domestic product over the medium-term. However, this was seen as too imprecise a way of controlling the money supply so that changes in monetary control were introduced in August 1981. The main thrust of the changes represented a movement towards a monetary base system which is central to the monetarists' view of the control of the money supply. The main changes were that MLR would no longer be posted and that control over the structure of interest rates would be lessened. The Bank of England's money market operations were also changed. These changes are considered fully in the next section.

M3 has been the main definition of money which has been used by the Government as a basis for monetary policy formulation and assessment. The significance of M3c has increased since the abolition of UK exchange controls in 1979 since foreign currency deposits can be held by UK residents and they can be quickly and easily switched into sterling and spent. The M4 and M5 definitions focus on the potential spending power in the economy but even they do not provide a complete picture. This is because foreign currency deposits are omitted. In addition, a complete assessment of potential spending power should include unused agreed overdraft facilities and credit card facilities. In the 1982 Budget, the Chancellor noted that other monetary aggregates, as well as M3 should be considered in policy making and secondly, he focussed on the fact that it had been difficult to achieve the monetary targets set.

Because M3 had been distorted by a number of factors, in 1982 the Chancellor, as we have already noted decided that targets would be applied to other aggregates which the Government believed reflected most accurately the underlying monetary conditions. The factors which distorted M3 included the abandonment of the corset which resulted in a return of lending business from outside the banking system with a consequent increase in M3. Also, from about 1979, the banks began to actively compete with building societies in the provision of mortgage finance. The result has been a movement towards the use of multiple targets. In the years ending April 1983 and 1984, the targeted aggregates were M1, M3 and M5 (formerly PSL2). In the years ending April 1985 and 1986, the targets were applied to M0 and M3. However, at the end of 1985, the Chancellor suspended the target for M3 for the year ending 1986 and announced the abandonment of the practice of overfunding to control the money supply. The Chancellor announced in the 1987 Budget that there would be no target for M3 although a target would be applied to M0. M0 has continued to be targeted each year.

We saw earlier that M3 can be broken down into its asset counterparts. The significance of this is that the authorities can control both the growth of bank deposits (the money supply) and also the lending which causes monetary growth. Monetary policy can, therefore, be used to influence the different counterparts to monetary growth as follows:

1. PSBR (Fiscal policy)
2. Public sector debt sales to the non-bank private sector. (Interest rate

policy)

3. Bank lending in sterling (Monetary control measures).
4. External and foreign currency finance (Exchange rate policy).

4.7.2 UK Monetary Policy Since 1971

The Competition and Credit Control arrangements were introduced in September 1971, to improve competition in the banking system, and to overhaul the system of credit control to enable the authorities to influence the growth of monetary aggregates quickly and effectively.

Although the Competition and Credit Control measures were introduced in September 1971, they were first published by the Bank of England in a consultative document in May 1971. The Competition and Credit Control measures provided for the application of a new reserve asset ratio to all banks; quantitative directives were abolished; the Bank of England's dealing tactics in the gilt-edged market were changed. In addition, the clearing banks agreed to abandon their collective agreement on interest rates.

The Competition and Credit Control measures required banks to maintain their reserve assets at a minimum of 12½% of their eligible liabilities (a ratio of 10% was applied to finance houses). Reserve assets comprised:

1. Balances at the Bank of England.
2. British and Northern Ireland Government Treasury bills.
3. Money at call with the London money market.
4. British government stocks and nationalised industries' stocks guaranteed by the Government, with one year or less to maturity.
5. Local authority bills eligible for re-discount at the Bank of England.
6. Commercial bills eligible for re-discount at the Bank of England (to a maximum of 2% of eligible liabilities). These comprised bills payable in the U.K. and accepted by London or Scottish clearing banks or accepting houses or British overseas banks or certain other banks having their head offices in the Commonwealth and with long established branches in London.

Eligible liabilities comprised:

1. Sterling deposits, with an original term of maturity of two years or less, from U.K. residents (other than banks) or overseas residents and all funds held temporarily on suspense accounts.
2. All sterling deposits (of whatever term) taken from banks in the U.K., less any funds lent to such banks.
3. All issues of sterling CDs (of whatever term) less all holdings of

such CDs.

4. Banks' sterling net deposit liabilities to their overseas offices.
5. Banks' net liabilities in foreign currencies

   LESS
6. 60% of net transit items.

The authorities could regulate the supply of reserve assets either by open market operations or by calling for special deposits. Because the reserve asset ratio applied to all banks, the authorities were in effect controlling the reserve asset base of the entire banking system so that individual banks were able to compete for deposits and lending business on equal terms, thus, credit was allocated more by price than by rationing. However, there were three main criticisms of this system. Firstly, not all reserve assets were fully under the control of the authorities. For example, commercial bills were not under full control but they were limited to 2% of eligible liabilities. Money at call was the second example. The theoretical argument had been expressed that at certain times it may have been possible for banks to manufacture reserve assets if they lent to the discount houses at call at the same time that the discount market purchased bank CDs. We have seen that the discount houses had separate credit control arrangements, so that the manufacture of reserve assets could only occur when the market was within the prescribed limits. However, the authorities kept such close contact with the market that in practice such a manufacture of reserve assets was unlikely to occur.

The second criticism related to the fact that although the authorities control the supply of Treasury bills, they may, in practice have found it difficult to regulate supplies because Treasury bills represent residual government borrowing. The authorities may at times have found it difficult to sell stocks so that issues of Treasury bills would have risen. Because the majority of bills are held within the banking system, the banking system's reserve asset base would have risen.

The third criticism was that the reserve asset ratio was applied to all banks. However, the operations and balance sheets of banks differ quite widely with the result that competition between dissimilar banks may have been distorted.

Although the use of quantitative directives was abandoned, the authorities retained the use of qualitative directives which were extended to all banks and deposit-taking finance houses.

We have already noted the change in the Bank of England's dealing tactics in the gilt-edged market in Chapter 2.

Under Competition and Credit Control the clearing banks agreed to abandon their collective interest rates agreement. Each bank now formulates its own base rate (to which overdraft rates are related) and deposit rate. Since this change base rates have generally been in line but this reflects the competitive environment in which banks operate. Prior to Competition and Credit Control, the clearing banks tied their deposit and overdraft rates to Bank rate which meant that if Bank rate moved in one direction then deposit and overdraft rates would automatically move in the same direction. The authorities also served notice that savings banks and building societies would continue to operate 'privileged circuits' within the financial system and that the increased competitiveness of banks would not be allowed to damage their operations. To this end, the authorities reserved the right to place restrictions on the rate of interest offered by banks on deposit accounts. The authorities used this power to restrict the interest paid on deposits of less than £10,000 to 9.5% during the period September 1973 to February 1975, to protect building societies from the effects of high interest rates.

The special deposits scheme was not only retained but was extended to all banks and to finance houses observing the 10% reserve asset ratio. Special deposits were deposits which were called for by the Bank of England which did not count towards the reserve ratio. Up until Competition and Credit Control, special deposits were expressed as a percentage of total deposits but with effect from September 1971, they were expressed as a percentage of eligible liabilities. The Bank of England paid interest on these deposits at Treasury bill rate, although on a small number of occasions in the past the rate was temporarily reduced. The use of special deposits facilitated the authorities open market operations where banks held a cushion of reserve assets over the minimum requirement. Without a call for special deposits, the initial sales of gilts may largely have been absorbed without pressure on banks' reserve assets. Thus it may have taken some time before such operations were effective and in the meantime it could have adversely affected the confidence of the holders of government debt. Special deposits made open market operations more effective under such conditions because banks' excess reserves were frozen.

In October 1972, Bank rate was replaced by minimum lending rate. Bank rate was market-determining which meant that the authorities could alter the level of interest rates, especially those of banks and building societies by altering Bank rate. Because Bank rate had tremendous political significance which was not warranted by its economic importance, the Bank of England decided that it would abandon its discretionary rate and replace it with a market-determined rate. Thus, minimum lending rate was designed to reflect the movement of interest rates and not to determine them.

Until May 1978, the calculation of minimum lending rate was linked to the Treasury bill rate in the following way. The authorities would take the average rate of discount at the Friday Treasury bill tender, add half a per cent and round up to the next quarter per cent. However, the authorities announced in May 1978 that this formula would no longer be used and it would in future be set at the authorities' discretion. The reason for the change was that from around the mid-1970s, the authorities had been pursuing quantitative targets for money supply growth, with the targets being pursued through interest rate changes. Because the Bank's open market operations had not, at times, been able to bring about the desired change in interest rates, the Bank decided that discretionary changes in minimum lending rate were required.

In November 1973, the authorities introduced the supplementary special deposits scheme (the 'corset') when rising interest rates failed to slow down the growth in the money supply. The scheme required each bank to lodge with the Bank of England, non-interest-earning supplementary special deposits, if its interest-bearing eligible liabilities exceeded a stipulated limit. Once a bank reached the stipulated limit, it would find it unprofitable to expand its business any further. In 1974, the rate of growth in the money supply slowed down and interest rates fell so that the authorities dropped the scheme in 1975. However, it was reintroduced in November 1976 after the money supply had once again increased dramatically. The scheme was again dropped in August 1977 after the rate of growth of the money supply had slowed down only to be reintroduced in June 1978.

Since the 1976 budget, the government has used monetary targets. Because of the difficulties of keeping monetary growth within the targets, the government, in November 1979, raised the minimum lending rate to 17%, its highest level ever, to underline its determination to secure monetary control. In order to increase the authorities' ability to control Sterling M3 (now M3), the Bank of England and the Treasury conducted a review of the methods of monetary control which was published in March 1980 in a Green Paper entitled 'Monetary Control'.

There were a number of reasons why the Green Paper was published:

1. The supplementary special deposits scheme led to disintermediation.
2. By the end of the 1970s it became generally accepted that the $12^1/_2$% reserve asset ratio was not necessary as an instrument of monetary control although the ratio was useful for the purpose of prudential control. It was generally felt that the Competition and Credit Control measures did not distinguish clearly between monetary and prudential aspects of control.

3. A number of financial commentators had for some time been advocating the adoption of a form of monetary base control and this was discussed in the Green Paper.

The main points of the Green Paper were as follows:

1. The Government expressed its intention to continue to formulate its monetary target in terms of Sterling M3 (now M3).
2. The Green Paper considered the main instruments for controlling the money supply. In their discussion of the existing arrangements, the Treasury and the Bank of England suggested that the supplementary special deposits scheme had neared the end of its useful life and should be phased out as soon as convenient. In addition, they considered that the maintenance of the reserve asset ratio appeared no longer necessary as a means of either influencing interest rates or affecting the rate of growth of banks' balance sheets. The Bank of England took the opportunity to state that the reserve asset ratio was not designed to control directly the level of credit created by banks but it was regarded as an element in the control of short-term interest rates. The proposal to lapse the ratio reflected a number of considerations such as the lack of distinction between monetary and prudential aspects of control, the distortion between the yields of reserve assets and other short-term assets and the reduction in the effectiveness of the ratio as a means of influencing short-term interest rates (by varying bank liquidity) because when faced with a tightening of liquidity banks would simply bid for more deposits rather than dispose of assets. The Treasury and the Bank of England proposed that the ratio be lapsed once consultations had been completed and new requirements on prudential liquidity agreed. At the same time that the Green Paper was published, the Bank issued a parallel consultation document which set out a proposed new framework for assessing the adequacy of banks' liquidity.
3. The Green Paper considered the possibility of a move towards a system of monetary base control. A variety of possible monetary base controls were considered in the Green Paper, some involving mandatory holdings of base money with others being based on conventional banking practice. The Green Paper also identified a number of technical problems which raised doubts that such a system would provide the desired control over Sterling M3 (now M3).
4. The Green Paper proposed that the cash requirement which applied only to the clearing banks be applied more generally and the Bank of England would be issuing a detailed discussion paper on this in due course. This cash requirement would become of more general use to

the Bank as a means of controlling the money supply by influencing the level of short-term interest rates on the money market.

5. The Green Paper discussed the use of indicator systems under which divergence in Sterling M3 (now M3) or the monetary base, from the desired trend, would automatically trigger a change in interest rates to correct the divergence. The main advantage of such a system would be that it would help to remove the 'bias towards delay' in adjusting interest rates. However, the main problem with a formal indicator system is that in certain situations it would be desirable that the authorities should have the power to 'override the trigger'.
6. The Green Paper suggested that the special deposits scheme be retained to guard against possible adverse effects of excess liquidity in the banking system.

The Bank of England also issued a discussion paper entitled 'The Measurement of Liquidity' which initially considered the two approaches to measuring banks' liquidity:

1. The first approach compares the available liquid assets with either total liabilities or certain categories of liabilities – a 'snapshot' approach. This measure of liquidity shows a bank's ability to survive a sudden withdrawal of deposits by making use of its liquid assets.
2. The second approach is essentially a dynamic extension of the snapshot approach. It assesses the ability of a bank to meet future commitments by examining known flows of funds.

The Bank proposed to introduce a test of liquidity which combines these two approaches. The test entails distinguishing between:

1. Liabilities and assets which are maturity-certain, e.g. fixed term deposits and loans.
2. Liabilities and assets which are maturity-uncertain, e.g. current account deposits or seven day deposits where notice is often waived and overdrafts.
3. Assets which have a fixed maturity but which can be realised sooner because they are readily marketable, e.g. Treasury bills or CDs.

The Bank proposed to establish for each bank an estimate of its likely need for liquid assets for each type of liability.

The characteristics of a liquid asset were noted by the Bank in its paper as follows:

1. its credit risk should be negligible
2. it should either be close to maturity or
3. it should carry minimal forced sale risk, i.e. if sold at short notice it

should produce cash at or close to its balance sheet value.

With these characteristics in mind, the Bank proposed that certain assets be classified as liquid assets for the purpose of its liquidity test.

These assets include:

Cash.

*Balances with the Bank of England (excluding special deposits).

*Call money with the London Discount Market Association.

*U.K. and Northern Ireland Treasury bills, local authority bills and bank bills eligible for re-discount at the Bank of England.

*British government stocks with less than one year to maturity.

Market loans to banks up to one month.

Loans to local authorities up to one month.

Non-eligible bills with less than three months to maturity.

CDs with less than three months to maturity.

British government stocks with between one and five years to maturity.

Northern Ireland Government stocks with less than five years to maturity.

Local authority and public corporation marketable securities with less than five years to maturity.

Gold.

Irrevocable undrawn standby facilities from other banks.

In order to give greater protection, the Bank proposed that banks should be required to hold part of their liquidity in the form of primary liquidity. Primary liquidity assets are those marked by an asterisk. The Bank suggested that 40% of each bank's liquidity needs should be in the form of primary liquidity. Special deposits would not be considered as liquid assets.

There were a number of developments after the publication of 'Monetary Control'. Essentially, the 'competition' element of the Competition and Credit Control measures remained unchanged but there were changes in the 'credit control' element as follows:

1. The supplementary special deposits scheme was abolished in June 1980.
2. The reserve asset ratio was reduced from $12^1/_2$% to 10% on 5th January 1981 and it was reduced further to 8% between 2nd-10th March, 1981 and again between 11th March and 30th April, 1981. The reductions to 8% in the ratio were also applied to the finance houses which observed the 10% ratio. The rationale for these reductions was to offset any possible upward pressures on short-term interest rates in the money market caused by tax payments and gilt sales.
3. During November 1980 the Chancellor announced that the Bank of

England would be discussing changes in its methods of operating in the short-term money markets to allow for greater flexibility in short-term interest rates and an increasing role for the market in the determination of the level of interest rates. In addition, access to the Bank's last resort lending facilities would be made less routine and relatively more expensive.

The Bank of England paper entitled 'Monetary Control: Next Steps' was published on 12th March 1981. The Bank of England stated in its paper that the London clearing banks' $1^1/_2\%$ cash ratio would be replaced by a new ratio, which would be applied to both recognised banks and licensed deposit-taking institutions, in each case above a minimum size, whereby they would be required to hold cash balances on special non-operational, non-interest-bearing accounts with the Bank of England. The London clearing banks would maintain such balances on their ordinary accounts at the Bank of England as would be necessary for their clearing activities. In addition, other recognised banks and licensed deposit-taking institutions with accounts at the Bank would also continue to maintain these accounts with balances appropriate to their business.

The Bank of England paper also noted that the Bank had begun, since the end of November 1980, to place greater emphasis in its money market management operations in bills rather than in discount-window lending. The paper stated that this change in emphasis had been facilitated by the reduction in the reserve asset ratio to 10% which released a large amount of bills for future sale to the Bank.

The Bank of England paper entitled 'The Liquidity of Banks' was published by the Bank at the same time as 'Monetary Control: Next Steps', as a follow-up to its discussion paper 'The Measurement of Liquidity'. In the paper the Bank stated that it had decided to remove the suggestion that banks should meet a primary liquidity requirement. In addition, the Bank stated that in assessing individual bank's liquidity positions, it would consider the quality of their liquidity assets.

The Bank of England Paper entitled 'Monetary Control - provisions' was issued by the Bank of England on 5th August 1981. It set out the new monetary control arrangements which took effect on 20th August 1981. The main elements of the system are as follows:

1. The reserve asset ratio was abolished.
2. The London clearing banks' agreement to hold $1^1/_2\%$ of their eligible liabilities at the Bank of England was lapsed. It was replaced by an obligation on all banks and licensed deposit-taking institutions to hold $^1/_2\%$ (now 0.45%) of their eligible liabilities with the Bank. This non-operational non-interest-bearing

requirement applies to institutions with eligible liabilities which average £10 million or more. In addition, the London clearing banks are required to hold voluntarily at the Bank operational balances for clearing purposes. The level of these balances are to be determined by the banks themselves. These changes have been designed to provide the Bank with non-interest-bearing funds equivalent to the amount provided by the $1^1/_2$% ratio on the London clearing banks.

3. The Bank discontinued the practice of continuously posting a minimum lending rate. However, the authorities have reserved the right to announce, in advance, the minimum lending rate which the Bank would apply to any lending in the market.
4. The aim of the Bank of England's money market operations was changed so as to keep interest rates at the very short end of the market within an undisclosed band. This band is moved from time to time but only with the approval of the Chancellor of the Exchequer. In setting the band, the authorities mainly take into account the growth of Sterling M3 (now M3) although such factors as the growth of other monetary aggregates and conditions in the foreign exchange market are also considered. The Bank no longer quotes rates but if it enters the market seeking to buy or sell bills, it responds to offers and bids from the discount houses.

The Bank makes public the rate at which it has transacted business. Thus, rates at the very short end of the market are directly under the Bank's influence leaving market forces to play a greater role in the determination of the structure of short-term interest rates. This should help to remove the 'bias towards delay' in changing interest rates.

Because the Bank of England's intervention in the money market continued to be conducted in the bill market, through the discount houses, the Bank ensured that there were enough bills. To ensure an adequate supply, the Bank increased the number of eligible banks. In order to ensure the efficient functioning of the bill and gilt-edged markets, the Bank sought undertakings from eligible banks that they would maintain secured money with members of the London Discount Market Association and/or secured call money with money brokers and gilt-edged jobbers. These funds were to normally average 6% of a banks' eligible liabilities (this was reduced to 5% in 1983). In addition, the amount of secured call money maintained with members of the London Discount Market Association was to be at least 4% of a bank's eligible liabilities on any day (this was reduced to $2^1/_2$% in 1983). This requirement for eligible banks to maintain secured money with members of the London Discount Market Association has subsequently been phased out.

5. The special deposits scheme was retained and will apply to all institutions in the monetary sector with eligible liabilities of £10 million or more.

6. Because of the various changes made in the framework of monetary control, the calculation of an institution's eligible liabilities was changed. Offsets are allowed in respect of:

   (a) funds lent to other institutions in the monetary sector; and

   (b) money placed at call with money brokers and gilt-edged jobbers in the Stock Exchange and secured on gilt-edged stocks, Treasury bills, local authority bills and eligible bank bills.

   The calculation of eligible liabilities is uniform for all reporting institutions except:

   (a) members of the London Discount Market Association whose calculation of eligible liabilities will be total sterling deposits other than from institutions in the monetary sector and from money-brokers and gilt-edged jobbers in the Stock Exchange.

   (b) Certain banks with money-trading departments who are allowed to omit from their calculation of eligible liabilities secured money placed at call by other banks with these departments, up to a limit set by the Bank of England.

7. Prior to 20th August 1981, the banking sector included institutions in the statistical list of banks and the list of discount market institutions. These lists were drawn up before the Banking Act 1979, and excluded a number of recognised banks, many licensed deposit-taking institutions and also the trustee savings banks. It was therefore necessary to define a new monetary sector which comprised:

   (a) all recognised banks and licensed deposit-taking institutions;
   (b) National Girobank;
   (c) the trustee savings banks;
   (d) those banks in the Channel Islands and the Isle of Man which decide to join the cash ratio scheme;
   (e) the Banking Department of the Bank of England.

   Because of the changes brought about by the Banking Act 1987, the Bank of England now provides a list of the institutions forming the monetary sector. It includes retail banks, accepting houses, other British banks, American banks, Japanese banks, other overseas banks and discount market institutions.

8. The Bank of England received assurances from those institutions which complied with the reserve asset ratio that they would not change the management of their liquidity, nor its composition, without prior discussion with the Bank.

The paper entitled 'The Measurement of Liquidity' was issued by the Bank of England on 20th July 1982 and it provides the framework for assessing the adequacy of liquidity of 'banks' (both recognised banks and licensed deposit-takers).

The measurement of liquidity is based on a cash flow approach. Thus, liabilities and assets are put into a 'maturity ladder', showing the net position in each time period. In the first time period on this ladder, sight and near-sight liabilities are compared with cash and near-cash assets in a similar way to a conventional liquid assets ratio. Marketable assets are put at the start of the ladder and not in accordance with their maturity date but the Bank will take account of any limitations in their marketability and susceptibility to price changes.

The paper notes the following particular features in the measurement of liquidity:

1. *Liabilities*

(a) All types of deposit are considered according to earliest maturity. The paper notes that the deposits of some banks differ, for example, retail and wholesale deposits, but the Bank of England will take this into account in its discussions with individual banks.

(b) Any known commitments to make funds available at some specified future date are put into the appropriate time band at their full value.

(c) It is unlikely that any undrawn overdraft facilities or any other commitments which are not due on a specified date will have to be met in full and so cannot be treated with precision. The Bank will take account of this.

(d) The measurement does not include contingent liabilities unless it is reasonably likely that the conditions necessary to trigger them will occur.

2. *Assets*

(a) Assets are measured according to their maturity unless they are nominally repayable on demand (e.g. overdrafts) or they are marketable or they are of doubtful value.

(b) The cash flow generated from lending which is nominally repayable on demand cannot be measured precisely and the Bank will agree the treatment of it with each bank.

(c) The Bank will treat marketable assets according to their marketability i.e. how quickly they can be sold for cash, whether any cost penalties may be incurred and whether there may be credit or investment risks which may adversely affect the value of these assets. These factors and others are allowed for by the application of discounts against their market values. Nil discounts will be applied to Treasury bills, eligible local authority bills, eligible bank bills, and government and government-guaranteed marketable securities with less than 12 months to maturity. A 5% discount will be applied to other bills and CDs with less than 6 months maturity and other government, government- guaranteed and local authority marketable securities with less than 5 years to maturity. A 10% discount will be applied to other bills, CDs and FRNs with less than 5 years to maturity and other government, government-guaranteed and local authority marketable debt with more than 5 years to maturity. The Bank will determine discounts on all other marketable assets.

(d) Any assets which have a doubtful value are excluded from the measurement of liquidity.

(e) Any contractual standby facilities given by other banks are included as equivalent to a sight asset.

Using this framework, the Bank will discuss with each bank the adequacy of their liquidity, taking into account their particular circumstances.

MLR was reactivated at 12% on 14th January 1985 which signalled a 1.5% rise in bank base rates on that day. This was done to demonstrate that the Government's resolve on its economic policies had not weakened and to stem the weakening of sterling against the US $ any further. This was the first time that MLR has been reactivated since the August 1981 changes in monetary control.

4.8.1 The Demand for Money

The demand for money and the determination of the rate of interest can be considered in terms of two main theories – 'real', non-monetary or loanable funds theory of interest and liquidity preference or monetary theory.

4.8.2 'Real' or Non-Monetary Theories of Interest

The real theories of interest were developed by classical economists and they form a cornerstone of the Monetarist theories of today. These theories state that the rate of interest is determined by the interaction of the supply of savings which are available for lending and the demand for these funds.

The volume of savings is determined by thrift whilst the volume of funds demanded for investment is determined by the productivity of capital. Thus, the rate of interest is determined by the 'real' forces of thrift and productivity.

In the real theory, money is not demanded for itself but merely as a medium of exchange, so that money is considered to be 'neutral'. Therefore, if people borrow money, the interest they pay reflects the demand for the goods and services which are purchased with the borrowed money. If people lend money, then the interest they demand reflects their willingness to forego the goods which they could otherwise have purchased. Because money is considered to be neutral, borrowing reflects the demand for money whilst saving reflects the supply of money and the rate of interest equates them, so that changes in investment and savings cause changes in the rate of interest. Diagram 4.5 shows saving (S) and investment (I) schedules with equilibrium rate of interest r0.

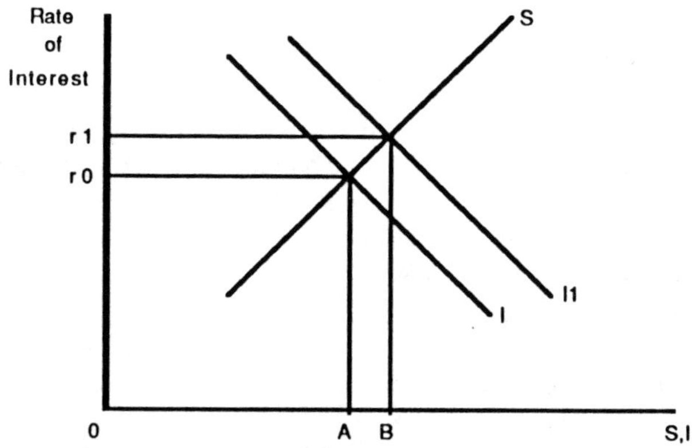

Diagram 4.5

Suppose the desire to invest increases, this is shown in Diagram 4.5 by a movement of the investment schedule from I to I1. The rate of interest will be bid up so that savings will be augmented by the attraction of higher interest rates and investment will fall because the cost of borrowing has increased. The rate of interest will continue to rise until it reaches r1 where saving equals investment. Real theory holds that interest rates change quickly and smoothly so that the volume of savings is always equal to the volume of investment.

Thus, real theory rests on two important assumptions - that investment is interest-elastic and that the rate of interest is perfectly free to change.

However, these assumptions break down in the real world. Empirical studies have casted doubt on the validity of the first assumption and the rate of interest is considerably influenced by monetary authorities thereby making the second assumption invalid.

4.8.3 Liquidity Preference or Monetary Theories of Interest

Liquidity preference theory was developed by Keynes and it challenges the classical theory that the interest rate will fluctuate so as to equate saving and investment.

Liquidity preference is the extent to which a person prefers to hold cash rather than part with it. An individual may keep his wealth in the form of money, financial claims or real capital. If he keeps his wealth in the form of money, he loses interest so that interest can be viewed as the reward for parting with money.

Keynesian theory distinguishes between three motives for holding money:

(a) The Transactions Motive

Individuals hold money to meet their day-to-day cash requirements. In other words, money is demanded for its medium of exchange function. The level of transactions balances depend mainly on the level of income and expenditure, and on institutional practices which includes, for example, how often people are paid, and whether banks will allow their customers to overdraw their accounts.

(b) The Precautionary Motive

Individuals hold money as a reserve to meet unforeseen contingencies - this reflects money's store of value function. The level of precautionary balances will depend upon what individuals judge to be adequate and they are likely to depend on the level of income.

Diagram 4.6 shows that at a given level of income the combined transactions and precautionary demand for money (Ltp) will be a vertical line because as we have already noted, their size depends on the level of income and not on the rate of interest.

The effect of changes in income on the combined curve is shown by a movement to the left or right. For example, a reduction in income will lead to a reduction in both the transactions and precautionary demand pushing Ltp to the left. An increase in income will push Ltp to the right.

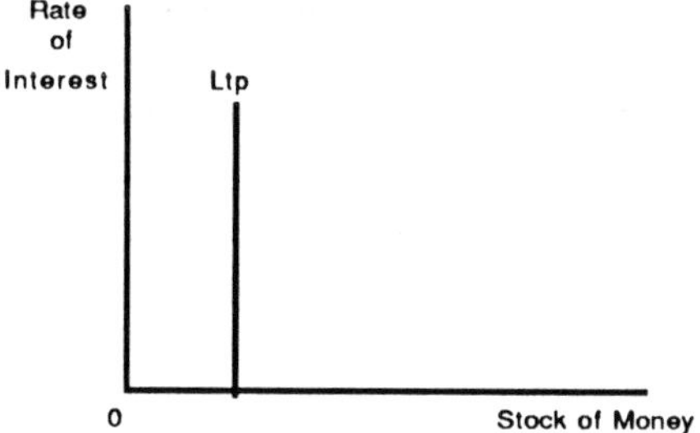

Diagram 4.6

(c) The Speculative Motive

Individuals hold money for speculative purposes, that is, they hold money in the expectation that prices of securities will fall or interest rates will rise. Investors hope to make a gain by buying and selling bonds at the right time. Thus, when interest rates are lower than considered normal (i.e. bond prices higher than normal) investors will sell bonds and hold more money because the cost of holding money is low (i.e. interest rates are low). When bond prices are lower than considered normal (i.e. interest rates are higher than normal) investors will buy bonds and hold less money because the cost of holding money is high. Notice that an increase in bond prices means that the rate of interest has fallen and vice-versa. This point can be illustrated as follows:

Suppose a bond costs £100 and pays £4 interest per annum - the rate of interest is;

$$\frac{£4}{100} \times 100 = 4\%$$

If the price of the bond goes up to £120, the rate of interest will be;

$$\frac{£4}{120} \times 100 = 3\ ^1/_3\%$$

Diagram 4.7 shows the speculative demand for money (Ls).

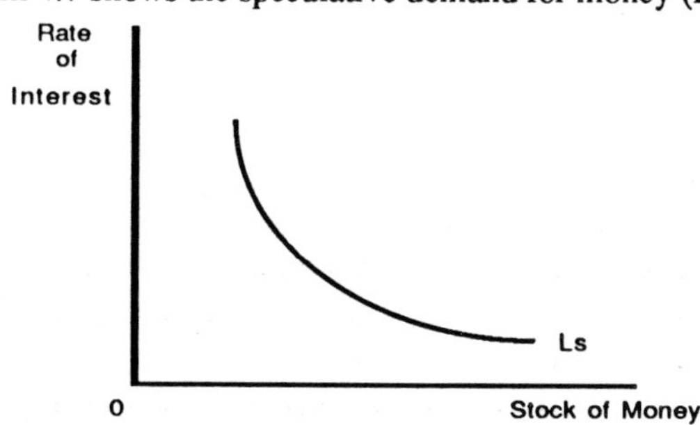

Diagram 4.7

The speculative demand for money is downward sloping from left to right because it is a function of the rate of interest.

Diagram 4.8 shows the total demand for money (i.e. Ltp + Ls) which is a function of income and the rate of interest.

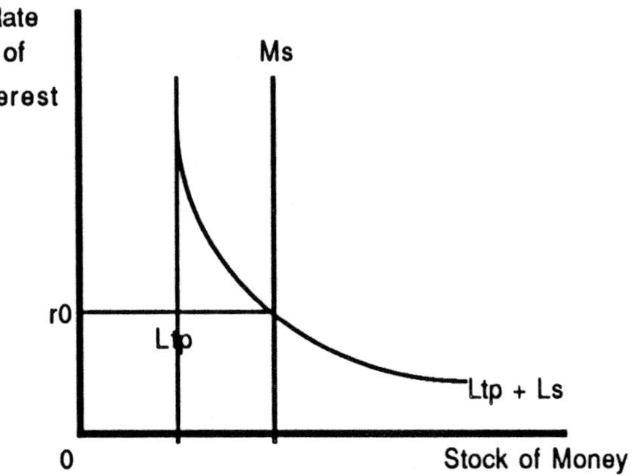

Diagram 4.8

Liquidity preference theory concentrates mainly on the demand for money, assuming that the stock of money (Ms) is determined independently by the monetary authorities. The rate of interest (r0) is the rate which equates the demand to hold money and the stock of money.

Extreme Keynesian theory sees the interest rate as being held at a certain level by speculative actions of bondholders. Fluctuations in saving and investment have no effect on the rate of interest because bondholders would buy or sell bonds to stabilise it but equilibrium would be restored through changes in the level of income. However, this extreme version of Keynes' theory is rejected by many economists and a modified version has been more widely accepted which states that changes in saving and investment cause changes in both the rate of interest and in income.

4.9 Summary

1. Money is an important economic indicator.
2. The amount of cash in an economy is regulated by the central bank.
3. Bank deposits are created when a bank receives a cash deposit from its customer; when it grants a loan to a customer; and when it purchases an investment.
4. Under a system of monetary base control, each bank has to keep a

minimum proportion of its liabilities in the form of base money which comprises balances with the Bank of England and may also include notes and coin held by banks and notes and coin in circulation.

5. The PSBR measures the amount that the public sector borrows from other sectors of the economy and overseas to finance any deficit that arises in its payments and receipts.
6. The PSBR is funded by:
   (a) By sales of debt to the non-bank private sector.
   (b) By external transactions.
   (c) By borrowing from the banking system.
7. Disintermediation is the use of savings and credit facilities outside the banking system.
8. Overfunding means that the authorities sell more public debt than is required to finance the PSBR.
9. The sale of public sector assets (privatisation) has been an important part of Government policy in recent years.
10. Monetary targets are currently applied to M0.
11. The current monetary control arrangements were introduced in August 1981.
12. There are two main theories of of the demand for money and the determination of the rate of interest:
    (a) Real, non-monetary or loanable funds theory.
    (b) Liquidity preference or monetary theory.
13. Liquidity preference theory distinguishes between three motives for holding money:
    (a) Transactions motive.
    (b) Precautionary motive.
    (c) Speculative motive.

Questions

1.* To what extent does the Bank of England now attempt to influence the general level of interest rates? Include in your answer an analysis of the Bank of England's operations in the money markets.

2.* Outline the major commercial factors which influence the distribution and growth of a commercial bank's assets. In what ways has the Bank of England influenced the structure of bank balance sheets in the United Kingdom during the last ten years?

3. Outline the present functions of the London discount market. To

what extent has the role of the discount market within the financial system changed since 1970?

4.* Outline the main changes in monetary control techniques that have occurred in the United Kingdom in the last two years. How have these changes affected the commercial banks?

(April 1982)

5. Outline the reasons for 'funding policy' as applied to government securities, the means by which it is carried out, and its effect on the banking system.

6.* Explain why the British Government needs to borrow (ignoring any need to borrow from abroad) and the impact of its domestic borrowing requirement on the banking system.

7. 'Monetary targets are pretty meaningless unless a broad definition is used' (Kaldor and Trevithick, 1981). In the light of this statement, discuss the problems which have occurred in the implementation of U.K. monetary policy in the last two years.

(Sept.1981 Paper)

8. Examine the relationship between the changes in a country's money stock and changes in its total output of goods and services.

9. Outline and explain the connection between the supply of money and the rate of inflation.

10. Compare and contrast the 'monetarist' and Keynesian viewpoints of how an increase in a country's money supply affects growth, inflation and the level of interest rates. Distinguish between short and long-run effects.

11. Distinguish between Keynesian and monetarist viewpoints on the motives for holding money. Why are these different approaches of importance for the conduct of monetary policy?

12. Distinguish between Keynesian and monetarist viewpoints on how an increase in a country's money supply affects;
    (a) the rate of inflation;
    (b) the rate of unemployment.

13. What effects do changes in a country's money stock have on its commercial banks?

14. For what reasons does a commercial bank need liquidity and how may it be provided? How has Bank of England supervision in this area evolved in the past two years?
(April 1983)

15. Define the measure of the money supply in the United Kingdom known as sterling M3. Explain how sterling M3 would be directly affected by each of the following:-
(a) an increase in sales of gilt-edged securities by the Bank of England;
(b) the payment by companies of value-added tax;
(c) an increase in sterling bank lending to the overseas sector.
(*Student note:* sterling M3 is now M3)

16. Discuss the factors which affect the level and pattern of money market interest rates in the United Kingdom. To what extent do changes in money market rates lead to changes in commercial banks' base rates?

17. In what basic ways do the U.K. monetary authorities currently seek to control the money supply? Briefly indicate how the methods of control have changed since June 1980.

18. Discuss in detail the main factors which cause changes in the money stock.

19. (a) What are the main ways in which a government may finance its borrowing requirement?
(b) Why is the way in which government borrowing is financed of importance to the banks?

20. (a) Define the measure of the money supply in the United Kingdom known as sterling M3.
(b) Discuss the view that changes in bank lending and only changes in bank lending cause changes in sterling M3.
(*Student note:* sterling M3 is now M3)

21. Explain in detail how an increase in government borrowing influences:-

(a) The money supply
(b) conditions in the money markets.

22. Assess the possible effects of an increase in government borrowing on:
(a) the money supply;
(b) long-term rates of interest.

23. Since 1984 the U.K. monetary authorities have set a target for the growth of the monetary aggregate MO, also known as the 'wide monetary base'.
(a) Define MO and explain the reasons for its introduction.
(b) Is the behaviour of MO alone sufficient to provide a clear picture of monetary conditions in the United Kingdom?

24. (a) What are meant by the terms 'PSBR' and 'overfunding'?(10)
(b) Discuss the importance of the PSBR and overfunding in relation to the control of the money supply. (15)

25. (a) What does the concept of liquidity mean in relation to: (i) an individual, (ii) a commercial bank?
(b) How do commercial banks provide for liquidity?

26. Outline the main ways in which a government can finance a budget deficit. How might the need to finance a rising deficit affect commercial banks?

27. Examine the effects of the following on the sterling M3 measure of the money supply:
(a) a reduction in the Public Sector Borrowing Requirement (PSBR);
(b) an increase in sterling bank lending to the UK private sector;
(c) a balance of payments surplus.
(*Student note:* sterling M3 is now M3)

28. (a) Define the measure of money supply known in the UK as sterling M3. (6)
(b) Why is the way in which government borrowing is financed crucial to the control of sterling M3? (11)
(c) What indicators other than sterling M3 do the authorities consider in assessing monetary conditions? (8)
(*Student note:* sterling M3 is now M3)

29. (a) How might a government reduce the size of its Public Sector Borrowing Requirement (PSBR)? (9)
    (b) Assess the effect of a reduction in the PSBR on:
    (i) the money supply;
    (ii) short-term and long-term interest rates (16)

30. Examine the influence of the Bank of England on:
    (a) interest rates in the London money market;
    (b) the structure of commercial banks' balance sheets.

31. (a) What is meant by the term 'Public Sector Borrowing Requirement' (PSBR)? (5)
    (b) Assuming the PSBR is zero, discuss the factors which could generate an increase in a country's money supply. (11)
    (c) Can the credit creation process be carried on indefinitely? (9)

32. (a) Explain how a government's public sector borrowing requirement (PSBR) might be:
    (i) reduced;
    (ii) financed. (16)
    (b) Why are the size and method of financing the PSBR of importance for commercial banks? (9)

33. (a) Define the measure of money supply known in the UK as M4.(7)
    (b) Discuss in detail the main factors which cause M4 to grow.(18)

CHAPTER 5

Interest Rates

5.1.1 The Role of the Rate of Interest

Interest is the price paid for borrowing money. Whenever money is borrowed a claim on the future comes into existence. For example, if a person borrows money, he may simply promise to repay whereas if a company borrows money, it may issue a financial claim on the future which may take the form of a bond or equity share. A financial claim, therefore, is a claim to the payment of a future sum of money and/or a periodic payment of money. The rate of interest can be seen as being a price which is determined by the interaction of the supply of and the demand for financial claims.

In Chapter 4 we considered the determination of the rate of interest by looking at two theories - the real (loanable funds) and the liquidity preference theories. The liquidity preference theory focuses on the price of liquidity (money) ignoring the real forces of thrift and productivity whilst the real theory focuses on these real forces so that it seeks to explain the determination of the rate of interest over the long-term. We can develop the role of the rate of interest further by considering more fully the demand for and supply of loanable funds in the economy and the setting of interest rates by banks.

The supply of loanable funds comes from individuals and firms. Individuals save for a variety of reasons such as saving for a 'rainy day' or to enable them to purchase some expensive commodity in the future. Companies save in the form of undistributed profits. It pays those with surplus funds to lend them out provided they obtain a rate of interest which covers the risk of the loan not being repaid. Banks play an important part in the channelling of these funds to individuals and firms who wish to borrow but we have already seen that the monetary authorities exert great influence over the supply of loanable funds.

The demand for loanable funds comes from individuals, firms and the government. Individuals demand loans for consumption and investment. They are willing to pay interest on these loans because they prefer to buy today rather than save and buy in the future. Expectations of increases in income over time together with expectations as to the future level of inflation play an important part in many peoples' decisions to borrow. Although the action of borrowing for consumption is sometimes referred to as impatience, there are some purchases that necessitate borrowing because it takes so long to save sufficient money to make an outright purchase, e.g., house purchase.

Firms borrow money to invest in capital goods which they expect will yield a return in excess of the cost of capital. By investing in capital, firms can raise production - this is called the productivity of capital. Businesses' demand for loanable funds is represented by the marginal productivity of capital. The marginal productivity of capital falls as each additional unit of capital is employed, so the decision as to whether to borrow money depends upon the productivity of the investment and the rate of interest. For example, if the investment is expected to yield a return of 5% per annum whilst the rate of interest on borrowed funds is 15% per annum, the borrowing of money to finance the investment would not be profitable. Thus, the lower the rate of interest, the greater the demand for loans because less productive projects will yield a return in excess of the cost of the funds which were used to finance the project. If rates of interest are extremely high, demand for loans will fall because there will be few projects which will yield a profit.

Government needs to borrow if their expenditure on the provision of goods and services is greater than its revenue.

A large number of empirical studies have been made regarding the demand for loanable funds. Most have concluded that the lower the rate of interest the higher the demand for loans. However, the studies generally show that the relationship between the demand for loans and interest rates is weak because there are other factors which affect the demand for loans apart from the level of interest rates. In a Bank of England discussion paper entitled 'Bank Lending and the Money Supply', published in July 1980, the Bank's researchers found that the most important factors which affected a company's demand for loans were wage costs, import costs, tax payments and stock building. In addition, studies also show that the demand for loans is fairly inelastic so that other things being equal, a reduction in interest rates leads to a less than proportionate increase in the demand for loanable funds. However, the increased use of sophisticated investment appraisal techniques such as discounted cash flow, and the high interest rates over recent years has probably resulted in making the private sector more conscious of changes in interest rates.

The price of loanable funds is essentially determined by the demand for and supply of loanable funds. However, such an approach would have to be modified to some extent for the following reasons. Often interest rates are not sufficiently free to move so as to equate the demand for and supply of loanable funds. For example, for administrative reasons, banks are reluctant to alter their interest rates every time the demand for loans changes. In addition, the monetary authorities exert considerable influence on the level of interest rates. The monetary authorities affect both sides of the market because they are borrowers on the one hand and they use monetary policy to influence the rate of growth in the money supply on the other.

The determination of interest rates by banks involves a number of considerations. The fundamental consideration for every bank is to equate the demand for and the supply of its funds. The difference between the rate of interest paid to depositors and the rate of interest charged on its advances provides a margin which should be sufficient to cover all its operating expenses and taxation, leaving a profit. However, in setting their interest rates, banks are influenced by a number of other factors:

1. Competition between banks and other financial institutions. Banks compete on both sides of their balance sheet i.e., the attraction of deposits and customers to lend to.
2. Monetary policy.
3. The level of interest rates in other countries.
4. The rate of inflation. If rates of interest remain unchanged an increase in the rate of inflation means that the real rate of interest falls and may even become negative. Thus, lenders demand a positive real return to offset the detrimental effect of inflation on their funds.

The factors noted above are of a general nature, applying to banks in all countries. However, as far as U.K. banks are concerned, an important consideration is that banks may be open to arbitrage operations (or roundtripping) if their rates do not move in line with wholesale money market rates. If the gap between these rates and bank base rates widens, large customers may find it profitable to borrow from banks and re-lend the money in the wholesale markets. On the other hand, if the wholesale rates fall below base rates, large customers may find it to their advantage to borrow from the wholesale markets rather than from the banks. Banks stem this type of activity by keeping their base rates in line with wholesale market rates.

5.1.2 Real and Nominal Interest Rates

A nominal rate of interest is one which is expressed in money terms whereas a real rate of interest is a nominal rate of interest which has been adjusted for the expected rate of inflation. For example, a nominal rate of interest of 15% adjusted for an expected inflation rate of 10% is equivalent to a real rate of interest of 5%. If the rate of inflation exceeds the nominal rate of interest, the real rate of interest becomes negative.

However, the main problem in calculating real rates is that we cannot calculate future rates of inflation in advance with certainty but despite this, the real gross redemption yields on index-linked gilt-edged securities provide a calculation of real rates of return. For example, 2% Treasury index-linked 1988 provided a real gross redemption yield of over 5% in 1984 and this had fallen to around 3-4% in 1986 and 2-3% in 1987. Similarly, the real gross redemption yield on 2.5% Treasury index-linked 2016 has been around 3-4% over recent years.

For some years nominal rates of interest in the U.K. (and also in the U.S.A.) have risen to high levels and these increases in nominal rates have been associated with higher rates of inflation. Table 5.1 shows inflation and interest rates over the period 1973-87.

Table 5.1 Inflation and interest rates 1973-85

(Annual averages: % per annum)

	1973-80	1981	1982	1983	1984	1985	1986	1987
Rate of growth in Retail Price Index	14.8	12.0	8.7	4.6	5.0	6.1	3.4	4.2
Yield on Treasury bills	11.3	13.0	9.96	9.04	9.33	11.48	10.94	8.38
Yield on long-dated government stocks	13.3	14.8	12.88	10.8	10.69	10.62	9.87	9.47
Yield on equities	5.9	5.9	5.7	4.8	4.6	4.5	4.0	3.5

(Source: Financial Statistics and Bank of England Quarterly Bulletin)

The figures show that throughout the 1970s the rates of return on both Treasury bills and government stocks were below the rate of inflation (i.e. the real rates of return were negative). However, in the 1980s the rate of inflation fell substantially thereby providing investors with a positive real return on their holdings of Treasury bills and government stocks.

There are a number of reasons why interest rates reached such high levels in the U.K. in the 1970s and early 1980s:

1. Interest rates became more volatile and there were a number of reasons for this:
   (a) In recent years the authorities focussed on controlling the growth of monetary aggregates rather than interest rates and this resulted in interest rates becoming volatile. The Bank of England is a marginal provider of funds so that if there is a shortage in the market, it will be in a monopoly position under such conditions. Thus, the Bank cannot control both the price and quantity so that if the Bank exerts control over

quantity then price will be determined by the market.

(b) In recent years interest rates became more volatile because the rate of inflation fluctuated. The rate of inflation reached over 25% in 1975, by 1978 it had fallen to under 10%, by 1980 it had once again increased to over 20% and it had fallen back down to 3% in 1986. These fluctuations in the rate of inflation led to an increase in volatility of interest rates.

(c) Interest rates became more volatile because the economic conditions in the 1970s and 1980s became less stable and this was reflected in the financial markets. In addition, the tremendous amount of interest-rate arbitrage between the two important financial centres of London and New York resulted in the two centres pulling each other's interest rates upwards. Similar considerations caused interest rates to rise steeply in the U.S.

2. In order to finance the gap between revenue and expenditure, the government has to issue debt. To sell this debt, rates of interest have had to be increased to make it more attractive to purchasers because of their expectation that inflation will continue in the future. However, a further attraction is the prospect of a capital gain if interest rates fall, (i.e. the price of gilt-edged securities rises). An added advantage to a holder of gilts is that there is no capital gains tax liability on stocks.

The effect of a fluctuating rate of inflation is that it creates greater financial uncertainty. Thus, companies have greater difficulty in trying to determine what their real cost of capital will be. It is probably this uncertainty which has contributed to the virtual disappearance of the long-term debt market in the 1970s and early 1980s (it is probable that the fall in company profitability in the 1970s also contributed).

5.2.1 The Level and Pattern of Interest Rates

The term structure of interest rates refers to the pattern of rates on securities which are similar apart from the term to maturity. It can be generally observed that interest rates on short-term securities are lower than on long-term securities. This can be demonstrated by a yield curve which shows the relationship between the yield and the maturity of fixed interest securities which are similar except for the term to maturity. A 'usual' shaped yield curve (curve A) is shown in Diagram 5.2. It shows that yields are lower on shorter maturities and higher on longer maturities. This is because the longer the term to maturity, the greater the risk and uncertainty so that the lender must be compensated for this by a higher return. Sometimes the yield curve slopes downwards from left to right (curve B) and this may occur for example when investors expect short-term rates to fall resulting in a sufficiently large increase in demand in the longer end of the market to push long-term rates below short-term rates. Thus, the yield curve does not remain the same over time and we will consider the reasons for this later in the chapter.

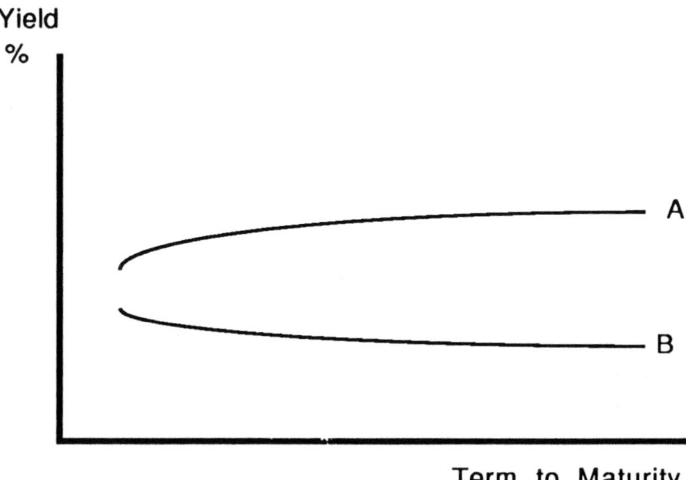

Diagram 5.2

5.2.2 The Reverse Yield Gap

This term relates to the fact that yields on equities are below the yields on gilt-edged stocks. Table 5.1 shows the Reverse Yield Gap which arose because investors turned to equities rather than fixed-interest stock during periods of higher levels of inflation. This is because equities provide investors with the prospect of increasing dividends and rising asset values of companies. Thus, the increased demand for equities pushed their prices to such a high level that their yields fell below those of gilt-edged stocks. The Reverse Yield Gap has widened over the last 20 years.

5.3.1 The Structure of Interest Rates

Although economists often speak of *'the'* interest rate, it is obvious that at any one time there are a number of interest rates. A first class company will be able to borrow more cheaply than a small newly-formed company. Government stocks and company bonds are issued at various interest rates. The reason why there are a variety of interest rates is that an interest rate is more than the price paid for the use of money. It also covers the risk of non-payment by the debtor, the administrative costs involved in making a loan, and it must compensate the lender for the loss of liquidity. The loss of liquidity factor involves two further considerations - the period of time for which the loan has been made and whether the debt can be sold to someone else before maturity. There are a spread of interest rates because loans differ as to the mix of each of these factors. In addition, the size of the loan is important. Thus, retail banks pay a lower rate on 7-day deposits compared with money market deposits where a minimum deposit of £10,000 is usually stipulated. Table 5.3 shows the yields on short-term money, British government securities and company securities.

Table 5.3 Yields (%) on May 30, 1986

Short-term money rates	
Treasury bills	9.56
Prime bank bills (3 months)	9.44
Trade bills (3 months)	10.13
Retail banks:	
7-day deposit	6.54
Call money	10.00
Inter-bank:	
Overnight lending	8.00 - 10.88
7 days	10.13 - 10.50
3 months	9.69 - 9.94
Sterling CDs (3 months)	9.63 - 9.75
British government securities	
Short-dated (up to 5 years)	8.50
Medium-dated (up to 10 years)	8.84
Long-dated (up to 20 years)	9.00
Company securities	
Debenture and loan stocks	9.94
Preference stocks	10.78
Industrial ordinary shares (dividend yield)	3.80

(Source: Financial Statistics)

It can be seen that yields differ because of the reasons noted above. For example, the return on British government stocks is slightly lower than on industrial debentures and loan stocks because of the lower risk of default and British government stocks are highly marketable. Bank 7-day deposit rates are lower than on similar deposits offered by building societies and finance houses because the former carries less risk of default. On long-term lending there is the additional risk associated with inflation - the erosion of the real value of the interest received and also the capital, so that lenders will seek a higher return on long-term fixed interest lending. We have noted that liquidity considerations are important so that for example, bank 7-day deposit rate is lower than the rates on term deposits because the former is more liquid.

The short-term money rates are very important because changes in these rates influence the level of interest rates in the long-term markets. We noted in Chapter 3 that the Bank of England influences rates in the very short end of the money market so that if rates rise in the very short end of the market other rates will also rise because of the highly competitive nature of the financial markets. The short-term money rates are particularly important indicators because they strongly influence the level of interest rates in all the financial markets. Thus, an increase in short-term money rates will tend to push up bank base rates because the banks increasingly rely on money market funds. In particular, the three-month LIBOR represents the marginal cost of funds to the banks so that changes in inter-bank rates influence the level of bank base rates. Table 5.4 shows the three-month inter-bank bid and offered rates and base rates between January and May 1986. The table shows that bank base rates are greatly influenced by the three-month LIBOR. Thus, the gradual fall in the three-month LIBOR has been matched by a gradual reduction in bank base rates over the period.

Table 5.4 Bank Base Rates and Three-month Inter-Bank Rates (%)

3-months Inter-bank		*Bank Base rate*	
Jan 31	12.81-12.94	Jan 9	12.5
Feb 28	12.25-12.38	Mar 19	11.5
Mar 21	11.13-11.31	Apr 9	11.0
Apr 25	10.25-10.38	Apr 24	10.5
May 30	9.69-9.94	May 27	10.0

(Source: Financial Statistics)

5.4 The Relationship between Short Term and Long Term Rates of Interest

The connections between short-term rates and long-term rates of interest are so strong that a large and permanent change in short-term rates will be associated with a change in the same direction in long-term rates. The link between the rates arises because borrowers and lenders alter their maturity-structures (or time-structures) to take advantage of any changes in interest rates. This applies to individuals, industrial and commercial companies and financial institutions. For example, suppose the monetary authorities bring about a reduction in short-term interest rates, lenders will prefer to lend money for longer-terms so as to take advantage of higher long-term rates whilst borrowers will prefer to borrow for shorter-terms. Because of the change in demand and supply in the long-term markets, long-term rates will tend to be pushed down. As the rates on short-term deposits falls, depositors will be more likely to place their funds in long-term securities such as gilts, and an increase in demand for these securities raises their price and lowers their yield.

It is not essential for holders of financial assets to switch from one end of the time scale to the opposite end, for example, from bank seven day deposits to very long-term government stocks. A mere movement along the time-scale by holders is all that is necessary to affect the term structure of interest rates. Thus, if short-term interest rates rise, a small shift of maturity structures by holders of financial assets will create a 'ripple' effect which will raise longer-term interest rates. The way in which movements in short-term interest rates become translated into movements in long-term interest rates depends on how competitive financial assets are. The more competitive and wide-ranging they are the smoother will be the ripple effect. This is certainly the case in the U.K. For example, the gilt-edged market provides investors with a wide range of maturities. Industrial and commercial companies issue many types of stocks and shares. The growth of financial intermediaries has resulted in the growth of financial assets which are varied and competitive.

The extent to which long-term rates move in response to changes in short-term rates depends much upon market expectations. Thus, a rise in short-term interest rates may have little effect on long-term rates if the market expects short-term rates to fall again shortly. However, a movement in short-term rates may well affect expectations so that the monetary authorities are able to influence the level of long-term rates by altering the level of short-term rates and the greater the change in market expectations the greater the effect on long-term rates.

In an earlier section we noted that normally the yield curve would be upward sloping but that it does not remain the same over time. We have already seen that one of the main determinants of the term structure of interest rates is market expectations regarding the future level of interest rates. Indeed the term structure of interest rates may change to such an extent that long-term rates may fall below short-term rates. This might occur where the market expects short-term rates to fall resulting in a sufficiently large increase in demand to push longer-term rates below short-term rates. In this situation, the yield curve would be downward sloping. Table 5.5 shows redemption yields on British government securities over recent years. It can be seen that for the period 1983-86 the yield curve was downward sloping.

Table 5.5 Redemption Yields on British Government Securities (%)

	Short-dated	*Medium-dated*	*Long-dated*
1981	14.65	14.88	14.74
1982	12.79	13.08	12.88
1983	11.19	11.27	10.80
1984	11.29	11.27	10.69
1985	11.13	11.06	10.62
1986	10.01	10.05	9.87
1987	9.36	9.57	9.47

(Source: Financial Statistics)

Occasionally, very short-term rates in the money markets rise to extremely high levels. This can occur where the banks and other institutions operating in the money markets require over-night money to enable them to balance their books. The price of over-night money can rise dramatically at such times.

5.5 The Relationship between Domestic, International and Eurocurrency Rates

We noted in Chapter 3 that the financial markets in London are highly competitive, and that the financial markets are international in character with London an important eurocurrency centre. Thus, there is a strong relationship between domestic, international and eurocurrency rates. In particular, rates for short-term funds in London and New York are highly competitive. For example, if interest rates rise in New York there will be a movement of interest sensitive short-term funds from London to New York. This will have the effect of pushing up short-term rates in London and because these exert a strong influence on the level of bank base rates, these will rise and other domestic rates will also rise. Interest rate differentials result in asset switching between financial centres and as we shall see in Chapter 8, such switching will affect exchange rates. However, for asset-switching to take place, the differential must be greater than any expected rate of appreciation of the domestic currency since an appreciation of the domestic currency will offset the benefit of the interest differential.

5.6.1 The Effect of Interest Rate Changes on the Banks

An increase in interest rates will affect the banks in the following ways:

1. When interest rates are high, retail banks' profits increase because of the 'endowment' element in retail bank profits. However, the banks may narrow the margin between deposit and lending rates as interest rates rise. The endowment effect may result in the government applying a windfall profits tax (as it did in 1981).

   Higher interest rates mean that their fixed-interest lending will be less profitable. On their wholesale business, the margin between bid and offered rates may remain unchanged as interest rates rise.
2. Banks may attract more interest-bearing funds due to a very short term increase in their competitiveness. This is because they are usually quicker to raise their interest rates compared with building societies, National Savings and their other competitors. However, the growth in current account balances will slow down due to switching to interest-earning accounts.

   Expectations are important because if investors believe that the rise in interest rates is temporary they may purchase fixed-interest securities (in particular gilts) with a consequent reduction in bank deposits.
3. High interest rates will tend to reduce bank lending. However, their advances may not fall greatly because lending tends to be interest-inelastic and there may be distress borrowing.
4. If the high interest rates reduce economic activity, then lending opportunities decrease and the difficulties that some bank customers may have of servicing higher interest payments may result in the banks increasing their bad debt provisions so that bank profits are adversely affected.
5. Banks will make a capital loss on their fixed-interest investments. The banks hold British government stocks and the prices of these securities will fall as interest rates rise.
6. The earnings from banks' overseas subsidiaries will be reduced by the rise in the exchange rate, as will the sterling value of banks' overseas residents deposits.

A reduction in interest rates will tend to have the opposite effect to that described above.

5.6.2 The Effect of Interest Rate Changes on the Domestic Economy

An increase in interest rates will affect the domestic economy in the following way:

1. High interest rates will adversely affect demand, output and employment through its deflationary effect on the economy. Higher interest rates increase industries' bank debt interest costs so that they may reduce their investment expenditure. Individuals may reduce the amount that they borrow for spending so that expenditure in the economy is reduced. In addition, higher mortgage rates will mean that consumer expenditure will be reduced.
2. Higher interest rates will tend to raise the exchange rate and reduce domestic output (see next section)
3. The very short term effect of high interest rates may be to push up the inflation rate, for example, because of the higher mortgage costs. However, the longer term effect will be to push inflation down because of the deflationary effect of high interest rates, the fall in the money supply and the reduced costs of imports.

A reduction in interest rates will tend to have the opposite effect to that described above.

5.6.3 The Effect of Interest Rate Changes on the Balance of Payments

An increase in interest rates will attract short-term interest sensitive funds which will have a beneficial effect on the capital account of the balance of payments. This will push up the exchange rate (assuming it is not fixed) making imports relatively more cheap and exports relatively more expensive. Domestic output may fall for two reasons. Firstly, the production of goods for export may fall because UK producers find it more difficult to sell abroad and secondly, imported goods may rise because they will be more competitive thus driving UK producers out of the domestic market. The balance of trade may be adversely affected but this depends on elasticity conditions. There will be increased outflows of funds on the invisible account as interest payments are made on the foreign capital.

A reduction in interest rates will tend to have the opposite effect to that described above.

5.7 Summary

1. Interest is the price paid for borrowing money.
2. The price of loanable funds is determined by the demand for and supply of loanable funds.
3. When setting their interest rates, banks are influenced by the following factors:
   (a) Competition.
   (b) Monetary policy.
   (c) Interest rates in other countries.
   (d) The rate of inflation.
   (e) Rates in the wholesale money markets.
4. A nominal interest rate is one which is expressed in money terms. A real rate of interest is a nominal rate of interest which has been adjusted for the expected rate of inflation.
5. The term structure of interest rates refers to the pattern of rates on securities which are similar apart from the term to maturity.
6. The Reverse Yield Gap relates to the fact that the yields on equities are below the yields on gilt-edged securities.
7. The structure of interest rates is determined by the size of the loan, the risk of non-payment by the debtor, administrative costs in making the loan, and compensation to the lender for the loss of liquidity (this depends on the term of the loan and whether it is marketable).
8. The connections between short-term rates and long-term rates of interest are so strong that a large and permanent change in short-term rates will be associated with a change in the same direction in long-term rates.
9. There is a strong relationship between domestic, international and eurocurrency rates.

Questions

1. What domestic factors affect the general level of interest rates in a country?

2. If a bank, operating in a modern community, is free to determine its own interest rates on deposits and advances, what factors influence it in doing so? What particular considerations, if any, apply to U.K. banks?

3.* Account for the large fluctuations in interest rates which have occurred in Britain in the 1970s.

4. Why, in practice, are there so many different rates of interest in a country such as the U.K.?

5. Briefly explain the difference between nominal and real rates of interest. Why did nominal interest rates reach such high peaks last winter, in countries such as the U.K. and the U.S.A.? (September 1980 paper)

6. What do you understand by the term 'yield curve'. Discuss the factors which influence the relationship between short-term and long-term interest rates. Illustrate your answer by reference to recent experience in the United Kingdom or any other country with which you are familiar.

7. Analyse the effects of a fall in the general level of interest rates on:-
   (i) the commercial banks
   (ii) the customers of the commercial banks.

8. Assess the likely effects of an increase in the general level of interest rates on:-
   (a) a country's economy;
   (b) the commercial banks.

9. Distinguish between nominal and real rates of interest. For what reasons might a country experience:
   (a) a high level of nominal interest rates;
   (b) high real rates of interest?

10. What do you understand by the 'term structure' of interest rates? Explain in detail the factors which influence the relationship between short-term and long-term interest rates.

11. Evaluate the effect of an increase in a country's interest rates on:
    (a) its commercial banks;
    (b) its balance of payments.

12. (a) What is meant by 'real' rates of interest and how are they calculated? (10)
    (b) Why have real rates remained high in most major economies

for the greater part of this decade? (15)

13. (a) What factors influence the general level of interest rates in a country? (10)
(b) Discuss the specific factors influencing:
(i) short-term interest rates in the London money markets;
(ii) UK commercial banks' base rates;
(iii) the yield on long-term gilt-edged securities. (15)

14. (a) Why are there so many rates of interest in a developed economy? (15)
(b) Describe how these different rates of interest are illustrated by the operations of a commercial bank. (10)

15. (a) Why and how does the Bank of England intervene in the money markets? (10)
(b) Discuss the view that the level of mortgage rates is primarily determined by the rate at which the Bank of England deals in 14-day bills of exchange in the money market. (15)

16. Analyse the effects of a rise in a country's interest rates on:
(i) the personal sector;
(ii) the corporate sector;
(iii) the commercial banks;
(iv) the capital account of the balance of payments.

17. (a) What is meant by the term 'yield curve'? (7)
(b) Examine:
(i) the factors which, in normal conditions, produce higher rates for long-term than short-term maturities;
(ii) the relationship between short-term interbank rates and commercial bank lending rates. (18)

CHAPTER 6

Monetary Policy

6.1.1 Objectives

The 1959 Radcliffe Report on the working of the monetary system set out the objectives of monetary policy in the U.K.:

1. A high and stable level of employment.
2. Reasonable stability of the internal purchasing power of money.
3. Steady economic growth and improvement of the standard of living.
4. Some contribution to the economic development of the outside world.
5. A satisfactory balance of payments.

6.1.2 Targets and Instruments of Monetary Policy

Monetary policy can be used to influence aggregate demand in two ways:

1. By bringing about a change in interest rates. The monetary authorities can influence investment and consumption by raising or lowering interest rates.
2. By controlling the money supply. The monetary authorities can reduce (increase) liquidity in the economy so that those wanting money to spend will find it more (less) difficult than before.

Thus, monetary policy has an effect on unemployment through its effect on aggregate demand. It also has an effect on investment and consumption and therefore, the rate of economic growth. Finally, it may be used to improve the balance of payments position by altering interest rates.

Monetary policy may be used to achieve policy objectives but the way in which monetary policy does so is by influencing intermediate targets such as the money stock, interest rates, credit, the level of expenditure and the exchange rate. To control intermediate targets, the monetary authorities influence operating targets such as the asset structure of banks or money market interest rates by the use of monetary policy instruments such as open market operations. For example, the stages of monetary policy may be as follows:

1. Instruments (open market operations)
2. Operating target (level of interest rates)
3. Intermediate target (control of growth of money stock and

expenditure)

4. Policy objective (reduce rate of inflation)

6.2.1 Effectiveness of Monetary Policy Techniques

The effectiveness of monetary policy techniques depends upon the central bank's relationship with the commercial banks. For monetary policy techniques to be effective the central bank must act as a banker to the commercial banks; it must have a monopoly of the note issue so that it is the only supplier of cash to the banks and the lender of last resort; and it must have the power to determine or alter the reserve requirement of banks, so as to make open market operations effective.

6.2.2 Problems Associated With the Use of Direct Controls

1. They distort competition between banks (i.e., between those that are subject to the direct controls and those that are not) and between banks and other financial institutions.
2. They inhibit competition between banks.
3. They lead to disintermediation.

6.2.3 Problems Associated with Controlling Interest Rates

1. It is difficult to estimate with any great accuracy the effect of changes in interest rates on the demand for credit.

2. There is the problem of time lags. The full effect of changes in interest rates occurs some time after the changes have been implemented. Thus, households and firms may not be able to reduce borrowing immediately interest rates rise because their expenditure is committed. The demand for loans is interest inelastic so that a rise in interest rates may lead to a less than proportionate fall in the demand for bank loans.

6.2.4 The Monetary-Fiscal Policy Mix

The government can influence the economy by the use of both fiscal and monetary policies so that it has the problem as to the emphasis it should place on each. For example, if the government wanted to reduce economic activity it could reduce the money supply. There would be less money in the economy so that interest rates would be pushed up. This may reduce investment and so retard economic growth. However, the government may place special emphasis on the attainment of economic growth so that it may prefer to raise taxation or reduce its expenditure thereby reducing the level of economic activity without seriously affecting investment. Governments must consider whether a certain policy instrument will have any adverse side effects on the attainment of other goals.

When a government seeks to attain the fulfilment of more than one policy objective, then generally one policy instrument will not be able to attain both. For example, if a government wishes to tackle a balance of payments deficit having adopted a fixed exchange rate and reduce unemployment, it can use a monetary-fiscal policy mix. Monetary policy can be aimed at attracting foreign capital by raising interest rates (so as to improve the balance of payments) whilst fiscal policy can be aimed at increasing aggregate demand (so as to reduce unemployment). However, expansionary fiscal policy may lead to an increase in imports thereby worsening the balance of payments situation whilst high interest rates would be an essentially short-term solution to the balance of payments problem. The government will be concerned, therefore, to ensure that the policy instruments used are effective and whether further policy instruments are needed.

6.2.5 The Monetarist and Keynesian View of Inflation

We have seen previously that the value of money is determined by its purchasing power. Inflation may be defined as the general upward movement of prices, so that during periods of inflation the value, or purchasing power of money will be falling. Deflation is the opposite to inflation - the general downward movement of prices with a consequent increase in the value of money.

The monetarist view of inflation is based on three components - the restated quantity theory of money which we considered earlier; the breakdown of the Phillips curve relationship; and the role of the exchange rate.

The relationship between the rate of unemployment and the rate of inflation was researched by Professor A.W. Phillips in the 1950s. Phillips used unemployment and wage rate statistics for the period 1863-1914 to produce a prediction table which forecasted the level of inflation at a given level of unemployment. The prediction table showed that as the rate of unemployment increases, the wage rate change decreases. These predictions have been tested and confirmed. Diagram 6.1 shows the relationship graphically (usually called the Phillips curve).

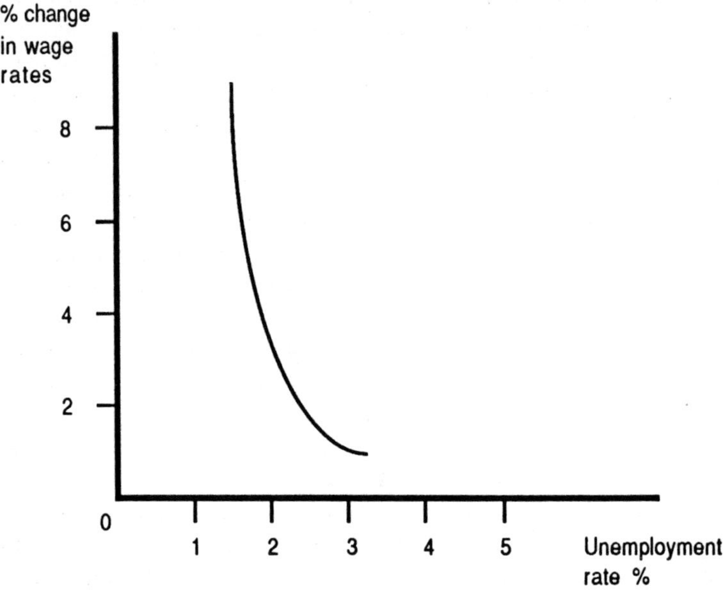

Diagram 6.1

Although the Phillips curve relates to unemployment and wage rate changes, the effect of wage rate increases can be related to the rate of inflation because if they are not matched by increases in output they would most likely be inflationary. The Phillips curve predicts that if unemployment is 1% then wages would rise by about 8% but it is unlikely that output would rise by such a proportion. Thus, the policy conclusion drawn from Phillip's work was that if inflation was to be controlled, the economy should be run with a margin of spare capacity. Keynesian economists saw this theory as confirming their view that it is excess-demand which causes inflation.

However, during the late 1960s and the 1970s, the Phillips relationship broke down. For example, in 1970 unemployment in the U.K. reached 4% yet wage increases exceeded 12%. Similarly, in 1980 unemployment reached 6.8% but most pay settlements were much higher. Various reasons have been put forward to explain the breakdown. When the 1966 statutory wage freeze was removed, large pay settlements were agreed at a time when unemployment was running at 2.4% so that trade unions found that their bargaining power was greater than was originally thought. In addition, about the same time social security benefits were increased so that strikes continued for longer periods, resulting in larger pay settlements.

The Phillips relationship shows the policy conflict between full employment and the control of inflation. Thus, inflation can be controlled but only at the cost of higher unemployment.

The monetarists adapted the Phillips curve to show that changes in the money supply will be split between changes in output and changes in prices. The monetarists argue that the economy works with a 'natural' rate of unemployment thus breaking the link between lower unemployment at the cost of higher inflation. Monetarists argue that workers consider the expected rate of inflation when wage bargaining so that they can maintain their real wages. Monetarists envisage a whole range of Phillips curves at different levels of expected inflation. In addition, the monetarists argue that there is a natural rate of unemployment (or NRU) which is the amount of unemployment at the point that the demand for and supply of labour are in equilibrium. At this point an increase in the money supply will affect prices and not output and employment. Thus, for example, trade union restrictive practices which reduce productivity will push the curve to the left so that there will be an increase in the NRU. Monetarists, therefore, consider that it is important to implement microeconomic policies designed to increase the efficiency of the labour market so as to reduce the NRU. This monetarist view has been criticised by other economists on a number of counts. Some economists argue that the Phillips relationship has not broken down but that the curve has shifted to the right. They argue that although figures for unemployment show an upward movement, there is still a shortage of labour because some unemployed are unemployable, some unemployed are nearing retirement age and so would be considered unsuitable for re-training. If the curve has moved to the right, the relationship would still hold but at higher levels of unemployment.

The third part of the monetarist view of inflation concerns the role of the exchange rate. Under a fixed rate of exchange each trading nation has little control over their domestic money supply so that it is the world money supply which is important. This is because to maintain a fixed exchange rate when it has a balance of payments deficit requires it to to buy its currency on the foreign exchange market and the fall in its reserves reduces the growth of the domestic money supply. In the case of floating exchange rates, each nation has control of its domestic money supply and, therefore, its inflation rate.

The non-monetarist view of inflation in the 1960s was based on 'demand-pull' which was supported by the Phillips curve. Demand-pull theory states that it is excess demand which causes prices to rise. In other words, the quantity of goods and services that consumers demand exceeds the supply of them. This disequilibrium is corrected by an upward movement in prices. Excess demand may arise in both the market for labour and the market for goods and services.

Let us consider the effect of excess demand in the labour market. Suppose the economy is working at full employment. Those firms with vacancies may tempt workers away from other firms by offering wages which are above the going rate. These firms will probably pass on the higher labour costs by raising the prices of their finished products. In these circumstances it is difficult to distinguish between cost-push (discussed below) and demand-pull because as wages rise, expenditure on goods and services increases; in addition, higher wages will be passed on in the form of higher prices.

An increase in demand in the market for goods and services will raise prices unless the increase in demand is offset by an immediate increase in production. If there is spare capacity in the economy, an increase in demand can be satisfied fully or partially by an increase in output.

We saw earlier that the Phillips relationship broke down in the 1960s and 1970s so that Keynesians focussed on the 'cost-push' theory of inflation. The cost-push theory states that increases in factor prices result in increases in prices of goods and services, so that prices rise independently of any excess demand. If firms' labour costs rise in excess of increases in productivity, they will raise their prices to cover the difference (unless, of course, businessmen are willing to absorb an increase in costs by a reduction in profit). As prices rise, trade unions will push for higher wages in order to maintain the standard of living of their members. Higher wage costs will, in turn, be passed on in the form of higher prices which will result in trade unions submitting bigger wage demands and so on. Such movement in wages and prices is known as a 'wage-price' spiral. A wage-price spiral is often exacerbated by a 'wage-wage' spiral. A wage-wage spiral occurs when some groups of workers try to maintain comparability or differentials. Suppose one group of workers negotiate a 20% pay rise which is tied to increases in productivity. A second group of workers may seek comparability even though they cannot justify it on the grounds of productivity. Such pay rises, not backed by increases in productivity, create inflationary pressures.

Cost-push inflation is not always generated domestically. Initially, the importation of goods at higher prices can result in inflationary pressures. For example, the U.K. imports much of its raw materials requirement so that increases in the cost of these inputs will quickly work through the system resulting in higher prices.

Keynesians have a concept which is similar to the monetarists' NRU.This is the *non-accelerating-inflation rate of unemployment* or NAIRUE so that if unemployment falls below this rate, it means that there is excess demand in the labour market which results in inflationary pressures.

6.2.6 Policy Implications Arising from Keynesian and Monetarist Theories

It is important to know whether Keynesian theory or monetarist theory is correct because if Keynesians are right, then the lack of emphasis placed by the U.K. government on monetary policy as a means of influencing the economy, for most of the post Second World War period has been correct. If the monetarists are right, then greater emphasis should have been placed on monetary policy with attention being directed at controlling the money supply rather than influencing interest rates.

Empirical observation has been used to test both these theories but the results have been inconclusive. This is because different studies have reached different conclusions because different researchers have used different assumptions. For example, some studies have used a narrow definition of money whilst others have used a wider definition. Some assume time-lags in the economy are short; others assume them to be long. Some take short-term interest rates; others use long-term interest rates. It is not surprising, therefore, that a variety of results and interpretations have emerged.

However, despite the lack of conclusive evidence one way or the other, in the 1970s policy makers tended to become increasingly aware of the importance of money in influencing economic activity so that most major countries adopted target growth rates for monetary aggregates. This increased use of monetary policy is not designed to take the place of fiscal policy but rather as a complement to it.

The adoption of a monetarist approach presents policy-makers with a number of problems. These include the choice of which money supply definition is to be used and how it is to be controlled. However, once the authorities control a definition of money its use as an indicator of what is happening in the economy ceases because its growth will be determined by supply (which is controlled by the authorities) rather than demand. In addition, forecasting may prove difficult because of varying time lags. Finally, there may be problems if the government is committed to increasing public expenditure by printing more money or by increasing public debt rather than by increasing its tax revenue.

Non-monetarists accept that monetary and fiscal policies can be used to reduce inflation but see the adoption of a monetarist solution as leading to extremely high levels of unemployment. Some have argued that the use of unemployment as a means of controlling inflation has lost much of its effectiveness and unemployment would have to rise to such a high level that it would be politically and socially unacceptable. The inadequacy of demand management policies has led many economists (especially 'Keynesian' economists) to argue for the adoption of an incomes policy and a smaller number of them have supported the use of some form of import controls.

Incomes policies (or wage-price policies as they are sometimes known) are advocated by many non-monetarists when there are cost-push pressures which result in inflation, so that if wage and price rises can be controlled then inflation can be controlled. Incomes policies have been tried by most Western countries since the Second World War. The main problem with incomes policies is that their effectiveness may be curtailed by wage drift. Wage drift occurs where the earnings of labour exceed the negotiated wage rates. So although the actual wage rate may be controlled by an incomes policy, the actual amount of take-home pay may be substantially greater through the offering of inducements to workers such as bonuses and guaranteed overtime pay which is paid even if the overtime is not worked. If the rise in earnings exceed the rise in productivity inflationary pressures will be added to.

6.2.7 Macroeconomic Objectives

Since the Second World War, successive governments have pursued a number of economic objectives - the maintenance of full employment; stability of prices; the achievement of a sound balance of payments; and a steady rate of economic growth. We can assess recent achievement by looking at the information shown in Table 6.2.

It can be seen from Table 6.2 that the Government has been successful in reducing the rate of inflation. Indeed, the rate of inflation fell to under 3% in 1986 before rising again. However, the rate of inflation is still higher than in West Germany and Japan, the U.K.'s major competitors. The rate of economic growth has improved after the recession of the early 1980s. However, U.K. growth rates have tended to be below the rates of growth achieved by other countries such as the US and Japan, although they compare quite favourably with European countries. The Government's record on reducing unemployment has not been a great success as shown by the figures in Table 6.2. European countries and North America have also had problems in reducing unemployment but they have been relatively more successful than the UK. However, more recently the total unemployed has fallen from over 3.25 million to around 2.5 million. The UK's balance of payments on current account was in surplus in the first half of the 1980s with North Sea oil revenues making an important contribution. However, a source of worry for the Government is the growing deficit in the non-oil visible trade balance. Indeed, the current account deficit was over £14bn in 1988.

Table 6.2 Values for Selected Policy Objectives

Year	*Annual change in RPI (%)*	*Annual change in GDP (%)*	*Unemployment as a % of working population*	*Balance of payments (current account £ m)*
1980	18.1	-2.4	6.0	+3,035
1981	11.9	-1.5	9.3	+6,743
1982	8.7	1.9	10.9	+4,480
1983	4.6	2.3	11.9	+3,753
1984	5.0	2.4	12.4	+2,009
1985	6.1	3.7	12.9	+3,275
1986	3.4	3.0	11.8	+46
1987	4.2	4.4	10.3	-1,679

(Source: Economic Trends)

6.3 Techniques of Monetary Policy

Central banks implement and advise their governments on monetary policy. The following instruments are available to them for the attainment of their policy objectives - discount rate; open market operations; reserve requirements; moral suasion; and direct controls.

1. Discount Rate

When the banking system is short of liquid funds, the central bank will lend to it at its discount rate. In other words, discount rate is the rate at which a central bank is prepared to act as a lender of last resort. The lending is normally made direct to banks but in the U.K., assistance is provided indirectly through the discount market. The central bank can influence the money market by changing the terms on which it is prepared to provide assistance by changes in its discount rate; by deciding whether assistance is to be provided by discounting assets or lending against collateral; by stipulating the type of collateral it will accept; by stipulating how frequently assistance may be sought; by placing limits on its lending.

A central bank's discount rate can become the pivot of the financial system through its direct influence on the rates of eligible securities. The rates on securities which are eligible as collateral will not be much higher than the discount rate otherwise it would be profitable for banks (discount houses in the U.K.) to borrow unlimited amounts from the central bank on the security of bills yielding a higher return. If central bank assistance was limitless and the yields on eligible securities were higher than the discount rate, banks (discount houses) would borrow from the central bank and the increased demand for securities would push their yields down.

Similarly, the rates on these securities would not fall far below the discount rate because discount rate would be a penal rate and banks (discount houses) would suffer a loss on the business covered by any borrowing at this rate. The influence of the discount rate can be spread to other financial assets because they are competitive with these money market assets.

The discount rate may be either market-determining or market-determined. In the former case, the discount rate is declared publicly and it is changed at the discretion of the central bank in order to influence the level of other interest rates. If the discount rate is market-determined it is related to some market-determined rate so that changes in the discount rate reflects changes in market interest rates. In the U.K. in October 1972, Bank rate (which was market-determining) was replaced by minimum lending rate (which was market-determined). The calculation of minimum lending rate was linked to the Treasury bill rate. However, in May 1978 the authorities announced that this formula would no longer be used and that it would in future be set at the authorities' discretion (i.e. market-determining). With effect from August 20th, 1981, the Bank of England discontinued the practice of continuously posting a minimum lending rate.

Sometimes a central bank's discount rate may have political significance and can be used to affect expectations. For example, because the U.K government found it difficult to keep monetary growth within the target it had set, in November 1979 minimum lending rate was raised to 17%, its highest level ever, in order to underline the government's determination to secure monetary control.

2. Open Market Operations

Open market operations can be conducted by central banks where there is a well developed financial structure, the national debt is relatively large, and the central bank has a large stock of government securities. The central bank can buy or sell securities in the market with a view to influencing interest rates and the money supply by altering the supply of financial assets. If open market operations are to be effective there must be an efficient and effective market in government securities. If the central bank purchases securities, this will add to demand so that prices will rise and yields will fall. Settlement of these purchases involves a transfer of cash from the central bank to the sellers of the securities which will increase the reserve assets of the banks thereby enabling them to increase their lending. This will increase the money supply and lower interest rates. Conversely, if the central bank sells securities, prices will fall and yields will rise. There will be a transfer of cash from the purchasers to the central bank and this will reduce the reserve assets of the banks. Banks will have to curtail their lending so that the money supply will be reduced and interest rates will rise.

The effect of open market operations on the banking system depends on the type of reserve requirement which banks are obliged to comply with. In some countries, the reserve requirement is expressed in terms of cash so that open market operations in short-term assets, such as Treasury bills, will alter the reserves of the banks. The central banks of these countries conduct most of their open market operations in the short-term markets. In other countries the reserve requirement includes short-term assets as well as cash so that open market operations in short-term markets will not affect the overall reserve position of the banking system but merely their composition. In these countries, open market operations must be extended to long-term securities which do not form part of the banks' reserve asset calculation, if the monetary authorities wish to affect the level of banks' reserve assets. In addition, the monetary authorities will be able to influence long-term interest rates directly.

In the U.K., the Bank of England actively participates in the market for long-term government securities - the gilt-edged market. The Bank of England can use open market operations in the gilt-edged market to influence the economy by affecting aggregate demand. If aggregate demand is excessive, the Bank of England can sell longer-dated stocks thereby mopping up excess liquidity. The money supply will be reduced and interest rates pushed up. We can show these changes by the use of a simple example. Let us suppose that the Bank of England sells £10,000 of stocks to the non-bank private sector who draw cheques on their current accounts. The Bank of England will present the cheques for payment and payment is effected by the Bank of England crediting its stocks (i.e. asset) account. The non-bank private sector will have increased their holdings of stocks and reduced their deposits with the banks. These changes are shown in Table 6.3.

Table 6.3 The Changes Resulting from the Sale of £10,000 of Stock by the Bank of England to the Non-Bank Private Sector

Bank of England

Liabilities		*Assets*	
Bankers' deposits	- £10,000	Stocks	- £10,000

Banks

Liabilities		*Assets*	
Deposits	- £10,000	Balances at the Bank of England	- £10,000

Non-bank private sector

Liabilities		*Assets*	
		Stocks	+ £10,000
No change		Deposits with banks	- £10,000

When aggregate demand needs to be stimulated, the Bank of England can buy stock so as to increase the money supply and reduce interest rates. Let us suppose that the Bank of England buys £10,000 of stocks from the non-bank private sector. The non-bank private sector will receive cheques from the Bank of England and these will be paid into their accounts with the banks. The banks will present the cheques for payment so that the Bank of England will complete the book-keeping entries by debiting its stock (asset) account and crediting bankers' deposits. The non-bank private sector will have reduced their holdings of stocks and increased their deposits with the banks. The changes are shown in Table 6.4.

Thus, open market operations can be used counter-cyclically. However, in the short-term, the Bank's tactics includes the stabilisation of the market so as to ensure that holders of long-term gilt-edged securities continue to hold their investments and continue to consider them highly reputable. To keep an orderly market the Bank will smooth out sharp fluctuations in price.

The effectiveness of open market operations as a means of controlling bank lending may be frustrated in the following circumstances. If the official control of reserve assets is ineffective, as, for example, when the government is running a large budget deficit or the banks hold or are able to obtain a cushion of reserve assets in excess of the minimum requirement. In addition, open market operations may be frustrated if the central bank has to issue new government securities as part of its funding policy.

Table 6.4 The Changes Resulting from the Purchase of £10,000 of Stocks by the Bank of England from the Non-Bank Private Sector

Bank of England

Liabilities		*Assets*	
Bankers' deposits	+ £10,000	Stocks	+ £10,000

Banks

Liabilities		*Assets*	
Deposits	+ £10,000	Balances at the Bank of England	+ £10,000

Non-bank private sector

Liabilities		*Assets*	
No change		Stocks	- £10,000
		Deposits with banks	+ £10,000

3. Reserve Requirements

Reserve requirements place a constraint on banks' asset structures. In the early stages of the evolution of a banking system most governments would apply a reserve requirement so as to ensure that banks were managed prudentially and to ensure that they were solvent so as to avert a run on the banks. As banking systems developed and became more stable, governments retained the use of reserve requirements as instruments of monetary control.

Reserve requirements entail banks maintaining certain assets in a specific form. The reserve requirements in many countries consists of cash ratios so that banks have to comply with a minimum ratio of cash to deposits. Cash may be defined narrowly as balances with the central bank or it may be widened to include notes and coin. In some countries the assets which are included in the calculation of the reserve requirement includes liquid assets.

If the monetary authorities control the supply of reserve assets, they will be able to control the money supply. Suppose banks find that their reserve assets have fallen to the minimum level permitted. They will have to stop increasing their lending because otherwise they will be increasing non-reserve assets or they will have to try to increase their deposits. Whichever of these two courses the banks take, they will drive up interest rates and cut back the growth in the money supply. If they wish to reduce their lending they will push up interest rates and if they wish to increase their deposits they will bid up the interest paid to depositors which will in turn push up the rates of interest charged on lending. Thus, by controlling the supply of reserve assets, the monetary authorities can put a constraint on the growth of the banking system.

The monetary authorities can restrain bank lending as follows:

(a) By open market operations which would use the reserve requirement as a fulcrum. The monetary authorities would restrict the quantity of reserve assets in circulation so as to influence the general lending operations of the banks.

(b) By altering the reserve ratio either directly by changing the ratio itself or indirectly by calling for special deposits.

The effect of both types of action would be to leave the banks short of reserve assets so that they can either switch their non-reserve assets into reserve assets or compete more actively for deposits thereby pushing up interest rates on deposits. However, if banks try to increase their holdings of reserve assets and the government does not create new reserve assets, they can only do so if the public or institutions outside the banking system are willing to sell some of their holdings. Thus, on the assumption that no new reserve assets are created and that the publics' holdings of reserve assets remain unchanged, a call for special deposits means that banks must reduce their total bank deposits in order to comply with the reserve asset ratio.

4. Moral Suasion

Moral suasion (or suggestion and request) is the use by a central bank of its influence in the financial community to persuade banks to curtail their lending or to alter its allocation. Central banks normally use moral suasion when the market fails in its important function of maximising social welfare. For example, when money is tight, it will go to those who are prepared to pay the highest price but this may not always be in society's interest. In these circumstances, the monetary authorities can intervene by requesting that banks place special emphasis in their lending to certain sectors of the economy (qualitative controls) thereby increasing the community's welfare. For example, a central bank may request banks to give priority in their lending to exporters and to industry and to restrain lending for importing and private consumption.

Moral suasion is more effective in those countries where the central bank is situated in close proximity to the financial institutions and there is regular communication between them. Thus, its use has been particularly effective in small countries such as the U.K., Switzerland and Norway where the important financial institutions can be easily brought together. Whereas, in the United States, for example, moral suasion is not so effective because of the large number of institutions which are spread over a very large area.

The advantage of moral suasion is that it is flexible since it does not require legal implementation. It can be used as and when required and if necessary it can be extended to cover financial institutions other than banks without a change in the central banks' statutory powers.

5. Direct Controls

Direct controls place restrictions on the banks' freedom to undertake certain activities, and the two most widely used are:

(a) Lending ceilings (or quantitative controls) - if the monetary authorities wish to slow down the rate of credit growth they can direct banks not to lend beyond a certain limit.

(b) Interest rate ceilings - these ceilings place a limit on the interest rates which banks pay on deposits. These ceilings may be used to curtail competition between banks and other financial institutions such as those engaged in the financing of the housing sector so that the authorities can ensure that the latter have adequate resources with which to continue their operations.

Direct controls are usually adopted when quick results are required so that if the authorities consider that the other means of influencing the banking sector may take longer to produce the desired results they may adopt direct controls. However, the main problem with direct controls is that over time they will probably lead to a misallocation of resources. In a free market, resources are allocated by price but where direct controls are applied, this interference in the market does not allow it to perform this important function efficiently. For example, if a lending ceiling is applied and credit is rationed, it is likely that some less worthwhile projects will receive finance whilst other more worthwhile projects do not.

A further form of direct control which is used widely is exchange control which regulates payments to and from foreign countries.

6.4 Summary

1. The objectives of monetary policy are:
   (a) The maintenance of full employment.
   (b) Control of inflation.
   (c) Economic growth.
   (d) A satisfactory balance of payments.
   (e) A contribution to the economic development of the outside

world.

2. Monetary policy can be used to:
   (a) Change interest rates.
   (b) Control the money supply.
3. Direct controls may:
   (a) Distort competition.
   (b) Inhibit competition.
   (c) Lead to disintermediation.
4. Problems associated with controlling interest rates include:
   (a) The imprecise effect on the demand for credit.
   (b) The problem of time lags.
5. Government can influence the economy by the use of a monetary-fiscal policy mix.
6. There are two main views of inflation: the Monetarist and the Keynesian view.
7. Keynesians argue that fiscal policy is more potent than monetary policy. Monetarists argue for the use of monetary policy to cure inflation.
8. The main economic objectives are:
   (a) The maintenance of full employment.
   (b) Stable prices.
   (c) A sound balance of payments.
   (d) Economic growth.
9. The techniques of monetary policy are:
   (a) Discount rate.
   (b) Open market operations.
   (c) Reserve requirements.
   (d) Moral suasion.
   (e) Direct controls.

Questions

1.* What are the objectives of monetary policy?

To what extent, in practice, is it possible to achieve them all simultaneously?

2.* Describe the basic techniques by which central banks operate domestic monetary policy and the relationship in which they must stand to the commercial banks if they are to do so effectively.

3.* What functions are usually carried out by central banks? What powers must they possess to carry out these functions effectively?

4.* What conditions are necessary for open market operations to be an effective means by which a central bank can influence lending by commercial banks? To what extent do these conditions obtain in Britain?

5.* What different techniques are available to the monetary authorities when seeking to control the money supply? Assess critically the effectiveness of each type of control.

6. Discuss the view that it is possible to control either the money supply or the level of interest rates but not both. What practical implications does this view have for the way in which monetary authorities seek to control the money supply?

7. What are usually regarded as the main objectives of monetary policy? Discuss the possible intermediate targets of monetary policy that the monetary authorities might set in order to achieve their objectives.

8. (a) Outline the principal features of monetary policy as operated in the UK since 1979. (15)
(b) To what extent have the overall goals of macro-economic policy been achieved in the UK since 1979? (10)

9. (a) What is meant by index-linking of financial assets? Include some examples of index-linked assets in your answer. (9)
(b) To what extent is index-linking likely to succeed in curbing inflation? How else might governments attempt to deal with the problem? (16)

10. Describe the following and discuss their role in the operation of monetary policy:
(a) gilt-edged securities (9)
(b) commercial (eligible bank) bills (9)
(c) the sale of public sector assets (7)

11. (a) Explain briefly why a country's monetary authorities consider the behaviour of the money supply to be important.(10)

(b) Discuss the problems which arise in modern economies in

defining the money supply. (15)

12. (a) Outline the Keynesian theory of liquidity preference. (9)
    (b) (i) Explain how the Keynesian theory of liquidity preference differs from the monetarist view of the demand for money. (8)
    (ii) Consider, from each of these two differing viewpoints, the possible impact on the economy of an increase in the money supply. (8)

13. (a) Outline the different techniques available to monetary authorities for controlling the money supply. (15)
    (b) Discuss the techniques for controlling the money supply which have been used in the UK during the 1980s. (10)

14. (a) State the main objectives of macro-economic policy and discuss whether, in practice, it is possible to achieve all these objectives simultaneously. (15)
    (b) To what extent have each of the main objectives in (a) been achieved in the UK in the past five years? (10)

15. In seeking to achieve the ultimate objectives of monetary policy, the authorities can set intermediate targets.
    (a) Discuss the intermediate targets that might be selected. (17)
    (b) List the techniques that could be used to achieve these targets.(8)

CHAPTER 7

Balance of Payments

7.1.1 The Structure of the Balance of Payments

The balance of payments statement of a country is a systematic record of all economic transactions between the residents of a country and foreign residents over a specified period of time (usually one year). It shows the country's trading position, whether it is a net foreign borrower or lender and changes in its official reserve holdings. Thus, a balance of payments statement is very useful to the financial authorities of a nation.

The construction of a balance of payments statement is based on the principles of double-entry book-keeping. Every transaction entails two book-keeping entries, a debit and a credit. For example, exports will be credits and the claims on the foreigners who have bought the exported goods will be debits (i.e. they are debtors). Similarly, imports will be debits and the amount due to foreigners in settlement of the imported goods will be credits (i.e. they are creditors). Table 7.1 shows the UK balance of payments in summary form for the year 1987.

Table 7.1 UK Balance of Payments Summary (1987)

		(£m)
Visible trade (balance)		-9,625
Invisibles (balance)		+7,946
Current balance		-1,679
Transactions in UK external assets	-75,326	
Transactions in UK external liabilities	+76,059	
Net financial transactions		+733
Allocation of SDRs and gold subscription to IMF		-
Balancing item		+946

(Source: Central Statistical Office)

A balance of payments statement is divided into two parts - a current account and a capital account.

7.1.2 Current Account

The current account records all transactions relating to a country's current income and expenditure. The balance on the account is called the current balance and Table 7.2 shows the U.K.'s current balance since 1975.

Table 7.2 U.K. Current Balance (£m)

	Visible Balance	*Invisible Balance*	*Current Balance*
1975	-3333	+1751	-1582
1976	-3929	+3016	-913
1977	-2284	+2172	-112
1978	-1542	+2507	+965
1979	-3449	+2845	-604
1980	+1353	+1682	+3035
1981	+3350	+3393	+6743
1982	+2324	+2156	+4480
1983	-863	+4616	+3753
1984	-4396	+6405	+2009
1985	-2190	+5465	+3275
1986	-8463	+8509	+46
1987	-9625	+7946	-1679

(Source: Central Statistical Office)

The current account is divided into visible and invisible items. Visibles comprise imports and exports of goods such as raw materials, food and manufactured goods and the balance on this part of the account is called the balance of trade. Table 7.3 shows the U.K.'s balance of trade since 1976.

Table 7.3 UK Visible Trade (£m)

	Exports (fob)	*Imports (fob)*	*Balance of Trade*
1976	25,191	29,120	-3,929
1977	31,728	34,012	-2,284
1978	35,063	36,605	-1,542
1979	40,687	44,136	-3,449
1980	47,147	45,794	+1,353
1981	50,668	47,318	+3,350
1982	55,330	53,006	+2,324
1983	60,698	61,561	-863
1984	70,263	74,659	-4,396
1985	77,988	80,178	-2,190
1986	72,678	81,141	-8,463
1987	79,622	89,247	-9,625

(Source: Central Statistical Office)

Invisibles comprise such items as shipping, banking, insurance, travel and tourism and we will look at these in greater detail in the following section.

7.1.3The Changing Pattern of the U.K. Invisibles Account

The existence of a large surplus on invisibles has been one of the most important features of the U.K. balance of payments. Indeed, this surplus has offset fully or partially a large and persistent deficit on visible trade.

The invisibles account can be split into three component parts – services; interest, profits and dividends; and transfers. Figures for these items over the period 1958-1986 are given in Table 7.4.

Table 7.4 Components of Invisible Balance (£m)

	1958	1968	1973	1978	1986
Services	+94	+342	+706	+3478	+5382
of which;					
General Government	-145	-287	-409	-733	-1405
Private sector and public corporations	+239	+629	+1115	+4211	+6787
Interest, Profits & Dividends	+293	+336	+1260	+827	+5076
of which;					
General Government	n.a.	-241	-199	-563	-1053
Private sector and public corporations	n.a.	+577	+1459	+1390	+6129
Transfers	-70	-238	-458	-1791	-2325
of which;					
General Government	-74	-179	-359	-1664	-2208
Private	+4	-59	-99	-127	-117
	+317	+440	+1508	+2514	+8133

(Source: Central Statistical Office)

The following trends can be gleaned from Table 7.4.

1. General Government

The General Government deficit has increased fairly dramatically over the years. The deficit can be broken down into expenditure on military, the

European Community, interest, profits & dividends, and other expenditure (including administrative and diplomatic services).

The U.K. is committed to maintaining a relatively large military presence overseas. This represents a considerable loss each year because there is only a small income from foreigners using bases in the U.K. to set-off against the U.K.'s expenditure. This deficit, therefore, is likely to continue to increase in future years.

The U.K.'s net contribution to the European Community has been increasing over the years. However, the UK Government has negotiated reductions in the U.K.'s contribution.

The deficit on interest, profits and dividends has increased substantially during the period 1973-1986 and this reflects the large amount of interest that was paid on increased official borrowing during this period.

Finally, the costs of maintaining embassies and consulates have increased and it is likely that they will continue to do so in the future.

2. Interest, Profits and Dividends

Interest, profits and dividends are receipts/payments which arise from investment which was undertaken in previous years. They are not additional investments otherwise they would be included in the capital account. Figures giving a breakdown of the private sector and public corporations surplus are shown in Table 7.5.

Table 7.5 Private Sector and Public Corporations

(£ millions)

	1968	1976	1978	1986
Direct investment	+239	+1351	+990	+4151
Portfolio investment	+116	+110	-149	+4042
Other (including overseas earnings of U.K. oil companies)	+222	+486	+549	-2064
Total	+577	+1459	+1390	+6129

(Source: Central Statistical Office)

The surplus increased during the period 1968-1973 and this was due to a buoyant world economy, especially during the years 1972 and 1973. During the period 1974-1976, the surplus again increased because sterling's depreciation resulted in an increase in profits of overseas subsidiaries of U.K. companies. During the years 1977-78 the underlying performance weakened and this was due in the main to a reduction in the overseas earnings of U.K. oil companies and sterling's appreciation. In the 1980s, the surplus increased rapidly and this was due to a big increase in the earnings from portfolio investment overseas which resulted from the removal of exchange controls in 1979.

3. Services

The private sector and public corporation surplus on services can be broken down into the following items (See Table 7.6).

Table 7.6 Private Sector and Public Corporations

(£ millions)

	1968	1976	1978	1986
Sea transport	+69	+228	+266	-1232
Civil aviation and travel	+11	+700	+958	-668
Financial and other (including for example overseas construction work)	+549	+1996	+2987	+8687
TOTAL	+629	+2924	+4211	+6787

(Source: Central Statistical Office)

Transport can be divided into two parts - shipping and civil aviation. Since the Second World War, the U.K.'s share of world shipping has fallen because other countries have developed their own merchant fleets which have often been heavily subsidised. Civil aviation has become an increasingly more important contributor to the U.K.'s invisible earnings. In the 1970s, a deficit on shipping has typically been offset by a surplus on civil aviation. However, in the 1980s, the deficit on shipping has increased rapidly reaching over £1 billion in 1986.

For some countries, such as Spain, travel and tourism is an important earner of foreign currency. Until the late 1960s, the U.K.'s net position on travel and tourism was usually adverse but during the 1970s the U.K.'s earnings from this item increased substantially. The main factor behind this increase has been the weakening of sterling. However, after 1978 sterling became stronger and this tended to discourage tourism in 1979 and 1980. Between 1980 and 1984 there was a deficit on travel but this turned into a surplus of £570 million in 1985. The balance on travel went back into deficit of £522 million in 1986.

The net surplus on financial services increased during the 1970s. Financial services covers the activities of insurance, banking, advertising and the licensing of foreign firms to use British inventions. These services have always made a significant contribution to the U.K. balance of payments. There has been a consistent increase in the earnings from financial and other services throughout the 1980s.

In the 1970s and 1980s services made the largest contribution to the invisibles surplus.

7.1.4 Capital Account

The capital account records transactions in a country's external assets and liabilities which include the flow of investment capital (direct and portfolio), loans between governments, overseas borrowing and changes in official reserves (see Table 7.7). Table 7.8 shows net transactions in UK external assets and liabilities since 1975.

Table 7.7 Summary of Transactions in UK External Assets and Liabilities (1987)

Transactions in external assets	*(£m)*
UK investment overseas:-	
Direct	-17818
Portfolio	+7950
Lending etc to overseas residents by UK banks	-49947
Deposits and lending overseas by UK residents other than banks and general government	-2796
Official reserves	-12012
Other external assets of central government	-703
Total transactions in assets	-75326
Transactions in external liabilities	
Overseas investment in the UK:-	
Direct	6099
Portfolio	12619
Borrowing etc from overseas residents by UK banks	53067
Borrowing from overseas by UK residents other than banks and general government	2656
Other external liabilities of general government	1618
Total transactions in liabilities	76059
Net transactions	+733

(Source: Central Statistical Office)

Table 7.8 Net Transactions in UK External Assets and Liabilities since 1975 (£m)

1975	+1599	1980	-2936	1985	-7748
1976	+595	1981	-6421	1986	-12585
1977	-3241	1982	-2905	1987	+733
1978	-3122	1983	-5035		
1979	-69	1984	-7100		

(Source: Central Statistical Office)

The capital account also records foreign aid payments made by the UK government and changes in foreign government sterling reserves. The latter balances were built up during sterling's role as a reserve currency.

7.1.5 Differences Between Direct and Portfolio Investment Overseas

Direct investment involves complete or nearly complete ownership with a view of direct management. Portfolio investment is the acquisition of a mixture of overseas stocks and shares with the holdings normally being minority holdings. Direct investment is undertaken, in the main by companies who set up subsidiaries abroad although individuals may undertake direct investment by investing in property.

The aim of portfolio investment is to give the investor yield and/or capital appreciation, depending on his requirements. The investor may hold the portfolio or he may obtain an interest in such a portfolio through a unit trust or investment trust.

7.1.6 Official Financing

The balance of payments always balances because the unadjusted balance on current account equals (with reversal of sign) net transactions in assets and liabilities. However, in practice there is invariably a discrepancy so that a balancing item is required. Table 7.9 shows the UK balance of payments summary for 1987 to illustrate this.

Table 7.9 U.K. Balance of Payments Summary (1987)

	(£m)	(£m)
Visible trade balance	-9625	
Invisibles balance	7946	
Current balance		-1679
UK external assets and liabilities:		
Transactions in assets	-75326	
Transactions in liabilities	76059	
Net transactions		733
Allocation of special drawing rights and gold subscription to IMF		-
Balancing item		946

(Source: Central Statistical Office)

The balance of payments always balances because the total currency flow on current account and transactions in external assets and liabilities (not including changes in official reserves and government borrowing), whether surplus or deficit, is matched by equal and opposite total official financing. Official financing may be undertaken in the following ways:

1. By drawing from or adding to the country's official reserve holdings.
2. By borrowing from or repaying loans to the IMF.
3. By using or repaying foreign currency borrowing facilities. These facilities are agreed between central banks and are used to combat short-term speculative capital flows.

7.1.7 Balancing Item

This relates to discrepancies between the total value of recorded transactions and the actual flow of money, i.e., it is the total of errors and omissions. If the balancing item is positive, then more money has flowed into the country than the estimated value of transactions show. If the balancing item is negative, then less money has flowed into the country than the estimated value of transactions show.

7.1.8 Changes in the U.K. Balance of Payments on Current Account

The U.K. current account was in deficit throughout most of the of the 1970s. We have already seen the major changes in the U.K.'s invisibles but as far as the U.K. visible balance is concerned one of the most important factors affecting it has been the price of oil. The large increases in oil prices in the early 1970s had a tremendous adverse effect on the U.K. visible balance. However, by the late 1970s, the U.K.'s production of North Sea oil began to rise very rapidly after many years of exploration, development and capital expenditure, so that by 1978 it began to make a significant contribution to the U.K. balance of payments. We shall consider the effect of North Sea oil on the U.K. balance of payments in the next section.

7.1.9 The Development and Production of North Sea Oil

The development of North Sea oil in the 1970s affected the capital account of the U.K. balance of payments. This was because of the direct investment of foreign oil companies in the UK. The result of this investment now is an outflow of funds in the invisibles section (interest, profits and dividends) of the UK balance of payments current account.

We have previously mentioned the effect of North Sea oil on the balance of trade. Table 7.10 shows the visible balance broken down into its oil and non-oil constituents.

Table 7.10 Components of UK Visible Balance 1978-1986 (£m)

	Visible balance		
	Oil	Non-oil	Total
1978	-1984	+442	-1,542
1979	-731	-2,718	-3,449
1980	+315	+1,046	+1,361
1981	+3,111	+249	+3,360
1982	+4,643	-2,312	+2,331
1983	+6,976	-7,811	-835
1984	+6,937	-11,321	-4,384
1985	+8,105	-10,283	-2,178
1986	+4,153	-12,407	-8,253

(Source: Central Statistical Office)

It can be seen from Table 7.10 that the UK became a net exporter of oil in 1980 and the supply on oil has been in the region of £7-8 billion during the period 1983-85, falling to about £4 billion in 1986.

On the other hand, the balance on non-oil trade has deteriorated sharply during the period 1982-86, reaching a deficit of over £10 billion in the years 1984-86. The effect of North Sea oil in the late 1970s and early 1980s was a rise in the sterling exchange rate and this resulted in a deterioration in the price competitiveness of UK producers. However, the sterling exchange rate has fallen in recent years and this has been partly due to the fall in the price of oil.

7.1.10 The Removal of Exchange Controls

The ending of exchange controls in October 1979 had the effect of increasing portfolio investment by financial institutions and in particular insurance companies, pension funds and unit trusts. This allowed them to diversify the content of their portfolios by the purchasing of foreign securities. Overseas portfolio investment increased rapidly from 1979 onwards as shown by Table 7.11.

The effect of the increased portfolio investment can now be seen in the invisibles section of the balance of payments. The earnings on portfolio investment overseas have increased rapidly since 1980 thereby having a beneficial effect on the interest, profits and dividends component of the invisibles balance. These earnings rose to over £6 billion in 1986.

Table 7.11 Total UK Private Investment Overseas 1976-1986 (£m)

	Direct Investment	*Portfolio Investment*	*Total UK Private Investment Overseas*
1976	-2,359	+90	-2,264
1977	-2,346	+12	-2,334
1978	-3,561	-1,073	-4,634
1979	-5,646	-909	-6,555
1980	-4,924	-3,230	-8,154
1981	-6,093	-4,300	-10,393
1982	-4,109	-6,720	-10,829
1983	-5,402	-6,520	-11,922
1984	-6,093	-9,550	-15,643
1985	-8,829	-18,300	-27,129
1986	-10,895	-20,410	-31,305
1987	-17,818	+7,950	-9,868

(Source: Central Statistical Office)

The figures in Table 7.11 also show an increase in direct investment overseas following the abolition of exchange controls. Much of this investment is undertaken by U.K. multinational companies and they have taken the opportunity to export capital overseas for the direct investment in plant and equipment.

7.2 Terms of Trade

The terms of trade measure the amount of imports that are obtained in return for exports. It is not possible to put this in a numerical form because of the diverse nature of trade so than one cannot add together, for example, tons of steel, barrels of oil, different types of machinery and other goods. It is, however, possible to measure changes in the terms of trade by using the following formula:

$$\text{Index of terms of trade} = \frac{\text{Price index of exports}}{\text{Price index of imports}} \times \frac{100}{1}$$

The price index of exports measures the change in the aggregate value of a selection of exports compared with its value at a given base date (i.e. the index value at the base date will be 100). Similarly, the price index of imports measures the change in the aggregate value of a selection of imports compared with its value at a given base date (i.e. the index value at the base date will be 100).

Suppose we wish to measure the terms of trade for country X for the year 1985, taking its base year as 1984. If the average price of exports rose by 4% and the average price of imports rose by 3%, the terms of trade would be:

$$\text{Terms of trade} = \frac{104}{103} \times \frac{100}{1} = 101$$

Thus, the terms of trade have improved because the country's exports will buy 1% more imports and so the country is better off.

If a country's terms of trade index is compared with the base year, and it exceeds 100 then its terms of trade have become more favourable; if the index is below 100 then its terms of trade have worsened.

If the terms of trade move in favour of a particular country it signifies that its export prices have become relatively higher compared with its import prices. This may have come about because export prices have risen or because import prices have fallen, so that the country will be able to import more for the same amount of exports.

However, the effect of changes in a country's terms of trade on its balance of trade depends upon elasticities of demand for and supply of goods being traded. Thus, changes in the prices of imports and exports will affect revenues and payments but the degree to which they are affected will depend upon elasticities. For example, if the prices of a country's imported goods rise but the demand for those goods is inelastic (which means that a rise in price leads to a less than proportionate fall in demand) then total payments for imports will rise and this will adversely affect the country's balance of trade. Similarly, if the prices of a country's exports rise and the demand for these goods in the overseas markets is inelastic, then its revenue would rise and this would improve its balance of trade. In fact, such a situation occurred during the oil price rises of the 1970s when the oil-exporting countries experienced an increase in their export price index which favourably affected their balance of trade (because the demand for oil was inelastic). Whilst oil-importing countries experienced an increase in their import price index which adversely affected their balance of trade.

7.3.1 Problems of a Balance of Payments Deficit or Surplus under a Fixed Rate of Exchange

If a country pegs its exchange rate at a certain level, then successive balance of payments deficits could lead to speculation that the problem will be rectified by devaluation. This often happened during the period 1944-1971 when countries adhered to the Bretton Woods adjustable peg system of exchange rates. For example, when the U.K.'s balance of payments moved into deficit during this period, there was a tendency for foreign holders of sterling to switch into safer currencies. This created an additional problem because the U.K. not only had to finance the deficit but it was also faced with a run on sterling.

Similarly, if a country has successive balance of payments surpluses under a fixed exchange rate system, it could lead to speculation that the country will revalue its currency. For example, in 1957 there was a run on sterling not because the holders of sterling feared devaluation, but because there was speculation that West Germany would revalue the Deutsche mark.

Since 1972, the adjustable peg system has been abandoned and exchange rates have been allowed to float (the European Monetary System is a regional exception to this). The main advantage of a floating exchange rate system is the claim that balance of payments problems are automatically countered by movements in exchange rates.

7.3.2 Solutions to Balance of Payments Deficits

The solutions to a balance of payments deficit depends on whether it is considered to be a short, medium or long-term problem.

Short-Term Solutions

1. Run down gold and foreign currency reserves.
   To meet future deficits every country builds up its gold and foreign currency reserves from surpluses in previous years.
2. Raising short-term interest rates.
   This will attract overseas funds which can be used to finance the deficit. However, such an action may have serious consequences in the long-term because if interest rates rise in other financial centres then there may be a movement of this 'hot money' to these more attractive centres. Such movements seriously affect the level of a country's reserves.
3. Borrowing from the International Monetary Fund.
4. Borrowing from central banks.
   Most central banks have entered into 'swap agreements' whereby if they become short of certain foreign currencies they will be able to borrow them from other central banks.
5. Borrowing in the eurocurrency market.
6. Gifts and grants.
   These are sometimes given by developed countries to less

developed countries as a form of aid to ease their balance of payments problems.

7. Exchange control measures.
   Where a balance of payments problem arises because of excessive overseas investment, a country can resort to exchange control measures. They are usually implemented by the central bank to restrict the availability of foreign currency for investment overseas.

Medium-Term Solutions

1. Borrowing on the eurobond or syndicated loans market.
2. Use of tariffs.
   A balance of payments problem can be improved by the imposition of tariffs with the aim of reducing imports by making them more expensive. For example, in 1965, the U.K. levied an import surcharge of 15% on imported goods. Although the use of tariffs is contrary to the principles of GATT, it does have a provision for the use of tariffs when all measures have failed. Even so, the use of tariffs must be temporary and they must be removed when the situation improves. Another deterrent against the use of tariffs is that it may lead to retaliation from other countries who feel that their exports are being penalised.
3. Use of non-tariff methods.
   Although these are contrary to the principles of GATT, there are two well practised examples:
   (a) The imposition of standards.
   A country can reduce its imports by stipulating that products meet certain minimum quality standards before they are allowed in. In addition, the standards may be changed continually so as to deter the seller from trying to comply with them. For example, the U.S. has precise safety standards and pollution laws relating to motor cars.
   (b) Public procurement policies.
   Government departments may be directed to purchase home produced goods only.

Long-Term Solutions

1. Borrowing on the eurobond or syndicated loans market.
2. Use of export incentives.
   In order to stimulate exports, a country could take measures to make exporting easier and more attractive. These measures might

include the provision of the following:

(a) insurance cover against risk of non-payment by the overseas customer.

(b) Export finance.

(c) Information as to general market conditions overseas, the degree of competition in these markets and details of tariffs and standards.

(d) Technical assistance in respect of export documentation and foreign exchange requirements.

There are limitations on the use of export incentives because a country has to be careful that it does not infringe international trading agreements.

3. Deflationary policy.

   If the balance of payments problem is largely attributable to inflationary pressures then excess demand can be dampened down by the use of deflationary fiscal and monetary policies. If a country's rate of inflation can be reduced below that of its competitors then its balance of payments should improve because its exports will become relatively cheaper and its imports will become relatively dearer. Often fiscal and monetary policies are supplemented by an incomes policy in order to try to keep wage increases in line with increases in productivity so helping to stabilise costs and prices.

4. Use of the exchange rate.

   A country may reduce the foreign exchange value of its currency to lower the price of its exports and to raise the price of its imports. It may do this by allowing its exchange rate to depreciate if it has adopted a floating exchange rate system or it may devalue its exchange rate if it has adopted a fixed exchange rate system. The use of the exchange rate is discussed in Chapter 8.

An alternative way of considering the solutions to a balance of payments problem on current account is to classify them according to whether they finance or rectify the problem. A current account deficit can be financed by:

1. Inflows of short-term and long-term private capital.
2. Official financing which can take the form of:

   (a) Net transactions with the IMF.

   (b) Foreign currency borrowing from overseas monetary authorities.

   (c) Foreign currency borrowing from the international money and capital markets.

   (d) Drawing on official reserves.

A current account deficit can be corrected by:

1. Deflation.
2. Depreciation/Devaluation.
3. Direct controls such as import tariffs or export subsidies.

7.4 Summary

1. The balance of payments statement of a country is a systematic record of all economic transactions between the residents of a country and foreign residents over a specified period of time (usually one year).
2. The current account records all transactions relating to a country's current income and expenditure.
3. The current account is divided into visible and invisible items.
4. The capital account records transactions in a country's external assets and liabilities.
5. The balance of payments always balances because the total currency flow on current account and transactions in external assets and liabilities (not including changes in official reserves and government borrowing), whether surplus or deficit, is matched by equal and opposite total official financing.
6. The balancing item relates to discrepancies i.e., errors and omissions.
7. The non-oil visible balance has deteriorated sharply in the 1980s.
8. The removal of exchange controls has resulted in a large rise in direct and portfolio investment overseas.
9. The terms of trade measure the amount of imports that are obtained in return for exports.
10. A balance of payments problem on current account may be financed (by inflows of private capital and borrowing) or corrected (by deflation, depreciation or direct controls).

Questions

1.* 'The external receipts and payments of a country, in total, must balance.' Explain this statement, illustrating your answer by reference to the United kingdom.

2. What do you understand by the 'invisibles' section of a country's balance of payments accounts? Assess the importance of and recent influences on the invisibles account of the United Kingdom or any other country with which you are familiar.

3. Describe the main items in a country's balance of payments, illustrating your answer by reference to one particular country.

4.* The figures below are taken from the annual balance of payments of Ruritania. Prepare:-

(i) Ruritania's balance of invisible trade.
(ii) Ruritania's balance of payments on current account.

Do these figures support the contention that Ruritania is a developing country, and not highly industrialised? Give reasons for your answer.

	Million Rurits
Banking earnings (net)	-30
Capital movements (net inflow)	+1280
Insurance earnings (net)	-20
Interest paid abroad	-1400
Interest received from abroad	+30
Manufactured goods:-	
exports (fob)	+120
imports (fob)	-2000
Raw materials and fuel:-	
exports (fob)	+3000
imports (fob)	-1000
Shipping earnings (net)	-80
Tourist earnings (net)	+100

Note:- there were no changes in Ruritania's official reserves during the year.

5.* (a) Distinguish between the concepts of balance of (visible) trade and terms of trade.

(13)

(b) Analyse how changes in the terms of trade help to determine a country's balance of trade.

(12)

6. In what ways can a deficit on the current account of a country's balance of payments be:
(a) financed:
(b) rectified?

7. Outline the effects on the UK balance of payments (both current

and capital accounts) of:

(a) the development and production of North Sea oil;

(b) the abolition of exchange control in 1979.

8. If the balance of payments always balances, how can a balance of payments deficit arise?

9. (a) Distinguish between a country's 'balance of trade' and its 'terms of trade'. (12)

(b) To what extent can a government influence its balance of trade and its terms of trade? (13)

10. (a) Identify the main components of the current account of the balance of payments. (8)

(b) Is it *necessarily* true that a current account deficit is unfavourable for a country:

(i) if it is temporary;

(ii) if it persists over many years? (17)

11. Explain, with regard to a country's balance of payments:

(a) how overall balance is achieved if the current account is in surplus; (12)

(b) why and how a country might seek to reduce its current account surplus. (13)

CHAPTER 8

Exchange Rates

8.1 The Operation of Foreign Exchange Markets

Bilateral trade agreements provide for each country being in equilibrium in its balance of trade with each of its trading partners rather than with its trading partners in aggregate (multilateral trade). Under bilateral trade agreements, any imbalance is corrected by the use of quotas or by placing a restriction on dealing in foreign currencies. Suppose countries A, B and C have such an agreement and country A has a deficit in its trade with B and a surplus with C. Ordinarily, the deficit and surplus would be netted out but under a bilateral trade agreement the government of A must get B to import more of A's goods otherwise A will have to reduce its imports from B. Similarly, the government of C must try to get A to increase its imports from C. The effect of bilateral trade agreements is to restrict trade between the parties to such agreements.

International trade arises because countries have a *comparative advantage* in the production of some goods and services but not others. A comparative advantage arises from differences in the amounts that every country has of each factor of production.

The exchange rate between two currencies is the rate at which they exchange for each other. For example, if the exchange rate between the pound sterling and the U.S. dollar is £1 = $2, then one pound will exchange for two dollars and one dollar will exchange for fifty pence.

Exchange rates arise because the currency of one country is not acceptable as a medium of exchange in another country. Thus, a British exporter will want to be paid in pounds because he could not use foreign currency to pay his workers or his other costs of production. The foreign buyer will therefore require pounds so that be can purchase the British exporter's products and he will offer his own currency in exchange. The foreign buyer will be a demander of sterling and a supplier of his own currency. Similarly, a British importer will require foreign currency in order to purchase goods from abroad and he will offer sterling in exchange. He will therefore be a demander of foreign currency and a supplier of sterling. Thus, the price or exchange rate in a free market is determined by the interaction of supply and demand.

We have already noted that an exporter is likely to want to receive payment for his goods in his own currency. The importer will, therefore, want to buy a bank deposit in the exporter's currency and he will use his own currency in payment. For example, a U.K. buyer of U.S. goods will use a sterling bank deposit to buy a U.S. dollar bank deposit. Such transactions are made in the foreign exchange market. The banks are, therefore, well placed to operate in the foreign exchange market and they deal on behalf of their customers and also on their own account. Other participants in the market include brokers who function as intermediaries bringing buyers and sellers together and central banks.

The U.K. foreign exchange market is centred on London and business is transacted by telephone and telex. Because of the improvements in communication since the Second World War, the foreign exchange market has developed into an international market, so that sterling and other major currencies are bought and sold in all the main trading centres.The main trading centres include London, New York, Singapore, Hong Kong, Tokyo, Zurich, Frankfurt and Paris.

Banks actively deal in the major currencies. They are willing to quote their buying and selling rates for delivery now (spot) or at an agreed future date (forward). There is a well developed forward foreign exchange market in certain major currencies such as US dollars, Deutsche marks and Swiss francs for example and deals can be made for delivery up to five years in the future. Some other currencies are bought and sold forward but limits are placed as to amount and delivery period. Forward rates are quoted at either a premium or discount to the spot rate, so that the forward rate is calculated by either subtracting the premium from or adding the discount to, the spot rate. The premium and discounts are based chiefly on differences in inter-bank interest rates for the eurocurrencies involved. Forward exchange rates are not forecasts made by banks of the level of spot rates in the future. Thus, an increase in eurocurrency interest rates will tend to push up spot rates and either increase the discount or decrease the premium on forward rates.

The Bank of England actively participates in the foreign exchange market. The Bank of England deals on behalf of government departments and overseas central banks and monetary institutions. The Bank of England also manages the Exchange Equalisation Account.

8.2.1 Factors Which Determine Exchange Rate Movements

1. The Current Account of the Balance of Payments

A current account surplus means that the demand for that country's currency will be greater than supply and the exchange rate will rise.

Let us assume that exchange rates are determined by supply and demand in free markets. Diagram 8.1 shows the determination of the exchange rate for the pound sterling and the U.S. dollar.

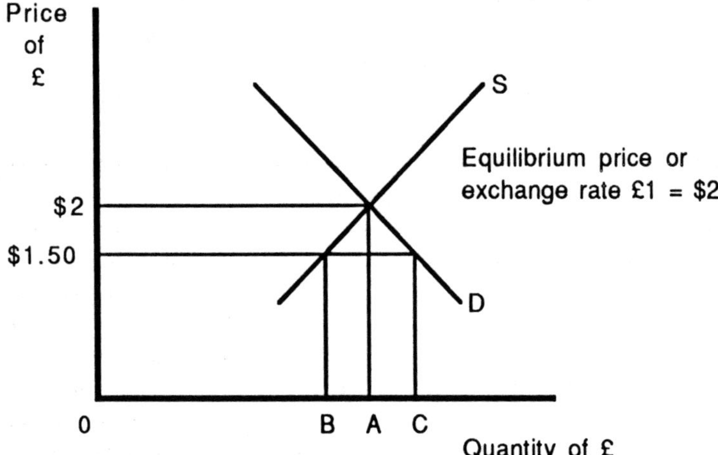

Diagram 8.1

The equilibrium price or rate of exchange is £1 = $2 and OA £s will be demanded. However, if the market price was say, $1.50 then OC £s would be demanded but only OB £s would be supplied, so the price would rise until it returned to its equilibrium price of $2.

Let us suppose that there is a change in tastes so that the British peoples' preference for U.S. goods increased. This will lead to an increase in purchases of U.S. goods and thus, the British will demand more dollars so that they can make payment. The demand curve for dollars will shift to the right (D1 to D2) as shown in Diagram 8.2.

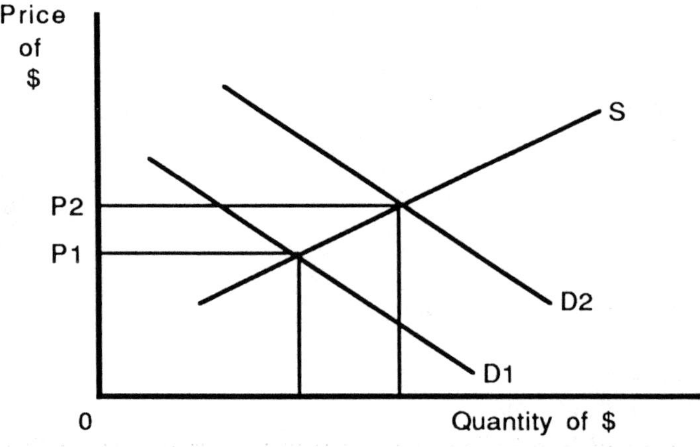

Diagram 8.2

Thus, the equilibrium price of dollars will rise from OP1 to OP2 (i.e. the dollar has appreciated whilst the pound has depreciated because more pounds are offered in exchange for dollars).

2. Relative Prices

A change in the price level of one country will affect the exchange rate. Let us assume that the U.K. is suffering from inflation but the U.S. is not. The sterling price of British goods will rise and so they will be more expensive in the U.S. Thus, the demand in the U.S. for British goods will fall. Buyers in the U.S. will require fewer pounds to settle with their British suppliers and so the supply of dollars will fall. On the other hand, U.S. goods will be more attractive in the U.K. in comparison with domestically produced goods because they have become cheaper and so more will be purchased. Thus, demand for dollars will increase (D1 to D2). The combined effects of the shifts in supply and demand are shown in Diagram 8.3. It can be seen that inflation in the U.K. leads to an appreciation in the value of the dollar (OP1 to OP2) and a corresponding depreciation in the value of the pound. If the price levels of both the U.K. and the U.S. increase by the same amount, then the relative prices of imports and domestically produced goods would be unchanged and so the exchange rate would be unchanged. However, if the price level of one country is rising faster than another, then the value of its currency will be falling relative to that of the second country.

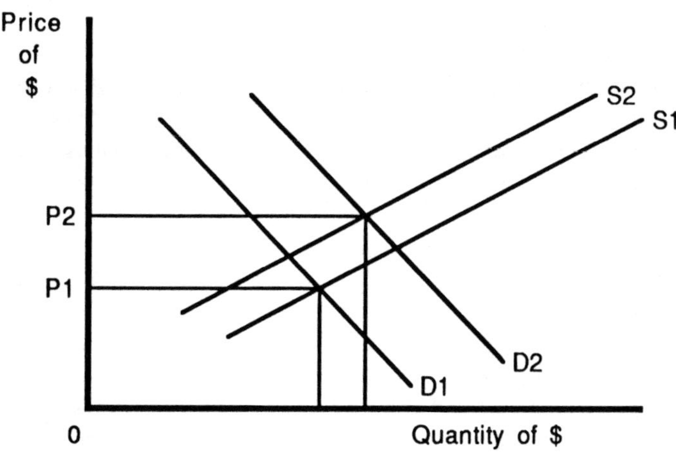

Diagram 8.3

The *theory of purchasing power parity* focuses on the relative purchasing power of currencies. This theory was developed by classical economists and it states that the exchange rate between two currencies is determined by their relative purchasing power in the country in which they circulate. For example, if goods costing £100 in the U.K. cost $1,000 in the U.S., then the rate of exchange would be 10 dollars to the pound (i.e. 1000/100). Thus, a change in a country's price level will affect its exchange rate, so that an increase in the rate of inflation in one country relative to other countries, will lead to a depreciation in its exchange rate. From our earlier discussion of the determination of exchange rates in free markets we can see that this theory has an element of truth. However, the theory implies that a rise in the internal price level of one country will lead to a proportionate fall in the exchange rate of the country. Thus, using our example above, if the price level in the U.S. doubled whilst the price level of the U.K. remained unchanged then other things being equal, the rate of exchange would be 20 dollars to the pound (i.e. 2000/100). The theory assumes that other things remain equal such as the maintenance of full employment, no change in tastes, no inventions but in the real world other things do not remain equal. As we have seen earlier, a change in tastes can alter a country's exchange rate without any change in its internal price level. Similarly, flows of capital from one country to another can affect the exchange rate.

The theory can also be criticised on the following grounds:

1. Not all goods and services in the domestic economy are traded.
2. Indirect taxes, subsidies and transport costs influence the internal price level of a country without affecting exchange rates in the way predicted from the application of the theory.
3. Exchange rates may vary for reasons other than changes in the internal price level. For example, the movement of capital will influence exchange rates but the theory does not take this factor into account. Similarly, an increase in national income may affect the exchange rate if the demand for imports rises relative to exports.

Despite the theory's shortcomings it does focus on the problem that countries with fixed exchange rates will have difficulty in keeping their exchange rates within their adopted par values if they have different rates of inflation. The participants in the European Monetary System keep their exchange rates at predetermined levels. Because the participants in the system have had widely divergent rates of inflation it has resulted in a number of realignments of currencies. This is because the alternative for those countries with higher rates of inflation would be to implement deflationary policies which would increase the level of unemployment. Because this policy option is politically unpalatable during a period of high unemployment, the only option open to these countries is devaluation.

3. The Level of International Interest Rates

A government can raise interest rates in order to attract short-term capital. However, if interest rates rise in other financial centres, the short-term capital may flow back to these other financial centres. Such movements of capital will affect exchange rates.

4. Other Economic Factors

Here we can include such factors as a country's balance of payments, the state of industrial relations, the level of the money supply and economic forecasts. Changes in these factors may influence the currency markets and exchange rates. For example, a fall in the price of oil will, other things being equal, detrimentally affect the balance of payments on current account of an oil exporting country and lead to a fall in the exchange rate of its currency. On the other hand, a fall in the price of oil will, other things being equal, beneficially affect the balance of payments on current account of a large oil importing country and lead to a rise in the exchange rate of its currency.

5. Political Factors

There are a whole range of political factors which may influence currency markets and exchange rates. These include political unrest, trade agreements between countries, changes in government policies and wars. For example, if the government decides to expand the economy by increasing its budget deficits then the expectation of higher rates of inflation, an increase in imports and a reduction in exports will lead to a depreciation of the exchange rate of its currency.

6. Central Bank Policy

A central bank may intervene in the foreign exchange market in order to even out excessive fluctuations in the exchange rate of its currency. If the value of its currency (i.e. the exchange rate) falls, the central bank may push the exchange rate back up by drawing on its foreign currency reserves in order to purchase its own currency in the foreign exchange market. On the other hand, if the value of its currency is rising, the central bank may use its own currency to purchase foreign currency reserves thereby pushing down the exchange rate for its currency.

8.2.2 Effects of Depreciation on the Balance of Payments Current Account

The depreciation of a currency will have an effect on both exports and imports. (Note that if a country adopts a fixed exchange rate system, then the effects of devaluation will be the same as for depreciation).

Effects on Exports

Suppose the rate of exchange between the pound sterling and the U.S. dollar is £1 = $2. This means that if a U.S. resident wishes to buy a British product costing £1 he would need to pay $2. Suppose that sterling depreciated so that it equalled $1.50 on the foreign exchange markets. The same product would now cost the U.S. resident $1.50. So the effect of depreciation would be to make U.K. exports cheaper and, therefore, more competitive so that more goods can be sold abroad resulting in an improvement in the balance of payments.

However, whether a depreciation will be successful depends on a number of considerations:

1. The immediate effect of a depreciation is that less foreign currency is received in exchange for the same exports. Thus, the U.K. would immediately be worse off because it would receive fewer dollars for the same amount of exports. Thus, the same amount of exports will purchase less imports. Using our example above, prior to depreciation the sale of the British product costing £1 to a U.S.resident would net $2 but after depreciation it would only net $1.50. Thus, each unit of export sales produces less revenue so that if depreciation is to be effective the volume of sales must increase by at least an amount sufficient to cover the initial reduction in revenue.
2. The effect of depreciation on the volume of export sales depends upon the elasticity of demand for its products in the overseas markets. If demand is elastic, then a fall in price will produce a more than proportionate increase in demand. But if demand is inelastic, then a fall in price will produce a less than proportionate increase in demand so depreciation is more likely to be successful when the demand for its products overseas is elastic.
3. Failure in export markets may be due to considerations other than price, such as quality, design, after-sales service, so that depreciation would not help directly in these instances.

4. The benefits of depreciation would be lost if a country's competitors also depreciated by the same amount or if they imposed import restrictions.
5. If the depreciation is to be effective, there must be spare capacity in industry to exploit the increase in competitiveness of its exports. If the demand for a country's exports increases after depreciation it must be able to meet the extra demand created. Thus, fiscal and monetary policies should be used to dampen down domestic demand so as to free resources for the production of export goods.

Effect on Imports

The effect of depreciation is to make imports more expensive. However, whether fewer imported goods are purchased depends on the country's elasticity of demand for its imports. If the demand for imported goods is inelastic, then an increase in price will lead to a less than proportionate fall in demand and so depreciation will be less successful. For example, the U.K. is highly dependent upon imported raw materials and food stuffs. These must be bought whether they become more expensive or not. Depreciation will only be successful if domestic substitutes can be found.

One of the most important problems associated with depreciation is that it can fuel inflationary pressures. For example, if a country imports a large amount of its raw materials and it is unable to provide domestic substitutes then its costs of production will increase. If the country imports a large amount of its food requirement and it cannot produce domestic substitutes then it will lead to an increase in its cost of living. This will lead to an increase in wage demands which will add to costs of production and in turn, the prices of finished goods will rise leading to a spiral in wages and prices. If the prices of exports go up as a result, the benefits of depreciation will be lost. It is important, therefore, that the government implements domestic policies which would check the inflationary pressures resulting from depreciation.

8.2.3 Exchange Equalisation Account (EEA)

The EEA was established in 1932, under the control of the Treasury, for the purpose of checking undue fluctuations in the exchange value of sterling. Initially, £150 million in sterling was made available for its operations. In 1939, the Issue Department of the Bank of England transferred its gold balances to the EEA and since then, it has been the custodian of the U.K.'s gold and foreign currency reserves and more recently SDRs.

The EEA's sterling capital, other than a working balance, is entirely invested in Treasury bills; it is in fact lent to the Exchequer. If the EEA purchases gold or foreign currencies it draws on its sterling capital and the amount the EEA has on loan to the Exchequer is reduced. In turn, the Exchequer has to cover this repayment by borrowing from the market (by issuing government debt). In effect the government borrows sterling in order to sell it in the foreign exchange market. On the other hand, when the EEA sells gold or foreign currencies it acquires sterling, which, in turn, is lent to the Exchequer. The Exchequer is then able to reduce its borrowing from the market. The EEA's working balance is lent to the Exchequer as interest free Ways and Means advances.

The EEA is free to operate in the forward exchange market but it does so only occasionally. It did, however, intervene in the forward exchange market prior to the devaluation of the pound in November 1967 and its operations resulted in a loss of over £350 million.

Although the U.K.'s reserves form part of the official financing section of the balance of payments, the EEA is not used by the authorities to balance the balance of payments.

The operations of the EEA have become muted since sterling was floated in 1972, but it is still used to smooth out severe fluctuations in sterling's exchange rate.

8.2.4 Trade-Weighted Indices

Trade-weighted indices (they are also known as indices of effective exchange rates) provide a measure of the value of a currency in terms of a number of currencies which are weighted according to their importance in trade with the country whose currency is being measured. For example, sterling is measured against a Bank of England index which until recently was based on trade-weighted changes from the exchange rates agreed by the Group of Ten countries in Washington in December 1971. In 1977 the weighting of the index was revised to take account of 1972 trade flows and it was again revised on February 2nd 1981, to take account of 1977 trade flows. The latter revision resulted in a lower weighting for the U.S. dollar and an increased weighting for the Irish punt, the yen, the guilder and the lira. Three smaller countries, Yugoslavia, Hong Kong and Taiwan were dropped from the calculations. In addition, the base was updated from December 18th 1971 equalling 100 to the annual average of 1975 equalling 100.

In January 1989, the calculation was changed again and the effective exchange rate index produced by the IMF now forms the basis of the

Bank of England index. The result has been a fall in the weighting of the US dollar and an increased weighting for European Community currencies. These changes reflect altering trade patterns. Also the base date has been changed to 1985 = 100.

The most popular trade-weighted index measuring the value of the U.S. dollar is the one compiled by Morgan Guaranty which like the Bank of England index is based on trade-weighted changes. Both indices are published each day and an example of them is shown in Table 8.4.

Table 8.4

July 3rd, 1986	Bank of England Index	Morgan Guaranty Changes %
Sterling	76.2	-15.2
U.S. dollar	113.6	+4.3
Canadian dollar	78.7	-12.0
Austrian schilling	127.3	+7.1
Belgian franc	95.6	-7.3
Danish kroner	86.5	-0.9
Deutsche mark	135.8	+15.0
Swiss franc	162.9	+19.1
Guilder	126.0	+9.5
French franc	69.4	-13.4
Lira	46.5	-17.7
Yen	211.1	+55.9

(Morgan Guaranty changes: average 1980-82 = 100)

8.2.5 Recent Exchange Rate Developments

During the period 1978 to mid-1980, exchange rates of the industrial countries remained fairly stable although there were a few exceptions, for example, the Pound sterling appreciated rapidly during this period. However, from mid-1980 the substantial and rapid swings in current account balances, differences in inflation rates and interest rates and differences in the financial policies of many countries resulted in large exchange rate movements in major currencies and of occasional pressures in the foreign exchange markets.

Between mid-1980 and mid-1981, the European currencies generally moved downwards, whilst the U.S. dollar and Japanese yen moved sharply upwards. The Pound sterling moved up until January 1981 and this was followed by a sharp fall which continued into 1982. On the other hand, the exchange rates between the currencies of the European Monetary System remained fairly stable despite fairly large differences in inflation rates. This stability resulted from a number of factors, such as official intervention in foreign exchange markets and a similarity in current account developments. There was only one realignment of currencies during the period end-1979 to mid-1981. However, from mid-1981 to mid-1982 there were three realignments and a further realignment in March 1983. There were no further realignments until July 1985.

Since 1980, the US dollar has strengthened significantly, having appreciated by some 30% during the period 1980-82 and it continued to appreciate throughout the period 1982-85. Sterling, on the other hand, weakened dramatically during the same period. In January 1985, the UK Government stemmed the further weakening of sterling against the dollar by reactivating MLR at 12% thereby signalling a rise in bank base rates.

The sterling/US dollar rate fell to a low point of 1.0357 on 26th February 1985 but sterling has strengthened since then rising from $1.158 at the end of 1984 to $1.8870 at the end of 1987. The sterling exchange rate index also improved during 1985 although it weakened once again during 1986. Table 8.5 shows the sterling/U.S. dollar exchange rate and the sterling exchange rate index.

Table 8.5 Sterling/US Dollar Exchange Rate and Sterling Exchange Rate Index

Last working day	*US$ to £*	*Sterling exchange rate index*
1977	1.9185	84.7
1978	2.0410	82.2
1979	2.2250	90.2
1980	2.3920	101.4
1981	1.9110	90.9
1982	1.6175	84.3
1983	1.4520	82.9
1984	1.1580	73.0
1985	1.4455	77.9
1986	1.4837	69.2
1987	1.8870	75.8

(Source: Bank of England Quarterly Bulletin - February 1988)

8.3.1 Exchange Rate Systems

The two extreme exchange rate systems are fixed and floating but there are a number of systems that come between these two extremes.

1. Absolute fixed peg

Under this system the rate of exchange is not allowed to fluctuate.

2. Fixed peg with small fluctuations

Under this system the rate of exchange is allowed to move narrowly, say 1% , either side of its adopted par value.

3. Adjustable peg

This system of exchange rates operated between 1944 and 1971. Rates of exchange are allowed to move 1% either side of parity but if there is a fundamental disequilibrium in a country's balance of payments then a new parity can be adopted by devaluation or revaluation.

4. Wider band float

This system allows greater flexibility by widening the band in which the exchange rate is allowed to fluctuate. This system was adopted under the Smithsonian Agreement in 1971.

5. Movable band

This is a more flexible version of the adjustable peg. If the rate gets jammed against the upper or lower limit, then the whole band can be moved.

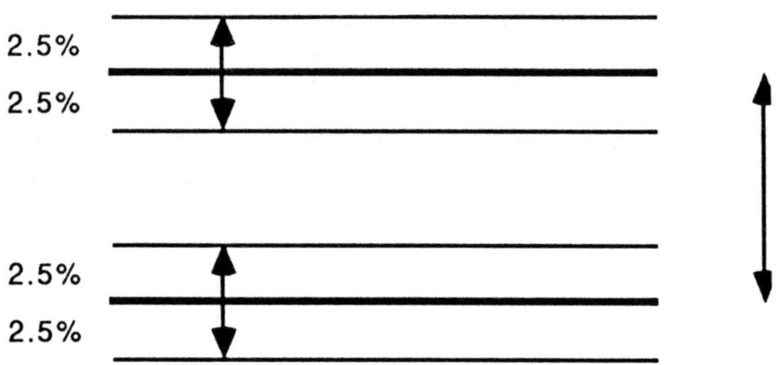

6. Crawling peg

Under this system, the rate of exchange is allowed to move with market pressures but only slowly.

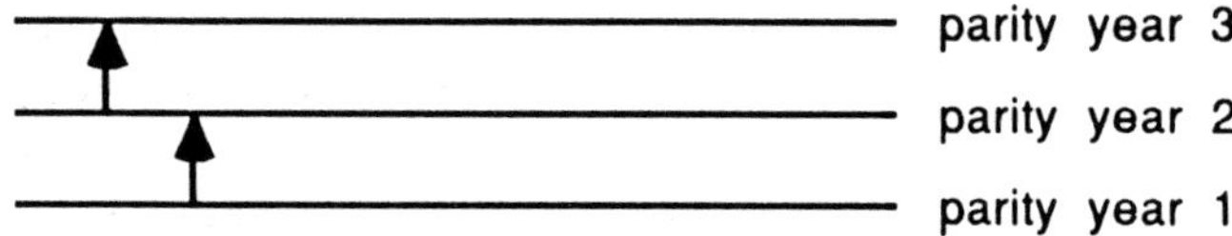

7. Managed float (often called a 'dirty float')

Under this system, the rate of exchange is allowed to float but the authorities intervene when it considers it politic to do so.

8. Free float

This system is the opposite extreme to the absolute fixed peg. The rate of exchange is determined by free market forces.

8.3.2 Fixed Exchange Rate Systems

Under a fixed exchange rate system, a country maintains the external value of its currency at a pre-determined level. The major trading nations of the world agreed at the Bretton Woods Conference in 1944 that they would abide by an adjustable peg system of exchange rates. So that if, for example, U.K. exports fell at the same time that purchases of imported goods increased, then the price of sterling would fall. If the rate threatened to fall below the lower limit of the band, then the Bank of

England would enter the foreign exchange market and buy pounds, thereby reducing their supply and pushing up the price back to its central rate. The Bank of England would use the Exchange Equalisation Account for this purpose. Similarly, if the demand for sterling increased so that its price threatened to move outside the upper limit of the band, then the Bank of England sold pounds so as to push the price down. The Exchange Equalisation Account is made up of the U.K's gold and foreign currency reserves so that a continuous balance of payments deficit under the adjustable peg system would have resulted in a substantial drain on the U.K's reserves and it would have to resort to borrowing to supplement reserves. For this reason, the IMF made funds available to nations suffering from balance of payments problems. As a result of the dollar crisis in 1971 many nations floated their currencies for a time. Under the Smithsonian Agreement in December 1971, most countries were persuaded to go back to fixing their rates but with a wider band of fluctuations. This agreement was abandoned approximately one year later and most major currencies are now floating, although the European Monetary System is a regional exception. However, monetary authorities still continue to intervene in the foreign exchange markets to smooth out sharp fluctuations or to mitigate the destabilising effects of speculative movements (hence the use of the term 'dirty float'). A number of countries still continue to peg their currencies. At the end of June 1985, thirty two currencies were pegged against the U.S. dollar, one against the Pound sterling, fourteen against the French franc and twelve against the SDR.

8.3.3 The Case for Floating Exchange Rates

1. The chief attraction of adopting a floating exchange rate is the claim that balance of payments problems will be automatically rectified by adjustments in the exchange rate. We have seen previously that where a country suffers inflationary pressures which have resulted in an adverse balance of payments then a depreciation in its currency will pull the balance of payments back towards equilibrium (the mechanism is of course subject to the considerations noted earlier). Similarly, if a country is experiencing deflationary pressures which result in a balance of payments surplus then its currency would appreciate and its balance of payments would move back towards equilibrium. A schematic representation is given in Diagram 8.6.

Diagram 8.6 Automatic Correction of a Balance of Payments Problem

1. Inflation	1. Deflation
2. Imports increase exports decrease	2. Imports decrease Exports increase
3. Balance of payments deficit	3. Balance of payments surplus
4. Supply of its currency increases Demand for its currency decreases	4. Supply of its currency decreases Demand for its currency increases
5. Price of its currency falls	5. Price of its currency rises
6. Imports fall (dearer) Exports rise (cheaper)	6. Imports rise (cheaper) Exports fall (dearer)
7. Balance of payments equilibrium	7. Balance of payments equilibrium

2. Because floating exchange rates automatically rectify a balance of payments problem, there is less need for a country to pursue stringent internal deflationary policies to improve its international payments position. The country is, therefore, free to implement policies of full employment without fear of inflation creating an adverse balance of payments because the automatic depreciation of the exchange rate will offset the effects of inflation. (On the other hand, the increased freedom in the management of the domestic economy might result in the country relaxing internal discipline still further).

3. With a floating exchange rate, there is less need for large reserves because the rate does not have to be supported.

8.3.4 The Case Against Floating Exchange Rates

1. The main problem with floating exchange rates is that uncertainty as to international receipts and payments is created. Thus, if a seller invoices his customer in foreign currency he will not be sure how much he will receive when he converts his foreign currency into domestic currency. However, such exchange uncertainty can be mitigated by the use of forward exchange contracts.
2. Floating exchange rates could discourage foreign investment because a movement in exchange rates could produce a capital loss when the investor realises his investment. Once again, the use of forward exchange contracts would mitigate the uncertainty.

These two criticisms of floating exchange rates were investigated by the Group of Thirty (this is a New York based study group consisting of eminent bankers supported by the Rockerfeller Foundation). Their findings, which were published in 1980 concluded that the major multinational corporations have found that the system of floating exchange rates has not been an impediment to trade and that it does not deter them from overseas investment.

8.3.5 The Case for Fixed Exchange Rates

1. Fixed exchange rates give certainty to traders and international investors and this certainty prevents speculation.

2. Fixed exchange rates impose some discipline on domestic monetary systems. For example, if a country's exports become uncompetitive and there is an adverse balance of payments, then the authorities will have to resort to deflationary policies to improve its international payments position.

8.3.6 The Case Against Fixed Exchange Rates

1. If a country has a persistent balance of payments problem then it could result in speculation that the country will rectify the problem by devaluation.

2. A country requires larger amounts of reserves to maintain its currency within its adopted par value.

8.4.1 The European Monetary System (EMS)

Ways of achieving full economic and monetary union of the European Communities were discussed by the Werner Committee in 1970. The outcome was the Werner Plan which aimed for full monetary union by 1980. The Werner Report considered that monetary union required the fulfilment of the following conditions:

1. Complete convertibility of currencies.
2. Completely fixed exchange rates.
3. Free movement of capital.
4. The eventual introduction of a common currency.
5. The setting up of a European central bank to manage the common currency and banking systems.
6. The taking of principal decisions on economic policy at Community level.

The movement towards full monetary union in the European Community raises a number of problems for member countries. In order to maintain fixed exchange rates, member countries would be required not to adopt monetary and economic policies which would conflict with the monetary and economic policies of other member countries otherwise their exchange rates would move apart. This entails the taking of decisions on important issues of economic policy at Community level. However, the surrender of autonomy by members over economic policy-making would appear to be a difficult political problem. Because of the problems associated with increases in the price of oil, exchange rate instability, inflation and an increasing membership of the Community, member countries have shown a greater concern for their own internal situation than that of the Community as a whole. Therefore, the harmonization of economic, monetary and fiscal policies of all members will be very difficult to achieve.

The commitment to completely fixed exchange rates by member countries entails the loss of the exchange rate weapon to help correct a balance of payments problem. Thus, a member country experiencing a balance of payments deficit would have to correct the situation by implementing deflationary policies which would result in an increase in unemployment. This problem is crucial for those member countries which are economically weak. The adoption of deflationary policies to cure a fundamental balance of payments problem would result in higher levels of unemployment and lower growth rates. An important issue for these countries would be the availability and effectiveness of Community schemes (such as the Regional Development Fund and EIB loans) to help overcome their economic weaknesses.

The first step towards monetary union was taken in April 1972 when the 'snake' arrangements were agreed.

8.4.2 The 'Snake'

The snake arrangements were introduced with the aim of securing greater exchange rate stability in European currencies after the breakdown of the IMF system. The parties to the initial agreement were the Benelux States (Belgium, Netherlands and Luxembourg), West Germany, France and Italy. Sweden joined in 1973, the U.K., Ireland, Norway and Denmark joined in 1976 (the U.K. having joined briefly in 1972). Italy left the system in 1973. France left in 1974, rejoined in 1975 and left again in 1976. The U.K. and Ireland left after participating in the arrangements for only one month and Sweden left in 1977. Although Norway never joined the European Community, she continued to participate in the arrangements until 1978 when the European Monetary

System was agreed.

The snake arrangements allowed a 2.25% margin of fluctuations on either side of the participating country's adopted par value vis-a-vis another (the snake). Each currency also had a fixed rate against the U.S. dollar with a 2.25% margin of fluctuation on either side of parity. This band of 4.5% was called the 'tunnel' and if the exchange rate between any two currencies threatened to move outside the tunnel both countries had to intervene to keep the snake in the tunnel.

Because of a number of currency crises in 1972 and 1973, the European currencies were floated against the U.S. dollar so that the snake was 'let out of the tunnel', so that by early 1974 none of the major European currencies were pegged against each other.

The snake arrangements were not very successful mainly because of destabilising speculative hot money movements which resulted from various currency crises.

8.4.3 The Development of the European Monetary System

The EMS developed out of the snake arrangements and the first stage came into force on March 13th, 1979. The EMS was agreed at a meeting of the European Council for Ministers on December 5th, 1978 and all members of the European Community agreed to participate in the system except the U.K. which opted out of the exchange rate system but agreed to participate in the other aspects of it.

The aim of the EMS is to increase exchange rate stability between member currencies and to promote greater co-operation in the conduct of their financial and economic policies. The EMS can be broken down into two parts:

1. the creation of a zone of exchange rate stability;
2. the provision of credit support facilities.

The numeraire of the system is the European Currency Unit (ECU) which is calculated by a formula which is based on a fixed amount of each Community member's currency which is weighted according to its importance in the Community (as measured by Gross Domestic Product). The currency amounts can be changed in the future by the Council of Ministers if the percentage weighting of a currency diverges too far from that country's relative importance in the Community. It was decided that the initial value and composition of the ECU would be the same as for the European Unit of Account.

The ECU performs the following functions:

1. As the denominator (numeraire) for the exchange rate mechanism.

2. As the basis for the divergence indicator (see below).
3. As the denominator for operations in both the intervention and the credit mechanism.
4. As a means of settlement between monetary authorities of the European Community.

Each currency has an ECU central rate and these rates determine a 'grid' of bilateral central rates between members' currencies. Adjustments can be made to central rates when necessary. Parities have been realigned on a number of occasions. Parities were realigned during September 1979, when the Deutsche mark was revalued by 2% against most currencies in the system and the Danish kroner was devalued by 3%. During November 1979 the Danish kroner was devalued by 5% against all member currencies. Parities were further realigned during March 1981 when the Italian lira was devalued by 6%, during October 1981 when the French franc and Italian lira were devalued by 3% and the Deutsche mark and Dutch guilder were revalued by 5.5%. During February 1982 the Belgian franc was devalued by 8.5% and the Danish kroner was devalued by 3%. During June 1982 the French franc was devalued by 10% against the Deutsche mark and the lira was devalued by 2.75%. There were further realignments in March 1983 and July 1985.

Each member must ensure its rate keeps within a band of $2^1/_4$% on either side of its central rate except for Italy which has a band of approximately 6% on either side of its central rate. If a member's exchange rate threatens to move outside its limits, it must intervene.

Each member has a divergence limit (known as its 'threshold of divergence') in respect of its ECU central rate. If a member's currency threatens to cross its divergence threshold then it is expected to take corrective action. The divergence indicator gives countries a forewarning that their currencies are getting out of line and triggers consultation about checking currency fluctuations. The divergence limits are calculated by using a complex formula and Table 8.7 shows ECU central rates and divergence limits at the beginning of August 1986.

Table 8.7

Currency	*ECU central rates*	*Divergence limit %*
Belgian franc	43.6761	+/-1.5338
Danish kroner	7.91896	+/-1.6408
Deutsche mark	2.13834	+/-1.1202
French franc	6.96280	+/-1.3701
Dutch guilder	2.40935	+/-1.5081
Irish punt	0.712956	+/-1.6669
Italian lira	1496.21	+/-4.0788

8.4.4 Credit Support Facilities

We have already seen that EMS members are expected to intervene by using their foreign exchange reserves to support their agreed parity rates. If a member's exchange rate comes under pressure three mutual support schemes are available under the EMS.

1. *The very short term facility*
   This facility provides, in theory, unlimited support for up to approximately ten weeks with an automatic renewal for a further three months if necessary. This facility can be extended even further by agreement.

2. *Short-term monetary support (STMS)*
   This facility provides assistance for up to nine months and ECU 14 billion have been made available. Each EMS member has a borrowing ceiling under this facility.

3. *Medium-term financial assistance (MTFA)*
   This facility is available to those members with balance of payments problems and ECU 11 billion have been made available. Assistance can be extended for two to five years and it is available subject to the sanction of the Council of Ministers of the European Communities and subject to any economic policy conditions that they may impose.

Both the STMS and MTFA existed under the snake arrangements but when the EMS was adopted the facilities were extended and enlarged from ECU 10 billion to ECU 25 billion.

The provision of these facilities is administered by the European Monetary Co-operation Fund. This Fund was set up in 1973 with the aim of facilitating the financing and settlement of claims and liabilities arising from intervention as a result of snake operations.

8.4.5 Pooling of Reserves

The EMS provides for the partial pooling of Community reserves. Community central banks (including the Bank of England, even though Britain is not participating in the exchange rate mechanism) deposit 20% of their gold reserves with the European Monetary Co-operation Fund, receiving equivalent amounts of ECUs in return. The deposit is renewed every three months to take account of changes in a member's gold and dollar reserves and also changes in the gold price. The ECU issue is then recalculated. For the purposes of the ECU calculation, gold is valued at the average market price over the preceding six months. Thus, whenever the price of gold increases (decreases) member's ECU reserve holdings rise (fall).

8.4.6 The Future Development of the EMS

On 17th April 1989, the Delors Committee published its report which aimed to provide a 'study and to propose concrete stages leading towards economic and monetary union'. The report notes a three-stage approach to economic and monetary union within the European Community. It envisages the creation of a new European central bank which would be responsible for a single monetary policy.

The report notes the following three stages:

1. Stage 1 where members work towards a convergence in economic policies.
2. Stage 2 where new European institutions, including a central bank, are created. Economic policy decision-making will begin to be taken at Community level.
3. Stage 3 where exchange rates become fixed, a common currency is adopted and monetary and exchange rate policy become the responsibility of the European central bank.

The report does not note a time-table for the implementation of the three stages.

Since publication of the report, the UK government has stated that it is reluctant to enter stage 1.

8.4.7 Britain and the EMS

We have already seen that Britain decided against joining the EMS exchange rate mechanism because it was felt that sterling's weakness together with Britain's inflationary problems would result in the instigation of deflationary policies which might be highly unpalatable when seen purely from the domestic point of view. Indeed, within the EMS, Belgium and Denmark, the two most consistently weak members of the scheme, were at times forced to push up their interest rates to well in excess of their inflation rates in order to maintain stability in their exchange rates against the Deutsche mark.

However, as far as sterling is concerned, instead of being a weak currency it was a high-flier in the foreign exchange markets during 1979 and 1980 and had Britain become a full member of the EMS it would have been under intense pressure to maintain sterling within the limits set under the scheme. On the other hand, after January 1981, the sterling exchange rate fell sharply and it continued to fall during the period up to 1985. It is this volatility in the sterling exchange rate which makes it difficult for Britain to become a full member of the EMS. Thus, the UK remains outside the exchange rate system of the EMS.

The economic arguments against Britain joining the EMS exchange rate mechanism can be summarised as follows:

1. The volatility of the sterling exchange rate. In recent years this volatility has been associated with changes in the price of oil.
2. The loss of the exchange rate weapon means that a balance of payments problem would have to be corrected by deflationary policies rather than by the use of the exchange rate.
3. Stability between sterling and the Deutsche mark may be difficult to achieve given their importance in the international financial system.
4. Sterling's entry into the mechanism may result in a much increased level of official intervention.
5. Finally, there is the problem of choosing the requisite exchange rate on entry.

8.4.8 Assessment of the Operation of the EMS

The European Commission's quarterly report to the Council of Ministers in March 1980, stated that in the first year of operation the EMS had cut exchange rate instability between European Community currencies by nearly two-thirds and that they were more stable than in any year since 1972. Member states' exchange rates vis-a-vis the ECU showed an average change of only 1.9% compared with an average of 5.2% per annum in the preceding six years. Indeed, during the period end-1979 to mid-1981, parities were realigned on only one occasion. However, after mid-1981, the maintenance of parities proved more difficult with the result that there were three realignments during the period mid-1981 to end-1982 and a further realignment in March 1983. There were no realignments of parities during 1984 and early 1985. However, there was a further realignment in July 1985.

The relative stability since 1983 has been helped by the strong US dollar (although more recently it has weakened) which shifted demand away from the Deutsche mark and reduced the upward pressures on the Deutsche mark relative to the other currencies in the EMS. In addition, countries within the EMS with high inflation rates introduced monetary and fiscal policies to reduce these high rates of inflation.

8.4.9 The Role of European Investment Bank (EIB) within the EMS

The EIB was created in 1958 by the Treaty of Rome in order to assist economic development within the Community. The Bank lends funds to public enterprises, public authorities with financial autonomy, financial institutions of any nationality provided the project for which finance is required is situated in a member State or in an associated country and to private firms.

Under the EMS arrangements, the European Council requested the EIB to make available, for periods of up to 5 years, loans of up to 1 billion European Units of Account to less prosperous countries fully participating in both the exchange rate and intervention mechanisms of the EMS, on special conditions. This facility will consist of loans raised by the Community itself but managed as regards appraisal of projects and administration by the EIB. The interest on these loans will be subsidised by 3% but the subsidy will be limited to a maximum of 200 million European Units of Account a year for 5 years. These loans are to be used for the financing of selected infrastructure projects and programmes.

Member States not participating fully in the mechanisms will not contribute to the financing of the scheme. Therefore, as far as the U.K. is concerned, it will not qualify for loans with an interest subsidy nor will it contribute towards interest subsidies for others so long as it continues not to participate fully in the EMS.

8.5 The Relationship between Exchange Rates and Interest Rates

We noted in Chapter 5 that changes in interest rates will affect exchange rates as a result of the movement of interest sensitive short-term funds. For example, a rise in interest rates (assuming a widening of the interest rate differential compared with other countries) will result in an inflow of short term capital and a consequent rise in the exchange rate. If interest rates rise as a result of monetary policy to reduce the money supply (rather than just to raise a low exchange rate) then the exchange rate may rise still further because of the increased confidence in the currency arising from the expectation of lower inflation in the future. A fall in interest rates would tend to have the opposite effect.

Interest rate differentials result in asset switching between financial centres, assuming that the interest rate differential is greater than the rate of any expected appreciation of the domestic currency. This is because if the domestic currency appreciates, the appreciation offsets the benefit of the interest differential.

8.6 Summary

1. International trade arises because countries have a comparative advantage in the production of some goods and services.
2. The exchange rate in a free market is determined by demand and supply factors.
3. The U.K. foreign exchange market is centred on London and business is transacted by telephone and telex.
4. Banks actively deal in the major currencies and two rates are quoted: spot and forward.
5. The Bank of England actively participates in the foreign exchange market.
6. Exchange rate movements are determined by:
   (a) The current account of the balance of payments.
   (b) Relative prices.
   (c) The level of international interest rates.
   (d) Other economic factors such as economic forecasts.
   (e) Political factors.
   (f) Central bank policy
7. Depreciation has an effect on both exports and imports.
8. The Exchange Equalisation Account is used to check undue fluctuations in the exchange value of sterling.
9. Trade-weighted indices provide a measure of the value of a currency in terms of a number of currencies which are weighted according to their importance in trade with the country whose currency is being measured.
10. The two extreme exchange rate systems are fixed and floating.
11. The arguments for floating exchange rates are:
    (a) Balance of payments problems are automatically corrected.
    (b) There is less need for a country to pursue stringent internal deflationary policies to improve its external payments position.
    (c) There is less need for large reserves.
12. The arguments against floating exchange rates are:
    (a) Uncertainty as to international receipts and payments is created.
    (b) The discouragement of foreign investment.
13. The arguments for fixed exchange rates are:
    (a) Certainty.
    (b) They impose discipline on domestic monetary systems.
14. The arguments against fixed exchange rates are:

(a) Could lead to speculation.
(b) Larger amounts of reserves are required.

15. The aim of the EMS is to increase exchange rate stability between member currencies and to promote greater cooperation in the conduct of financial and economic policies.
16. The numeraire of the EMS is the ECU.
17. The EMS provides for credit support facilities.
18. Britain has decided against joining the EMS exchange rate mechanism.
19. Changes in interest rates affect exchange rates as a result of the movement of interest sensitive short-term funds.

Questions

1.* What steps has the European Community taken towards European monetary union and how successful have they been?

2. (a) Outline the principles and methods of operation of the European Monetary System (EMS). (12)
(b) Do you think the EMS will help to achieve the goal of monetary union in Europe? (13)

3.* What do you understand by the theory of purchasing power parity? Discuss the implications of this theory for the operation of the European Monetary System (EMS).

4. Discuss the relative merits of fixed and floating exchange rate systems.

5.* Outline the principles on which a central bank operates in the foreign exchange market when:-
(a) it is formally committed to maintaining the exchange rate of its currency within narrow limits, and (b) it is not.

6. In what sense do a country's balance of payments' accounts always balance? How will the operation of a freely floating exchange rate regime affect the balance for official financing?

7. Discuss the factors which determine changes in the foreign exchange rate of a country's currency.

8. In the absence of official intervention in the foreign exchange

market, what factors are likely to influence changes in a country's exchange rate?

9. For what reasons and in what ways might the monetary authorities seek to affect the level of a country's exchange rate?

10. Outline the main features of the European Monetary System (EMS). What do you consider to have been the successes and failures of the system?

11. Discuss in detail the effects of a rise in a country's exchange rate on its balance of payments.

12. Following the breakdown of the so-called Bretton Woods system in the 1970s most major currencies were allowed to float. To what extent have the theoretical advantages of floating exchange rates been borne out in practice?

13. Other things being equal, what are the likely effects of the following on a country's exchange rate:
    (a) an increase in the domestic inflation rate;
    (b) a reduction in domestic interest rates;
    (c) a general expectation that oil prices will fall;
    (d) a rise in the country's budget deficit?

14. (a) What are the objectives of the European Monetary System (EMS)? (9)
    (b) Outline the economic arguments for and against full UK entry into EMS. (16)

15. (a) Explain the significance to a country of the performance of its balance of payments on the current account. (9)
    (b) Is an adjustment of the exchange rate sufficient to rectify a sizeable deficit on a country's current account? What other measures could be introduced? (16)

16. (a) For what reasons might a country's central bank intervene in the foreign exchange markets?
    (b) To what extent is intervention by a country's central bank likely to succeed in affecting the exchange rate of that country's currency?

17. (a) What factors determine long-term movements in a country's exchange rate? (9)
(b) Discuss the case for and against a return to a worldwide system of fixed exchange rates. (16)

18. Analyse the impact of the following on a country's exchange rate, assuming in each case that other factors remain unchanged:
(i) a major pay increase in the manufacturing sector;
(ii) a relaxation of monetary policy involving lower interest rates;
(iii) the emergence of political and social unrest;
(iv) the government exceeding its spending targets.

19. In April 1987 the Chancellor of the Exchequer indicated a policy of keeping the pound near its then existing level (approximately $1.60 and DM2.90).
(a) What are the advantages of keeping a stable exchange rate? (7)
(b) How could this policy be achieved:
(i) in the short term;
(ii) in the long term? (14)
(c) Has the Chancellor's objective of keeping the pound stable been achieved? (4)

20. (a) To what extent does the theory of purchasing power parity explain a change in a country's exchange rate? (13)
(b) Examine the consequences of a depreciating exchange rate on a country's
(i) current account of the balance of payments; (9)
(ii) inflation rate. (3)

21. During the Spring of 1988, the UK experienced strongly rising bank and building society lending and an appreciating exchange rate.
(a) Why were the authorities concerned by the rise in credit? (7)
(b) What are the main economic advantages and disadvantages of a rising exchange rate? (9)
(c) Discuss the policy dilemma for the authorities confronted by a simultaneous rise in credit and an appreciating exchange rate. (9)

22. (a) Outline the main objectives of the European Monetary System (EMS). (5)
(b) What economic conditions are essential for the objectives of the EMS to be achieved? (8)
(c) Discuss the case for and against full entry into EMS. (12)

CHAPTER 9

International Liquidity

9.1.1 The Nature of International Liquidity

International liquidity consists of those assets which are accepted internationally to settle debts between nations which arise from international trade and capital movements. It consists of balances of gold, currencies such as the U.S. dollar, Pound sterling, Deutsche mark, reserve positions in the International Monetary Fund and Special Drawing Rights (SDRs).

For an individual nation its own liquidity position is of importance and it will depend upon its stock of gold and foreign currencies held in reserves, its ability to raise loans from institutions such as the International Monetary Fund and central banks and from the international capital markets.

9.1.2 U.K. Official Reserves

Table 9.1 shows the official reserves of the U.K. These comprise gold, convertible currencies and SDRs held in the Exchange Equalisation Account together with the U.K.'s reserve position in the International Monetary Fund (IMF).

Table 9.1 UK Reserves $ millions

End of	*Total*	*Gold*	*Special drawing rights*	*Reserve position in the IMF*	*Convertible Currencies*
1979	22,538	3,259	1,245	-	18,034
1980	27,476	6,987	560	1,308	18,621
1981	23,347	7,334	1,043	1,513	13,457
1982	16,997	4,562	1,233	1,568	9,634
1983	17,817	5,914	695	2,168	9,040
1984	15,694	5,476	531	2,110	7,577
1985	15,543	4,310	996	1,751	8,486
1986	21,923	4,897	1,425	1,820	13,781
1987	44,326	5,792	1,229	1,579	35,726

(Source: Bank of England Quarterly Bulletin - May 1988)

The reserve position in the IMF represents an automatic drawing right on the Fund and is equal to the U.K. quota less holdings of sterling by the IMF. The basis of valuation of the U.K. reserves have changed periodically. Until end-March 1979, gold is valued at $42.222 per fine ounce, SDRs at SDR1 = $1.20635 and convertible currencies at middle or central rates. In 1979, gold was valued at the average of the London fixing price for the three months up to end-March, less 25%; from end-March 1980 it is valued at that price or at 75% of its final fixing price on the last working day in March, whichever is the lower. From end-March 1979, SDRs and convertible currencies are valued at the average of their exchange rates against the U.S. dollar in the three months to end-March, or alternatively from end-March 1980, of their actual U.S. dollar values on the last working day of March whichever is the lower. From July 1979, convertible currencies include European Currency Units.

9.1.3 The Importance of International Liquidity

A trading nation must maintain reserves in order to settle any balance of payments debts. Since the Second World War, the demand for international liquidity has outstripped the limited supply of reserves, so that international trade has been financed by a shrinking amount of international money. The gap between the demand for and the supply of international liquidity has become known as the 'liquidity gap'.

In the domestic economy, a shortage of money can easily be rectified by the monetary authorities printing more money. However, in the world economy there is no monetary authority that can provide this service. The closest example to this is the International Monetary Fund with its issue of SDRs.

The problem of liquidity has been exacerbated by the size of many nations balance of payments deficits which resulted from increased oil prices during 1973-74 and 1979-80. However, this additional problem has been alleviated to some extent by recycling international liquidity from the oil exporting nations to the oil importing nations.

9.2.1 Gold

Britain adopted the gold standard in 1816. The gold sovereign became the legal standard unit and in 1821, the Bank of England was legally required to redeem its notes in gold bars or coin. In the next sixty years or so, the gold standard was gradually adopted by most developed nations because they had confidence in gold as a unit of value and so the settlement of international debt was facilitated.

The adoption of a gold standard requires the fulfilment of three conditions:

1. Free mintage of gold into legal coins of the realm. A person possessing a bar of gold would be able to have it turned into coins by the mint, without charge.
2. Free importation and exportation of gold.
3. Legal paper money should be fully convertible into gold by the central bank.

The gold standard lasted in Britain until 1918 whereupon it was suspended until 1925 when the gold bullion standard was introduced. Under this system there was limited convertibility in that individual bank notes were no longer convertible but a gold bar of 400 ounces could be bought for about £1,555.

In 1913, the gold bullion standard was abandoned because of large outflows of gold. When Britain went on the gold bullion standard, it adopted an unrealistically high exchange rate. Because sterling was overpriced, the resulting balance of payments deficits produced large outflows of gold. By 1931 Britain's balance of payments problems were so serious that the pound's convertibility into gold was suspended.

The advantage of a gold standard is that no balance of payments problem arises because of the link between a country's stock of gold and its money supply. Because of the convertibility of bank notes into gold, a country's stock of money will depend on its stock of gold. If a country's stock of gold increases, then its stock of money increases and vice-versa. The automatic correction of a balance of payments problem is shown in Diagram 9.2.

Diagram 9.2 Automatic Correction of the Balance of Payments Problem

Balance of payments deficit	*Balance of payments surplus*
1. Export of gold	1. Import of gold
2. Less money	2. More money
3. Domestic prices fall	3. Domestic prices rise
4. Domestic incomes fall	4. Domestic incomes rise
5. Exports increase, imports decrease	5. Exports decrease, imports increase
6. Balance of payments equilibrium	6. Balance of payments equilibrium

The reasons for the failure of the gold standard were as follows:

1. For those countries with a balance of payments deficit, the automatic

adjustment in the balance of payments would be at the expense of production and employment. A balance of payments deficit results in an outflow of gold and a reduction in the money supply leading to a fall in incomes and prices. This deflationary movement produces unemployment and many nations who were unwilling to see this occur, failed to ensure that there was a reduction in the money supply. They could do this because bank credit became an important part of the money supply so that the movement of gold abroad did not necessarily lead to a reduction in the money supply if bank credit was expanded.

Similarly, many nations with balance of payments surpluses failed to expand their money supply with the increased stock of gold because of their fear of inflation or merely to keep their balance of payments surplus.

2. The gold standard often had an adverse effect on a nation's economic growth. An expanding economy requires an increasing stock of money but this depends on the stock of gold. Those countries with balance of payments deficits would suffer gold outflows resulting in a shrinkage of their money supply which would seriously hamper their economic growth.

3. The normal functioning of the gold standard could be frustrated if a country decided to increase its interest rates. If a country had a balance of payments deficit, it could increase its money supply by raising its interest rates. The foreign money which would be attracted by the higher interest rates could be converted into gold so that the money supply could be increased.

4. Many countries adopted unrealistically high or low exchange rates. We have seen that sterling was overpriced during the period 1925-1931 and this led to balance of payments problems. On the other hand, the French franc was undervalued during this period so that France had a series of balance of payments surpluses which resulted in a very large stock of reserve assets. In 1931, France decided to convert its reserves into gold and this was probably the major contributory cause of Britain's suspension of convertibility of the pound into gold.

The next development was the gold exchange standard. The gold exchange standard evolved out of the gold standard but the essential difference was that a nation's reserves consisted of both gold and convertible currencies. This system was set up at Bretton Woods in 1944 with the aim of securing the advantages of the gold standard but without its rigidity. The member nations of the IMF agreed to link their exchange rates to the U.S. dollar which was convertible into gold and they were only allowed to deal in gold at the official price. They also undertook not to increase their gold reserves. Central banks were no longer obliged to buy or sell gold with their own currencies and national currencies were no longer backed by gold internally. Between 1934 and 1971, the United States held down the official price of gold at $35 an ounce. However, in 1968, a meeting of central bankers took place in Washington and agreement was reached on the establishment of a two-tier price system, according to which central banks would continue to transfer gold between themselves at the official price, whilst its price in the free market was left to find its own level. They also agreed not to sell their gold in the free market because if the market price was higher than the official price, central banks could make enormous profits by arbitraging the two prices.

The development of the two-tier price system was the result of the sterling devaluation in that year which resulted in a weakening of the U.S. dollar which in turn led to speculation that the United States would increase the official price of gold.

The continued weakness of the U.S. dollar in the late 1960s and early 1970s culminated in the announcement of its inconvertibility on 15th August 1971 so that the direct link between exchange rates and gold was severed. In addition, the U.S. Government decided to raise the official price of gold to $42 an ounce.

The movement towards the demonetisation of gold increased after the dollar crisis, and the IMF's policy, with much support from the United States, has been to try to phase gold out as an international monetary asset. In April 1978, the Second Amendment of the IMF's articles allowed members to deal in gold without restriction so they are now able to increase their gold reserves and to buy and sell in the free market at prevailing prices. These changes have meant that national authorities have been able to revalue their gold stocks at market prices. In January 1980, it was estimated that the world's central banks' holdings of gold, valued at market prices, made up about 70% of their total monetary reserves. This proportion was last seen in the 1950s. However, the U.K. has not benefited because its policy of switching reserves out of gold into the U.S. dollar has resulted in its gold reserves shrinking as a ratio of convertible currencies from 8:1 in 1961 to 1:15 in 1979.

The next important development was the gold price explosion in the late 1970s. In early 1978, the London gold price was under $200 an ounce, by early 1980 the price had reached $850 before falling back to below $300 for a time in 1982. Most of the price rise occurred during late 1979 and early 1980. There were a number of reasons for this increase in price. Firstly, the movement towards gold was in the main the result of the continued weakness of the U.S. dollar. Curiously enough, the dramatic rise in the price of gold probably helped to stabilise the dollar because the U.S. gold stocks, valued at market prices, were almost enough to settle the United State's total overseas debt. Secondly, at the end of 1979 there was a tremendous amount of uncertainty which led to a strong speculative demand for gold. Thirdly, much demand for gold came from the OPEC countries because of their wish to diversify the content of their reserves. Table 9.3 shows the London gold price since 1977.

Table 9.3 London Gold Price

End-year	*US$ per fine ounce*	*End-year*	*US$ per fine ounce*
1977	164.95	1983	381.50
1978	226.00	1984	308.30
1979	524.00	1985	327.00
1980	589.50	1986	390.90
1981	400.00	1987	486.50
1982	448.00		

(Source: Bank of England Quarterly Bulletin - February 1988)

The changes in the standing of gold in the international monetary scene at the end of the 1970s indicated that it was making a come-back and indeed, there were some who were calling for a remonetisation of gold so that it could return to a central role in the monetary system. However, whether or not gold could make a come-back depends on how well it is able to fulfil the functions of money.

1. *As a Unit of Account*

   The role of gold as a 'numeraire' was overthrown by the use of SDRs. In recent years the SDR has widened its unit of account function so that it is difficult to see gold making a return as a unit of account.

2. *As a Means of Exchange*

   It is not likely to make a come-back as a means of exchange because it is highly unlikely that nations will return to gold coins as the principal circulating medium.

3. *As a Store of Value*

The strongest case for gold is as a store of value. Over a long period of time it has at least maintained and probably increased its purchasing power. It has outperformed currencies, bonds and equities. In addition, the purchase of gold does not depend on luck or judgement because one gold bar is like another.

However, in the short-term, the price of gold has been highly unstable so that if it was to take on a greater role as a reserve asset, then it is likely that central monetary authorities would have to intervene in the markets to maintain stability. This would require tremendous resources because there are not only the large physical gold markets in London and Zurich, there are also the vast speculative futures markets in gold in Chicago, New York, Hong Kong and Singapore and a smaller futures market in London which was launched during 1982.

The role of gold in the international monetary system has been boosted by a mechanism built into the European Monetary System under which member countries profit from an increase in the price of gold.

In the late 1970s a number of financial commentators advocated the sale of gold by the United States to reduce the excessive supply of dollars in the international monetary system. It was argued that this could be done because of the increased value of the United States' gold reserves (at market prices). The dollar would have been strengthened because of a reduction in the supply of dollars and a strengthening in the U.S. balance of payments because gold sales count as trade. However, in the early 1980s, the dollar strengthened significantly, as we shall see in the next section.

9.2.2 International Reserve Currencies

The most important of the reserve currencies is the U.S. dollar which has made the greatest contribution to international liquidity since the Second World War so that at present it accounts for about 70% of world currency reserves. The role of the dollar as an international reserve currency was given impetus by successive U.S. balance of payments deficits which fed dollars into the international payments system. However, by the late 1960s the strength of the dollar was being questioned as a result of the U.S. balance of payments problems. The dollar had always been convertible into gold but the dollar crisis of 1971 led to the declaration of the dollar's inconvertibility on August 15th, 1971. There were a number of reasons for this crisis:

1. Dollar balances outside the U.S. had grown to enormous levels whilst the U.S. gold reserves which backed these balances had fallen so that the convertibility of the dollar became suspect. During 1971, sales of dollar balances for gold were so great that the U.S. had to suspend convertibility to preserve its reserves.
2. The dollar had become central to the world monetary system so that the U.S. dollar could not unilaterally devalue or revalue its currency. Under the Bretton Woods system a country suffering from a balance of payments deficit could devalue its currency but because of the importance of the dollar this option was not open to the U.S. Had the U.S. tried to remove the deficit through deflation this would have resulted in an unacceptably high level of unemployment.

After the dollar was made inconvertible there was a period during which major currencies were floated and most currencies appreciated vis-a-vis the dollar. However, in December 1971 at a meeting of the Group of Ten countries in Washington, it was agreed to implement a new exchange rate system. The Group of Ten comprise the United States, United Kingdom, West Germany, France, Italy, Japan, Netherlands, Canada, Belgium and Sweden. The agreement, more commonly known as the Smithsonian Agreement, allowed currencies to move within a band of $2^1/_4$% on either side of their agreed par value rather than 1% either side under the Bretton Woods system.

However, this system lasted approximately one year because of successive speculative crises during early 1973 which led to a further devaluation of the dollar and a general floating among the major currencies of the world. The great increase in the price of oil about the same time precluded any return to fixed exchange rates.

The dollar continued to weaken in the latter half of the 1970s. Continuing U.S. balance of payments deficits resulted in a depreciation of the dollar on the world's foreign exchange markets. In late 1979, the dollar weakened still further as a result of the Iranian crisis which led to the U.S. freezing Iranian dollar balances lodged with U.S. banks both at home and abroad. The result of the continued weakening of the dollar in the latter half of the 1970s has been the movement towards a multiple currency reserve system. For example, in 1979, it was estimated that holdings of Deutsche marks in the currency reserves of the world's central banks amounted to about D.M.50 billion of which D.M.20 billion was deposited in West Germany and D.M.30 billion in foreign banking centres. The increase in the Deutsche mark's reserve role during the latter half of the 1970s was partly due to the lessened reserve role of sterling whose share of world wide currency reserves had fallen to about 2% at the end of 1978, from over 10% in 1970. The principal non-dollar currencies held in official reserves are the Deutsche mark, the Swiss franc, the Japanese yen, the Pound sterling, the French franc and the Netherlands guilder.

During March 1980, the U.S. Government unveiled an anti-inflation package and this resulted in an immediate strengthening of the dollar against other major currencies including the Deutsche mark, Japanese yen and Swiss franc. In consequence these countries raised their interest rates, removed barriers to capital inflows and sold dollars to support their own currencies. Their policies were in fact a complete reversal of those adopted during the late 1970s when their currencies were rapidly appreciating vis-a-vis the dollar.

From 1980 onwards, the US dollar strengthened significantly, having appreciated by some 30% during the period 1980-82. The US dollar continued to appreciate during the period 1982-85. The continued appreciation of the dollar resulted from an increase in demand from investors for dollar-denominated assets. This demand resulted from relatively high returns on investments in the United States and the uncertainties in the international financial system. However, recent problems for the US include the large federal budget deficit and the deterioration of the balance of payments on current account. Since 1980 the movement towards multiple currency reserves has been reversed and the US dollar still retains its dominant position in international liquidity. Many commodities which are traded continue to be priced in dollars and transactions are settled by the payment of dollars.

In September 1985 the first step towards managed floating of exchange rates was taken by the major countries at a meeting (in the Plaza Hotel) and the agreement is referred to as the *Plaza agreement*. At the meeting it was felt that the gyrations in exchange rates were damaging and that the U.S. dollar was far too high. Thus, it was considered to be the right time for the authorities of major countries to give a clear lead to the markets. This agreement was instrumental in securing a fall in the U.S. dollar during the period up to 1987.

In 1987, a further step forward was taken in securing managed floating, the so-called *Louvre agreement*. The aim of this agreement was to promote a period of stability so as to give time for the major economies to adjust to the changes in exchange rates which had occurred.

These tentative movements towards managed floating have been aided by low world inflation and a consensus among major countries for the need for firm monetary and fiscal policies in pursuance of sound economic policies.

9.2.3 Sterling Balances

After the Second World War, sterling's share of world currency reserves amounted to over 50% but during the period 1960-80 disposals of sterling by overseas holders during balance of payments crises, combined with the very large increase in world dollar reserves resulted in the share falling to about 2%. Table 9.4 shows the exchange reserves in sterling over recent years.

The exchange reserves in sterling held by central monetary institutions includes government and government- guaranteed stocks, Treasury bills and other banking and money-market assets held by central banks and international organisations such as the IMF. These investments are held because they are readily marketable. The other banking and money-market assets include deposits (including sterling certificates of deposit) by non-residents with U.K. banks together with local authority bills and temporary loans to local authorities. However, the table does not cover all overseas holdings of sterling which may be regarded by countries as part of their reserves, for example, overseas holdings of equities are not included.

Table 9.4 Exchange Reserves (£m)

	Exchange Reserves in Sterling held by Central Monetary Institutions				Banking & Market liabilities to other holders
	Total	Govt stocks	Banking and Money-Market liabilities	Non-interest - bearing notes	
1981	4,755	2,555	1,527	673	13,461
1982	5,561	2,922	1,930	709	17,629
1983	6,628	3,169	2,762	697	21,408
1984	7,755	3,207	3,872	676	26,825
1985	9,327	4,690	3,933	704	31,236
1986	9,585	5,199	3,930	456	37,160
1987	13,951	6,569	6,653	729	44,301

(Source: Central Statistical Office)

The banking and money-market liabilities to other holders includes private balances held by individual non-residents and multinational companies.

Because these funds flow into the U.K. through the foreign exchange market, any liquidation of these balances will lead to a reduction in the exchange rate for sterling and/or a reduction in the official reserves. The exchange rate for sterling would fall because sterling is traded for other currencies. However, if the authorities intervene in the market and use the Exchange Equalization Account to buy up the pounds on offer then the exchange rate will be supported. However, it is important to note that the extent to which the exchange rate can be supported will be determined by the size of the official reserves. These balances can, therefore, be a problem because of their size and also because they are short-term in nature. The volatility of sterling balances can cause large and undesirable changes in the exchange value of sterling.

The sterling balances became an important problem for the U.K. during the mid-1960s when the balance of payments position had deteriorated to such an extent that holders of sterling balances became worried that they would suffer capital losses if sterling was devalued. This led to a flight from sterling into other currencies which served to worsen the U.K. balance of payments position and put tremendous pressure on the exchange rate for sterling. The result was that sterling was devalued in 1967. Because of the undesirable impact that the sterling balances could have on the U.K's balance of payments and exchange rate various measures were introduced to try to deal with this problem.

In 1966 currency 'swap' arrangements were organised whereby the Bank for International Settlements and a group of central banks agreed to provide swap facilities (i.e. sterling would be exchanged for foreign currencies) to the U.K. whenever a reduction in sterling balances threatened to reduce the U.K. official reserves. A further measure was introduced in 1968 to deal specifically with the problem arising from the movement out of sterling by countries in the overseas sterling area (these were countries that pegged their exchange rates to the pound sterling and maintained their reserves in sterling). This measure, known as the Basle facility, was organised through the Bank for International Settlements and provided for credit facilities of $2 billion. In addition, the U.K. obtained agreement from sterling area countries to maintain their sterling reserves at a certain level and in return, the U.K. agreed to a dollar guarantee to compensate them in the event of a loss resulting from a fall in the sterling exchange rate. However, because confidence in sterling increased during the following few years, the guarantee arrangements were little used and were terminated in 1974.

In the early 1970s, sterling balances increased largely as a result of a movement into sterling by OPEC countries. However, by 1973 sterling balances had once again become a problem as a result of the U.K. balance of payments deficits which resulted from higher oil prices. This led to a movement out of sterling and a consequent fall in the sterling exchange rate. U.K. official reserves fell as the authorities tried to support the exchange rate. In the following years there were a series of sterling crises which resulted, in 1976, in an agreement between the Bank of England and foreign monetary institutions that official sterling reserves would be held down to the level of working balances sufficient to cover day-to-day transactions. At the end of 1976 these balances amounted to approximately £2.6 billion compared with approximately £5 billion in 1981 and almost £14 billion in 1987. Since 1976, private sterling balances have increased rapidly from approximately £3.5 billion to approximately £12.5 billion in 1981 and £44 billion in 1987.

9.2.4 Borrowing Facilities at the IMF

Members' borrowing rights are governed by the size of their quotas. Members borrow in tranches of 25% of their respective quota up to 125% of their quota. The Fund's attitude to the first tranche (known as the 'reserve tranche') is very liberal. However, conditions on further borrowing become progressively stricter as each tranche is taken up, and any borrower will have to undertake to take steps to improve its balance of payments position - perhaps through the imposition of an incomes policy or control of its money supply. The term 'borrowing' in this connection is a misnomer because a member buys currencies which it needs and pays for them by putting an equivalent amount of its own currency into the 'pool'. Thus, the more a country borrows, the greater will its currency feature in the 'pool'. At the end of April 1985, outstanding purchases in respect of regular facilities totalled SDR 5.5 billion.

Other IMF supplements to international liquidity include the following.

1. Stand-by arrangements

This facility has been available to members since 1952 and it takes the form of an assurance from the IMF that certain quantities of credit would be made immediately available to them for a particular period without further negotiation. Such arrangements are useful in curbing speculation in a currency because of the knowledge that IMF assistance will be available if the need arises. A member requesting stand-by arrangements will normally give the IMF its assurance that it will take steps to tackle its economic problems.

2. The General Agreement to Borrow (GAB)

This agreement was made in 1961 between the ten major member nations of the IMF - the Group of Ten. They agreed to lend stated amounts of their currencies to the Fund. These could be drawn by other members of the Fund but only when the IMF needed supplementary resources to smooth over an international monetary problem. This agreement was implemented in the late 1960s when Britain's heavy borrowing requirements from the IMF made certain currencies in the 'pool' scarce. The GAB was used to replenish the Fund's holdings of those currencies. At the present time, the total amount available to the Fund is equivalent to some SDR 18.5 billion.

3. Compensatory Financing Scheme

This scheme was introduced in 1963 and from August 1979, members have been allowed to borrow up to 100% of their quota to meet delays in receiving export receipts arising from international factors beyond the member's control. The strings attached to this facility are not as strict as for upper tranches of normal borrowing. There has been an increase in the use of this facility since the liberalisation of the scheme in 1979. At the end of April 1985 outstanding purchases under this scheme amounted to approximately SDR 7.5 billion which represents about $^1/_3$ of total purchases from the Fund.

4. Buffer Stock Facility

This facility was introduced in 1969 and allows members to draw 50% of their quota to cover their subscriptions to approved international buffer stock schemes. This facility has been used in respect of only two commodity agreements - the Fourth International Tin Agreement and the 1977 International Sugar Agreement (although the Fund has authorised its use in connection with cocoa buffer stock agreements). The strings attached to this facility are similar in their strictness to the Compensatory Financing Scheme. In 1985 outstanding purchases amounted to approximately SDR 0.2 billion.

5. Extended Facility

This facility was introduced in 1974 to provide extra borrowing of up to 65% of members' quotas. The repayment period is between four and eight years. This facility is intended for countries with critical balance of payments problems which will take many years to correct. The strings attached to this facility are very strict. The amount outstanding on April 30, 1985 was approximately SDR 6.5 billion.

6. Supplementary Financing Facility

This scheme was introduced in 1979 as a supplement to higher tranche borrowing and is available under stand-by arrangements or extended arrangements. This scheme is designed to provide supplementary financing to members with serious balance of payments problems which are large relative to the size of their economy and IMF quotas. The facility is agreed subject to the applicant complying with policies stipulated by the Fund. Resources are provided by fourteen lenders including the Saudi Arabian Monetary Agency, the United States and the Deutsche Bundesbank and the total amount available under this facility is SDR 7.8 billion. The amount of outstanding borrowings under this facility on April 30, 1985 was SDR 6.3 billion. This facility ensures that the Fund has adequate resources and this has been an important consideration since the ending of the oil facility. The oil facility was used in 1974 and 1975 by the Fund as a means of supplementing its resources. It entailed the borrowing of funds from those countries with a balance of payments surplus to aid those countries needing assistance because of the large oil-price rises in 1973.

7. Enlarged Access

This allows for enlarged access to the Fund's resources. Although it was introduced as a temporary measure, the Interim Committee decided to continue it in 1985. On April 30, 1985 the amount outstanding under this facility was SDR 8.9 billion.

8. Special Drawing Rights

These are considered fully in the next section.

9.2.5 Special Drawing Rights

Special Drawing Rights were introduced by the IMF in January 1970, as a means of supplementing international liquidity. They do not exist in note form but are created through book-keeping entries. Thus, member nation's special drawings accounts are credited. New allocations of SDRs were to be made annually but they were suspended after the 1972 issue and were only resumed in 1978. The allocations of SDRs are based on members' quotas. All members participate in the scheme.

At the end of 1978, there were 9,315 million SDRs in existence. A further 4,033 million were created in January 1979, 4,033 million in January 1980 and a further issue of 4,053 million was made on 1st January 1981 which brought the total of SDRs to SDR 21,434 million. There have been no further issues of SDRs since 1981. Until 1974, their value was linked to the dollar and thus to gold and so they were often referred to as 'paper gold'. In 1974 it was decided to value SDRs according to the value of a weighted basket of 16 currencies. Currencies were weighted according to their prominence in international trade and the weights in the basket were to be amended every five years to take into account changes in the importance of the different currencies (see Table 9.5).

Table 9.5 Percentage Weight of Each Currency in the 'Basket'

Currency	*Valuation basket 31.12.80* %	*Interest basket* %	*Valuation basket as from 1.1.81*
U.S. dollar	33	49	42
Deutsche mark	12.5	18	19
Japanese yen	7.5	11	13
French franc	7.5	11	13
Pound sterling	7.5	11	13
Italian lira	5		
Netherlands guilder	5		
Canadian dollar	5		
Belgian franc	4		
Saudi Arabian rial	3		
Swedish krona	2		
Iranian rial	2		
Australian dollar	1.5		
Spanish peseta	1.5		
Norwegian krona	1.5		
Austrian schilling	1.5		
	100.0	100.0	100.0

However, in 1980, the IMF decided to simplify the SDR calculation by reducing the weighted basket to five currencies. This change took effect from 1st January 1981 and was made to enhance the attractiveness and marketability of the SDR and SDR-denominated assets. For example, banks taking SDR-denominated deposits will be able to match their currency liabilities more easily because of the well-developed foreign exchange and money markets in the five currencies. The currencies of the five member countries were chosen on the basis that they accounted for the largest exports of goods and services during the period 1975-9 (see Table 9.5).

The weighting of the currencies reflects their prominence in both international trade and official reserves. The IMF intends to review both the currency composition of the basket and also the weighting attached to each currency after a period of five years.

Any country using SDRs must pay interest which is paid over to those countries holding more than their allocation. Initially, the interest rate was set at 1.5% but in 1974 it was decided to link the rate to short-term rates in five major financial centres by the use of a weighted currency basket (see Table 9.5). The rate of interest was set at 80% of the combined interest rate of the basket. However, with effect from May 1st 1981, the IMF adjusted the SDR interest to the full market rate. Because these changes have made the SDR more attractive, the IMF removed the reconstitution requirement with effect from April 30, 1981. Until this change the use of SDRs was limited in that a member's holdings were not allowed to fall below a five yearly average of 15% of its allocation. Thus, 85% of a member's allocation represented unconditional liquidity and the remaining 15% represented a short-term borrowing facility. However, the IMF removed this limitation because it no longer considered it necessary to have a compulsory holding.

The IMF expects SDRs to be used when a member nation runs into balance of payments problems or it is losing a substantial part of its reserves. If a member wishes to use its allocation of SDRs, it may do so in one of two ways. It may use the indirect method under which the member (applicant) notifies the IMF of its intention to use its SDRs and the Fund will nominate a country with a substantial balance of payments surplus to provide the applicant with foreign exchange or gold in exchange for the applicant's SDRs. The SDRs would be added to the donor's reserves so maintaining their original level but with a different composition. At some later date, the applicant must repay the foreign currencies or gold to the donor country. Alternatively, the direct method may be used.Since SDRs have become more acceptable, many nations are willing to accept them directly in settlement of debt.

The Fund permits additional uses of SDRs such as buying and selling forward, borrowing, lending, pledging and the use of SDRs in swaps or the making of donations. These additional uses are reviewed annually by the Fund.

The role of SDRs can be assessed in the light of their functions:

1. As a Unit of Account

The IMF expresses its statistics of international liquidity - gold, foreign exchange, reserves - in terms of SDRs. A number of other international and regional organisations use the SDR as a unit of account e.g., the Arab Monetary Fund, the Asian Clearing Union, the Economic Community of West Africa, the Islamic Development Bank and the Nordic Investment Bank. The SDR has been used for many years in the calculation of Suez Canal toll charges. However, in recent years the SDR has increased its commercial role. Examples include the taking of SDR-denominated deposits by banks, SDR-denominated issues in the eurobond and syndicated credit markets and issues of SDR-denominated certificates of deposit. The commercial application of SDRs has been boosted by the introduction of the simplified SDR calculation on 1st January 1981.

2. As a Means of Exchange

Apart from member countries, the Fund has the authority to permit the holding of SDRs by a range of official holders. In 1981 there were ten 'other holders' which included central banks, the Bank for International Settlements and international development institutions such as the World Bank and its affiliate, the International Development Association. The number of official holders rose to fourteen by 1985. Their use as a means of payment is limited because there are only a few 'other holders' and because they cannot be used by commercial firms.

3. As a Store of Value

At the Jamaica Interim Committee meeting in 1976 it was decided to make the SDR the principal reserve asset in the international monetary system and to reduce the role of gold. This change and other changes to the IMF's articles have come into effect and are known as the Second Amendment. Although the store of value function of the SDR has been enhanced in recent years, it still remains limited.

Because of the SDR's limited role, as a means of exchange and a store of value, its role as an international reserve asset must necessarily be limited and it is likely that its progress in this direction will be slow. Since the Second Amendment, the IMF's policy regarding gold has been to phase it out as an international monetary asset. Indeed, the IMF has conducted gold sales and any profit accruing on the transactions was placed in the IMF Trust Fund and distributed to the poorest members. The Trust Fund was established in 1976 with the aim of providing additional balance of payments assistance, on cheaper terms, to developing country members. The Trust Fund's resources came from the profits resulting from the sale of the the IMF's gold. The sale of 25 million ounces of gold took four years and was completed in May 1980. The sales realised profits of U.S. $4.6 billion and 104 less developed countries received U.S. $1.3 billion. The remainder was made available for loans. These funds were lent out over four years so that by 1981 the objectives of the Trust Fund were fulfilled and the IMF took steps to terminate it. The terms of the loans are between six and ten years.

Their role as a reserve asset is also limited because there are not many in existence. However, recent issues have certainly helped in this respect. Its role may, however, be widened with the implementation of a substitution account in the future.

The merits of SDRs are as follows:

1. They increase world liquidity.
2. They reduce the need for any single country, like the U.S.A., to run a balance of payments deficit to increase world liquidity.

The success of SDRs depends on their acceptability. Many developed nations feel that excessive issues of SDRs may fuel inflation so that new issues should be strictly controlled. Indeed, they are able to do this because they control the voting in the Fund (whether any new issues should be made is decided by a weighted 85% majority of members). However, less developed countries feel that existing world liquidity is distributed towards developed nations and they feel that the increased use of SDRs could redress the imbalance. Less developed countries must therefore allay the fears which the developed countries have regarding SDRs.

The SDR is also used as a currency peg. In 1985 there were twelve countries pegging their currencies to the SDR so that the value of their currencies was fixed in terms of the SDR.

9.3 The Role of the International Banking System in the Financing of World Current Account Deficits

During the period 1979-80, there were large swings in the current account balances of major groups of countries. During the period 1978-80 oil exporting countries enjoyed an increase in their current account surplus of almost $110 billions. On the other hand, the industrial countries' current account balance shifted detrimentally from a surplus of $31 billions in 1978 to a $44 billions deficit in 1980. The non-oil developing countries' current account deficit increased from $37.5 billions in 1978 to $82.1 billions in 1980.

These swings in current account balances have been due in the main to changes in terms of trade and to a lesser extent to the recession in industrial countries which led to a fall in the growth in world trade. The terms of trade of the oil exporting countries increased by 28% and 42% in 1979 and 1980 respectively, whereas over the two years, the terms of trade of the industrial countries fell by 9.5% and those of the oil importing less developed countries fell by some 8.5%.

These substantial movements in current account balances have had a great impact on the flows of capital and reserves. The rise in oil prices and the subsequent rise in the national savings of oil exporting countries resulted in an increase in external investment by these countries. These investments were channelled by banks to borrowers in industrial countries and non-oil developing countries. The non-oil developing countries substantially increased their borrowing from the international banking system (particularly through the syndicated loans market) even though interest rates were high.

In 1978 the banks reporting to the Bank for International Settlements borrowed $58 billions from industrial countries, $7 billions from oil-exporting countries and $17 billions from non-oil developing countries. In 1980 borrowed funds from industrial countries and oil exporting countries had risen to $98 billions and $38 billions respectively, whilst borrowing from non-oil developing countries had fallen to $6 billions. We have already noted that these funds were used by the banks to lend to industrial and non-oil developing countries. Thus, the banks lent $46 billions to industrial countries in 1978 and this rose to $87 billions in 1980. Lending to non-oil developing countries was $31 billions in 1978 and this rose to $47 billions in 1980.

The recycling of international liquidity in 1979 and 1980 occurred at the same time that the major industrial countries placed greater emphasis on reducing inflation. These countries adopted a policy of reducing monetary growth which led to higher interest rates and this had the effect of increasing the cost of borrowing.

The early 1980s saw the beginning of the international debt problems of developing countries. Between 1981 and 1984, the developing countries experienced a dramatic fall in their net borrowing from the international financial markets. This was because creditors believed that borrowing countries would find it difficult to service their debt obligations. This led to a drying up of sources of market finance for the developing countries. For example, market borrowing of these countries was $125 billion from banks and other private creditors in 1981-82 and this fell to $20 billion in 1983-84. The situation was even tighter than these figures suggest because much of this borrowing relied on agreement to debt rescheduling.

The reduction in new lending, together with the flight of capital from these countries led to arrears, debt rescheduling, the increased use of IMF credit and a rundown of reserves. However, by 1984 their current accounts improved and these countries resorted less to IMF credit, although rescheduling continued.

Thus, since the early 1980s, the flow of funds through the international financial markets has been influenced by the international debt repayment problems of some developing countries. However, the flow of funds was aided by international cooperation between the IMF, international banks, the debtor countries and other international agencies. This cooperation involved rescheduling of debts, IMF standby or extended arrangements and new credits from international banks.

From 1982, banks lending to problem debtor countries have been strengthening their balance sheets by increasing their capital relative to their exposure to these countries' debts. During the period 1982-86, banks have reduced their loans to problem countries as a percentage of their total assets. Banks have also increased their bad debt provisions in respect of these loans. For example, in 1986 National Westminster Bank increased its provisions by approximately £0.5 billion and Midland Bank by almost £1 billion. In 1987, Lloyds bank made provisions of £1,066 million against doubtful Third World loans.

9.4.1 The International Monetary Fund

The International Monetary Fund (IMF) was set up at a conference at Bretton Woods, U.S.A., in 1944. The conference was organised by the United Nations in an attempt to bring some order into international trade and payments after the chaos that had developed after the abandonment of the gold standard in the 1930s. During the 1930s, the nations of the world experienced problems of depression and unemployment which were so great that they resorted to protectionism through the erection of tariff barriers.

The IMF comes under the aegis of the United Nations, although in practice its operations are virtually free from interference. Ultimate responsibility for the management of the Fund rests with a Board of Governors whose membership includes members' finance ministers or central bank governors. Because of the size of the Board and the fact that it meets annually, the day-to-day management is delegated down to an Executive Board. The twenty two executive directors on the Executive Board represent either one of the five large member countries or a group of smaller countries.

The structure of the IMF is completed by the Interim Committee which was set up in 1972 (and was originally known as the Committee of Twenty) to supervise the international monetary system. This committee meets approximately two times a year and membership is on the same basis as for the Executive Board.

Membership of the Fund includes virtually all countries of the world except Switzerland and the Comecon countries (except Romania). In 1985 there were 148 members.

The functions of the IMF are as follows:

1. to engender international monetary co-operation;
2. to provide a 'pool' of international liquidity which can be used by members experiencing balance of payments problems or when their currencies need support;
3. to supplement international liquidity through issues of Special Drawing Rights (SDRs).

When the Fund was set up, members agreed to maintain their exchange rates within 1% on either side of their adopted par value against the U.S. dollar. Countries were allowed to change their par values by devaluation or revaluation but only if there was a fundamental disequilibrium in their balance of payments. By 1971, it was decided that the 1% stipulation was too restrictive and so it was increased to 2¼% under the Smithsonian Agreement in that year.

During the 1970s the par value system broke down so members are now free to peg their exchange rate at a certain level or allow them to float. However, the IMF still carries out its obligation to monitor members' domestic policies to ensure that they do not conflict with the Fund's objective of maintaining order in international trade and payments.

We can now go on to consider the operation of the Fund. Each member agrees a quota with the Fund. This is a unit which determines members' borrowing rights, voting powers and contributions to the

Fund. The size of a members's quota is calculated through complicated formulae which take into account:

1. the size of the member's national income;
2. the degree of its involvement in international trade;
3. the size of its gold and foreign currency reserves.

When the Fund was set up, each country agreed to contribute to a 'pool' of currencies from which members could make drawings. Contributions (subscriptions) are made in accordance with the size of members' quotas. Originally, the subscription was split - 25% gold and 75% national currency, but the gold requirement has now been dropped so that the 25% is now paid in reserve assets. When a member country runs into balance of payments difficulties and finds its reserves inadequate it can borrow from the 'pool' of currencies.

The IMF provides for a regular review of the adequacy of quotas. They were increased in 1959 by 50%, in 1965 by 25%, in 1970 by 35% and in 1976/7 by 32.5%. However, not all members' quotas increased by these amounts. For example, the U.K.'s quota rose by 125 million SDRs in 1976/7 but this represented a fall from 9.6% to 7.5% of the total.Quotas were again increased in 1978 raising total quotas to almost SDR 40 billion. The Seventh General Review of Quotas became effective in 1980 and it provided for an increase of 50% in general quotas. There were a number of selective quota increases e.g., Saudia Arabia's quota was more than doubled which raised its quota from 1.74%of total quotas to about 3.5%. The Seventh General Review of Quotas raised total quotas from SDR 39,766.5 million to SDR 60,025.6 million. The Eighth Quota Review in 1983 increased quotas by just under 50%. Table 9.6 shows IMF quotas on April 30, 1985.

Table 9.6 IMF Quotas (April 30, 1985)

Country	*Amount (SDR million)*	*%*
United States	17,918.3	20.1
United Kingdom	6,194.0	6.9
West Germany	5,403.7	6.1
France	4,482.8	5.0
Japan	4,223.3	4.7
Canada	2,941.0	3.3
Italy	2,909.1	3.3
India	2,207.7	2.5
Netherlands	2,264.8	2.5
Belgium	2,080.4	2.2
Australia	1,619.2	1.8
Other countries	-	41.6
Total	89,301.8	100.0

We can next consider the voting rights of members. Each member is allocated 250 votes plus one vote for each 100,000 SDRs of its quota. Operational decisions are passed by a simple majority of votes but important issues may require a 70% or 85% majority depending on the importance of the issue. However, voting provisions are rarely used in practice, most decisions being made by consensus.

9.4.2 Repayments to the IMF

The repayment of loans to the IMF includes an interest and service charge. The IMF will normally stipulate the currency or currencies in which the repayment (re-purchase) can be made. The currency or currencies chosen will be the one(s) in great demand by other members and in which the Fund's holdings are low. Loans are normally repaid over a period of three to five years and a repayment schedule is agreed between the borrower and the Fund.

9.4.3 The Role of the IMF

By the end of the 1970s, the IMF no longer enjoyed a dominant position in the management of the world's economic and monetary affairs. Arrangements like the European Monetary System, which could ultimately lead to a European Monetary Fund, reduced the role of the Fund. In addition, support for the U.S. dollar was organised through agreements between central bankers.

Thus, it was the developing countries who became the Fund's main customers in the 1970s, particularly because of the debt problems resulting from the oil price rises of the early and late 1970s. But even these countries looked for alternative sources of finance because of the tough strings attached to IMF support. In this connection we have seen previously the important part played by the syndicated loans market in recycling funds to the developing countries.

The go ahead for the development of the substitution account was given at the annual meeting of the Fund during 1979. It was hoped that the scheme could be implemented in the early 1980s. However, at a meeting of the Fund's Interim Committee in early 1980 it was decided to defer the introduction of this scheme for the time being. Under the scheme, countries wishing to diversify their reserve holdings would be able to deposit their unwanted currencies and receive in return an interest-bearing claim on the IMF denominated in SDRs. The IMF would invest all deposits in U.S. Treasury bills. This scheme would give greater security to those countries with large reserve dollar holdings at a time of monetary uncertainty.

The oil price rises of the late 1970s meant that the IMF had to increase its resources in order to meet its members' financing requirements. The IMF was helped by an increase of 50% in quotas in 1980 which resulted from the Seventh Quota Review. However, despite this increase, the continuing demands upon the IMF from members meant that the Fund had to search for new sources of borrowing. In 1981, the IMF arranged to borrow a further 8 billion SDRs from Saudi Arabia and 1.3 billion SDRs from the central banks and official agencies of 16 countries including the Bank of England, either directly or through the intermediation of the Bank for International Settlements. In 1983, the Eighth Quota Review increased quotas by almost 50%.

More recently, the international debt repayment problems of some developing countries has resulted in these countries having to resort to IMF assistance as market sources of borrowing dried up.

9.5 Summary

1. International liquidity consists of those assets which are accepted internationally to settle debts between nations which arise from international trade and capital movements.
2. The IMF's policy with regard to gold has been to try to phase it out as an international monetary asset. However, gold still accounts for about 70% of central banks' total monetary reserves.
3. The U.S. dollar accounts for about 70% of world currency reserves. Other currencies held in official reserves include the Deutsche mark, the Swiss franc, the Japanese yen, the Pound sterling, the French franc and the Netherlands guilder.
4. The Plaza and Louvre agreements represented moves towards managed floating of exchange rates.
5. Sterling balances have grown rapidly in the 1980s.
6. Borrowing facilities at the IMF include:
   (a) Stand-by arrangements.
   (b) The General Agreement to Borrow.
   (c) Compensatory Financing Scheme.
   (d) Buffer Stock Facility.
   (e) Extended Facility.
   (f) Supplementary Financing Facility.
   (g) Enlarged Access.
   (h) Special Drawing Rights.
7. The international banking system was important in the recycling of surpluses to the non-oil developing countries. However, the

resulting international debt problems led to rescheduling of debts and banks have made large bad debt provisions in respect of Third World loans.

8. The functions of the IMF are as follows:
   (a) to engender international monetary co-operation;
   (b) to provide a 'pool' of international liquidity which can be used by members experiencing balance of payments problems or when their currencies need support;
   (c) to supplement international liquidity through issues of Special Drawing Rights (SDRs).
9. By the end of the 1970s, the IMF no longer enjoyed a dominant position in the management of the world's economic and monetary affairs.
10. More recently, the international debt repayment problems of some developing countries has resulted in these countries having to resort to IMF assistance as market sources of borrowing dried up.

Questions

1.* Appraise the differing roles now played in the international monetary system by gold and by Special Drawing Rights (SDRs).

2. Assess the role played by Special Drawing Rights (SDRs) in the contemporary international financial system. Do you agree that they will eventually become the principal international reserve asset? Give reasons for your answer.

3. What changes has the International Monetary Fund undergone in the 1970s?

4. (a) Define sterling balances.
   (b) What problems have arisen from the growth of sterling balances.

5.* What problems have been posed for international liquidity requirements by the large balance of payments surpluses accruing to oil producing countries in recent years? To what extent have the Eurocurrency markets helped in overcoming these problems?

6.* Outline the role of gold in the world monetary system today.

7. Comment of the significance of gold as a monetary asset.

8. Assess the present role in the international monetary system of:
   (a) gold;
   (b) special drawing rights (SDRs);
   (c) the U.S. dollar.

9.* (a) Outline the main changes that have occurred in the composition of international liquidity since 1971.

    (b) To what extent has the existence of floating exchange rates reduced the need for international liquidity?

10. What do you understand by the concept of international liquidity? Assess the importance of the International Monetary Fund (IMF) in ensuring an adequate supply of international liquidity in recent years.

11. Outline the ways in which the International Monetary Fund (IMF) has assisted countries experiencing balance of payments difficulties in recent years. How effectively has IMF support served the needs of such countries?

12. Identify the components of international liquidity and discuss the advantages and disadvantages of each of them in its role as a component.

13. Discuss the contribution to international liquidity made over the past ten years by the following:
    (a) the International Monetary Fund;
    (b) commercial banks.

14. (a) For what reasons, and in what form, do governments hold international reserves? (11)
    (b) What options are open to a country whose international reserves are inadequate for its financing needs? (14)

15. (a) What is meant by measuring changes in a country's exchange rate on a 'trade-weighted' basis? (6)
    (b) What are the fundamental factors underlying currency performance? (6)
    (c) Between late 1980 and early 1985, the index of the US dollar's trade-weighted exchange rate rose by almost 70%. To what extent did this appreciation, and subsequent developments, reflect the

fundamental factors underlying currency performance? (13)

16. (a) What do you understand by the concept of international liquidity? (8)
(b) Examine the contribution of the following to international liquidity, indicating any major changes which have occurred in the past decade:
(i) gold;
(ii) foreign exchange holdings;
(iii) syndicated bank lending. (17)

17. (a) International liquidity can be defined in both a narrow and a broad sense. Identify the components of each of these definitions.(10)
(b) Select any three of the components of international liquidity, and discuss their advantages and disadvantages in performing that role. (15)

CHAPTER 10

Eurocurrency Markets

10.1 Eurocurrencies

The eurocurrency market is an international money market. Eurocurrency deposits are deposits held by banks in one country in the currency of another. Thus, eurodollar deposits are dollar deposits held by banks outside the U.S. The first and most important of the eurocurrency markets was the eurodollar market which originated in the early 1950s.

10.2 The Role of the Eurocurrency Markets

At this stage we can examine the way in which a eurocurrency deposit originates. Suppose a French company has a $1 million demand deposit with a New York bank (perhaps acquired through trading with the U.S.). The French company may decide to convert its demand deposit into a fixed term deposit with a London bank. The transaction is completed when the demand deposit is transferred to the London bank's correspondent bank in New York. It is now a eurodollar deposit. If the London bank cannot immediately employ the deposit by lending it to one of its customers, it could deposit it with another bank in the inter-bank market. So far, two eurodollar deposits of $1 million each have been created. Thus, eurodollars have been created in excess of the deposit held in New York.

The development of the eurocurrency market can be traced back to the early 1950s when the U.S.S.R. and other East European countries switched their dollar deposits from U.S. banks to Western European banks because they feared that their deposits may be blocked by the U.S. Government. The development of the market was given impetus by the happening of three events; in 1957 the use of sterling acceptance credits for trade in which no U.K. resident was a party, was prohibited by the British authorities; in 1958 many countries made their currencies convertible into U.S. dollars; and in 1959 the U.S. authorities implemented tight credit controls which resulted in many U.S. companies seeking dollar finance outside the U.S.

The market continued to grow in the 1960s especially in eurodollars because successive U.S. balance of payments deficits fed dollars into the world economy. Also Regulation Q of the U.S. Federal Reserve Board placed restrictions on the rates of interest which U.S. banks could pay for deposits. Because short-term interest rates were generally lower in the U.S. than elsewhere, branches of U.S. banks in London offered higher rates (where Regulation Q did not apply) and lent these deposits back to their head offices in the U.S.

Transactions in the eurocurrency market are invariably for large amounts and maturities range from overnight up to five years, although most deals are arranged for periods of two days to three months. The market is highly competitive and it is not subject to any controls from monetary authorities.

The eurosterling market is a small market (less than 2% of the eurocurrency market). The main centres of the eurosterling market are Paris, Brussels and Amsterdam. Until October 1979, U.K. exchange control measures greatly influenced the market so that during the period when exchange control measures were in force, eurosterling interest rates were generally higher than domestic interest rates. This differential in rates existed because exchange control stopped the flow of sterling from the U.K. to the eurosterling market. Following the abolition of exchange controls the market grew fairly rapidly although more recently the growth of the market has slowed down. Since the abolition of the Bank of England's supplementary special deposits scheme in June 1980, the domestic and eurosterling markets have been brought more closely together so that the interest rate differential is virtually non-existent. Thus, the eurosterling market can be viewed merely as an extension to the domestic market.

The characteristics of the eurocurrency markets can be summarised as follows:

1. The markets are unregulated. The lack of official regulation from monetary authorities has resulted in tremendous growth since its origins in the 1950s for the following reasons. As we noted earlier, banks can use the eurocurrency markets to side-step restrictions placed on their domestic business. Governments have increasingly used the eurocurrency markets to finance current account imbalances (see Chapter 9). Finally, multinational companies are able to borrow from the eurocurrency markets when borrowing from the domestic market has been restricted.
2. The markets aid bank balance sheet management in two ways. Firstly, they provide liquidity and secondly, they enable banks to match their assets and liabilities according to maturity and currency.
3. The markets allow for the short term investment of surplus foreign currency funds. They can be invested until required without the need for conversion into domestic currency and without carrying an exchange rate risk. Bank commission is saved by not converting into

domestic currency.

4. The competitiveness of interest rates (see section 10.4).

10.3.1 The Sources and Uses of Eurocurrency Funds

The following are both suppliers and users of eurocurrency funds; governments, central banks, international organisations, commercial banks and multinational companies. The eurocurrency market consists of a number of markets such as the inter-bank eurocurrency market, dollar CDs and eurodollar commercial paper. Inter-bank transactions account for a large proportion of the total transactions in the market. Lending is normally unsecured with lenders reducing their risk of loss by placing a limit on the amount that they are willing to lend to each borrower.

10.3.2 The International Capital Market

Until the 1960s, it was customary for those seeking longer-term finance to raise funds on the capital markets of London, the U.S. and other countries. However, in the early 1960s there developed a new capital market which is essentially a long-term extension of the short-term eurocurrency market and today it consists of two parts - the eurobond market and the syndicated loans market.

1. Eurobond Market

The first eurobond issue was a dollar fixed rate bond raised in Europe as a result of steps which the U.S. authorities had taken to curb the raising of capital in New York by non-residents of the U.S. Bonds can be denominated in a variety of currencies but the bulk of issues have been made in U.S. dollars although other currency issues have been important when the dollar has weakened. Eurobond issues are syndicated which means that they are underwritten by a number of banks. Each issue has a bank acting as a lead manager (or there may be a small number of co-managers) which is responsible for advising the borrower on the terms of the proposed issue and for completing the various formalities involved in the issue. For this service, the manager charges a commission which is calculated as a percentage of the face value of the issue. On completion, the issue is advertised in various newspapers.

The main types of bond which are issued include fixed rate bonds, floating rate notes and drop-lock bonds. Fixed rate bonds are repaid in full at maturity and provide for fixed annual interest payments. Floating rate notes are similar to fixed rate bonds except that the rate of interest floats at a predetermined margin over a reference rate (usually LIBOR). Finally, drop-lock bonds are floating rate notes which automatically convert into fixed rate bonds when the reference rate falls to a certain specified level.

The borrowers on the market include governments, international institutions such as the World Bank and multi-national companies. The bond market is predominantly a source of finance for more developed countries. A limited secondary market exists where eurobonds can be traded and this is centred mainly around London and Luxembourg.

2. Syndicated Loans Market

The syndicated loans market or syndicated eurocurrency credit market as it is sometimes known, is essentially a source of medium-term finance. The market has been growing rapidly since the early 1970s. Like the eurobond market, credits are syndicated amongst a number of banks, with the credit being advertised in various newspapers. The market has been particularly useful as a source of medium-term finance to non-oil less developed countries. Since the early 1970s, the syndicated loans market has played an important part in the recycling of surpluses, especially of OPEC countries to non-oil developing countries.

10.4 Eurocurrency Interest Rates

Interest rates are highly competitive compared with domestic interest rates for the following reasons.

1. Banks do not have to comply with reserve asset requirements.
2. Wholesale banking business can be conducted on finer margins because the banks operating in the eurocurrency markets are not concerned with the costs of maintaining large branch networks and they deal in large amounts.
3. The market is highly competitive and banks deal with first class borrowers and and lenders.
4. The existence of economies of scale in wholesale banking allow the banks involved in the eurocurrency markets to pay more for their deposits, but due to the lower margins, they can be highly competitive on the terms of their loans.

The existence of exchange controls results in a wider interest rate differential between eurocurrency rates and domestic interest rates so that eurocurrency rates are generally higher than domestic interest rates. This is because the movement of funds from the domestic market to the eurocurrency market is restricted. The removal of exchange controls and other restrictions on domestic business may virtually eliminate the interest rate differential, for example, as in the eurosterling market.

Eurocurrency interest rates are important determinants of spot and forward rates in the foreign exchange markets. We saw in Chapter 8 that forward rates are quoted at a premium or discount to the spot rate. The premiums and discounts are based chiefly on differences in inter-bank interest rates for the eurocurrencies involved. A rise in eurocurrency interest rates will tend to push up spot rates and either increase the discount or decrease the premium on forward rates.

10.5 Control of the Euromarkets

Since the late 1970s, there has been increasing criticism of the euromarkets on a number of accounts. Central bankers have become increasingly worried about the market's role in facilitating the movement of hot money between financial centres. Eurocurrency funds are extremely sensitive to interest rate movements and scares about exchange rates, so that hot money flows may create additional problems for a country trying to cope with its domestic situation. In addition, deficit countries have been able to borrow at fine rates on these markets, thereby avoiding the strings which would have been attached to any IMF assistance.

Banks operating in the euromarkets face a number of risks. The first arising from the mismatching of assets and liabilities. Where long-term loans are backed by short-term funds, a sharp rise in interest rates could result in serious difficulties for banks which get locked in for a period of time. Secondly, there is the problem of country risk. Because of the rapid increase in oil prices in the 1970s, a number of countries have built up substantial external debt. There is the danger that these countries may not be able to meet debt repayments. In addition, there is the problem of political instability in borrowing countries. The problem for banks is to ensure that they do not lend excessively to such countries so that if a country defaulted, loan losses would not undermine the bank's viability. The final problem relates to capital adequacy - whether bank's would be able to stand large loan losses.

During April 1980, the Bank for International Settlements (which monitors the euromarkets) stated that it would monitor the activities of the euromarkets more closely and that it would set up a standing committee to report twice a year to central bank governors, on the state of the market or more frequently if conditions warrant it. The Bank for

International Settlements also urged that domestic authorities should call for consolidated bank balance sheets which would show the full extent of a bank's involvement in international banking and improve their assessment of each bank's exposure to high risk countries and on monitoring the extent to which banks mismatch. However, there were no proposals for reserve requirements to curb the growth of the market.

In December 1987, the Bank for International Settlements issued a paper which considered proposals for the application of similar minimum capital requirements for banks in the major economies. In addition, the proposals also aim for more equal competition between banks in different countries by removing the distortions caused by different definitions of capital. Under the proposals, banks will have to maintain a ratio of capital to assets of at least 8%. It is expected that these proposals will be in operation by 1992.

On 8th January 1987, the Bank of England issued a notice on the convergence of capital adequacy in the UK and the US. The notice stated that the Bank of England and the US Federal Banking Regulatory Authorities agreed proposals for a common measure of capital adequacy. The agreement for such proposals was the result of arguments based on both prudential and competitive aspects of international banking and the introduction of new financial instruments.

The proposals are for a common system of measurement and a common minimum primary capital requirement. The system of measurement is risk-related so that credit risk is weighted according to the nature of the obligor. The primary capital ratio will be applied to each institution authorised by the Bank of England or the US Banking Regulatory Authorities. The primary capital ratio is the ratio of primary capital to total weighted risk assets and a common ratio will apply to banks in both the UK and US. In addition, there will also be a minimum primary capital ratio for each individual institution and this will be set to reflect the institution's strengths and weaknesses.

10.6 Financial Innovation in International Banking

In recent years there has been an increase in the rate of innovation, deregulation and structural changes in international financial markets. The increase in financial innovation has resulted from changes in regulation of markets, the use of new technology, volatility of markets, movements in current account balances and ever increasing levels of competition between financial institutions operating in the international financial markets.

Such innovation has repercussions for central banks in that they will have to respond more quickly to changing circumstances and the internationalisation of financial markets may require central banks to co-operate more closely.

Disintermediation

Multinational companies have increasingly turned to the international securities market for finance rather than borrow from large international banks. Such a development will tend to reduce the quality of international banks' assets with the result that they may not be able to respond to sudden, unforeseen liquidity requirements.

The Growth of New Instruments

The effect of the increase in innovation has been to make the international financial markets more efficient by the introduction of new financial instruments for borrowing and for reducing risks associated with exchange rate and interest rate volatility. On the other hand, these changes may make the international financial markets less stable if for example, the new instruments are underpriced so that the cost does not fully cover the risks involved in the borrowing; the new instruments may be less liquid as in the case where a large number of holders seek to dispose of their holdings of the new instruments issued by a particular debtor.

Securitisation

There has been an increase in securitisation. This refers to the growth of credit in the form of marketable debt instruments such as Note Issuance Facilities (NIFs), eurobonds, and floating rate notes (FRNs).

NIFs are medium term arrangements which allow a borrower to issue short-term paper, called euro-notes, which are underwritten by commercial banks. There are also NIFs, which are not underwritten and these are known as euro-commercial paper. The underwriting arrangements of the short-term paper means that banks will purchase any paper that the borrower cannot sell or to provide the borrower with standby credit. If bank borrowers issue this type of paper they are short-term certificates of deposit. The NIF commitment is usually for a period of 5-7 years whilst the paper is issued for maturities of 3-6 months on a revolving basis. The first publicly announced NIF was arranged in 1981 for New Zealand.

NIFs are used by banks, governments and state entities, and

multinational companies. The notes are generally held by bank investors.

Monetary Policy

The innovation, deregulation and structural changes in international financial assets has had a great impact on the conduct of monetary policy in some countries. The implications for monetary policy are as follows:-
1. The use of monetary policy to influence the availability of credit is circumscribed and therefore greater emphasis is placed on the price of credit, i.e. interest rates.
2. The greater freedom of international capital flows has resulted in greater emphasis being placed on the exchange rate aspect of monetary policy.
3. There may be greater uncertainty with regard to the timing and impact of monetary policy.
4. Monetary aggregates become increasingly distorted and less useful as indicators on which monetary policy decisions can be based.

10.7 Summary

1. The eurocurrency market is an international money market.
2. Eurocurrency deposits are deposits held by banks in one country in the currency of another.
3. The characteristics of the eurocurrency markets are as follows:
   (a) They are unregulated.
   (b) They aid balance sheet management.
   (c) They allow for the investment of surplus foreign currency funds.
   (d) Interest rates are highly competitive.
4. The following are both suppliers and users of eurocurrency funds; governments, central banks, international organisations, commercial banks and multinational companies.
5. The international capital market consists of two parts - the eurobond market and the syndicated loans market.
6. Eurocurrency interest rates are highly competitive.
7. The euromarkets have been criticised on the grounds that they facilitate the movement of hot money between financial centres and they enable countries to borrow at fine rates, thereby avoiding the tough strings which would be attached to IMF assistance.
8. In recent years there has been an increase in the rate of innovation, deregulation and structural changes in international financial markets.

Questions

1. (a) Define Euro-Sterling
   (b) What problems have arisen from the growth of Euro-currencies?

2. Account for the growth of the euro-currency markets. Is there a case for the international control of these markets?

3. For what reasons are rates of interest paid on deposits in the euromarkets usually higher than comparable rates paid on domestic deposits? How far does this factor explain the rapid growth in the euromarkets?

4. What factors have contributed to the rapid growth of the eurocurrency markets in recent years? To what extent has this growth been a cause of concern to the world's monetary authorities?

5. What is a eurodollar? Why are changes in eurodollar interest rates of importance to the foreign exchange markets?

6. Identify the main types of lenders and borrowers in the eurocurrency markets and discuss the characteristics of the markets which have attracted these participants over the past decade.

7. Examine the relationship between rates of interest for a currency in the domestic money markets and the euromarkets. Other things being equal, what effect would a change in domestic interest rates have on:
   (a) the spot foreign exchange rate?
   (b) the forward exchange rate?

8. (a) To what extent are the factors which stimulated the rapid growth of the eurocurrency market during the 1970s still relevant? (13)
   (b) Why has the rate of growth in bank lending through the eurocurrency market slowed considerably in the 1980s? (12)

9. (a) What is meant by bank lending in 'eurocurrencies'? (7)
   (b) Consider the impact of the following on the eurocurrency bank lending market:
   (i) the debt problem of the developing countries;

(ii) securitisation;
(iii) liberalisation in the domestic markets. (18)

10. Examine the impact of the international debt problem on:
    (i) the syndicated bank lending market;
    (ii) the IMF;
    (iii) the commercial banks.

11. (a) Discuss the factors which determine the level of eurocurrency interest rates. (13)
    (b) Why are changes in eurodollar rates of importance to the foreign exchange markets? (12)

APPENDIX A

Suggested Answers to Examination Questions

Chapter 1

1. 1. In a developed community money consists in the main of bank deposits because there will be a well developed banking system.
   2. Thus, in a developed community, the amount of notes in the money stock will be fairly stable over the short-term so the monetary authorities can aim their control at bank deposits leaving the issue of notes to be determined largely by demand and supply.
   3. In a less developed community, the money supply consists in the main of notes rather than bank deposits because the banking system is less well developed.
   4. In less developed countries, the monetary authorities will seek to control the note issue as well as bank deposits because the note issue forms a greater proportion of the money stock.
   5. For example, in the U.K., notes and coin represent approximately 10% of the M3 definition of the money stock. In their evidence to the Radcliffe Committee, the authorities stated 'that Government's function in issuing notes is simply the passive one of ensuring that sufficient notes are available for the practical convenience of the public'.

2. The first part of the question should present no problem provided that you have remembered the qualities of money. The second part is more difficult as it involves the practical application of the theory outlined in the first part. A note should be made as to the use of the pre-war gold Franc as being highly acceptable to the seafaring community because gold enhances acceptability and stability of value. The main problem, however, is how to evaluate the value of the 'little known monetary standard' in terms of, say, U.S. dollars or sterling.

   The final part is more straightforward. These tokens either fulfil the functions of money in a very limited way or not at all. Their use as a medium of exchange is limited, they do not act as generalisers of purchasing power and they only act as a store of value in a limited way in that they provide a means of saving for a large electricity bill.

3. 1. The functions of money should be mentioned and an explanation of the extent to which the different financial assets fulfil these functions.
   2. The medium of exchange function is fulfilled by notes, coin and bank current account balances.
   3. Quasi-money assets do not function directly as a medium of

exchange but they can be quickly turned into cash or sight deposits. They function more as a store of value.

4. In more developed countries there is the additional problem of whether to include money market instruments.

5. To take account of these type of problems, the U.K. monetary authorities have definitions covering narrow and broad money. The narrow definitions include M0, M1 and M2 and the broad definitions include M3, M3c, M4 and M5.

6. In the case of less developed countries, money will consist in the main of notes and coin. In addition, the question as to whether or not to include money market instruments or quasi-money assets is less of a problem because of the more rudimentary nature of the financial system.

4. After stating and explaining the functions of money you must consider how the value of money is determined. It is important to consider the rate of inflation and deflation as the functions are affected to different degrees at different levels. You must mention the index-linking of financial assets as an example of a device to overcome the inability of money to fulfil its functions.

5. The answer to this question is straightforward covering acceptability and characteristics of money - see text (section 1.1.1 and 1.1.2).

6. This is covered in the text - section 1.1.1.

7. (a)

1. State the functions of money.

2. Money may fail to fulfil the functions when there is a loss of confidence arising from inflation.

3. Consider index-linking (see section 1.3.6).

(b)

1. Explanation of index-linking is required.

2. Give examples, Index-linked NSCs and index-linked gilt-edged stocks.

8. 1. The value of money is determined by its purchasing power. Changes in prices affect the value of money.

2. In the past having an intrinsic value made commodity money more acceptable.

3. Representative money has no intrinsic value.

4. Token money is convenient and secure. Both representative money and token money are acceptable as money.

5. During inflationary times having an intrinsic value makes money a better store of value.

9. (a)

1. The principal liabilities of the commercial banks are sight and time deposits. The principal liabilities of building societies are deposits, ordinary shares and term shares. A brief description of these liabilities is required.

2. Only bank sight deposits completely fulfil the medium of exchange function. The other liabilities have to be converted into notes and coin or a bank sight deposit.

(b)

1. A discussion of the returns on bank and building society accounts is required. Banks current accounts do not earn interest on credit balances. The tax treatment should be mentioned - both pay interest net of basic rate tax.

2. Mention should be made of higher interest term deposits offered by both banks and building societies.

3. Interest-earning deposits fulfil the store of value function better than non-interest-earning deposits during inflationary periods.

4. A discussion of real rates of interest is required. In recent years the real rates of return have been positive.

(c)

1. A definition of M3 should be given, emphasising that only bank deposits and notes and coin are included.

2. Building society retail deposits are included in M2.

3. A discussion of M4 is required to stress that building society shares and deposits are included in a wider monetary aggregate.

10. (a) See section 1.3.1.

(b)

1. Mention should be made of the course of inflation over the past three years.

2. During inflationary periods non-interest earning deposits suffer a fall in their real value. Thus, over the last three years, the store of value function will not have be satisfactorily fulfilled by these deposits.

3. Interest-earning deposits have fulfilled the store of value function because the interest earned has mitigated the effects of inflation. Indeed, over the last three years there have been positive real rates of return.

Chapter 2

1. 1. A full discussion of financial intermediation is required (section 2.1.1).
   2. A description of the different types of financial intermediaries is required (section 2.1.2).
   3. Banks are the principal financial intermediaries because:
   (a) size of their balance sheets;
   (b) their liabilities form part of the official money supply calculations;
   (c) other financial intermediaries hold accounts with them.

3. 1. A definition of liquidity should be given and it should be stressed that on realisation there is no capital loss.
   2. Liquidity is required:
   (a) to cover withdrawals;
   (b) to settle outstanding balances with other commercial banks;
   (c) to cover bad debts and losses on investments.
   3. Discussion of liquid assets should be according to whether the bank is retail or wholesale. A retail bank will hold liquid assets whilst a wholesale bank will rely relatively more on matching and irrevocable undrawn standby facilities with other banks.

Chapter 3

2. A discussion of each of the following markets is required - local authority, inter-bank, sterling CDs, finance house and inter-company.

3. When answering this question, it is important that the assets are discussed in turn, according to size - commercial bills, sterling CDs, British government stocks, local authority debt (stocks, bills and loans) dollar CDs, Treasury bills and cash deposits with the Bank of England.

Chapter 4

1. A full discussion of the Bank of England's operations in the money markets is required (see section 2.8.3). A full discussion of the August 1981 changes is, therefore, necessary.

2. The distribution and growth of a commercial bank's assets will be influenced by:
   1. liquidity/profitability - a discussion of liquid assets/advances is required;
   2. growth of deposits;
   3. demand for bank loans;
   4. growth of bank loans will be affected by risk and the level of each

bank's own capital.

The second part of the question requires a discussion of the effects of the Bank of England's monetary policy particularly the asset ratios imposed since Competition and Credit Control and including the August 1981 cash ratio and call money ratio, also the use of the special deposits scheme and the corset. The effect of overfunding, the reduction in banks holdings of Treasury bills, and the raising of interest rates to reduce the growth of bank advances should also be discussed.

A discussion of the Bank's changes in prudential regulation is required covering both liquidity and capital.

4. The changes in monetary control since 1980 are fully covered in the text (see Chapter 4)

The effect of these changes on the commercial banks include;

1. the removal of the corset allowed by the banks to lend more freely, particularly with regard to mortgage lending;

2. the discontinuance of the practice of continuously posting a minimum lending rate allowed the banks a greater degree of competition in the setting of interest rates and allowed the setting of base rates to be more flexible and sensitive to changes in the market;

3. the Bank's changes in its intervention in the discount market has led to greater competition in the acceptance credit market;

4. the abolition of the reserve asset ratio will give the banks more freedom in their composition of their liquid assets.

6. 1. The government needs to borrow in order to finance a budget deficit.

2. If the government borrows from the non-bank private sector, the deposits of the non-bank private sector with the banks will fall and bankers' deposits at the Bank of England will fall. When the government spends the money it has borrowed deposits at the banks will be restored (as will bankers' deposits).

3. If the government borrows from the banking system by selling gilts then bankers' deposits will fall and banks' holdings of gilts will rise. When the government spends the money it has borrowed, non-bank private sector deposits with the banks will rise (as will bankers' deposits).

4. The government may borrow from the banking system by issuing Treasury bills. An explanation of how the banks are affected is required.

Chapter 5

3. The salient discussion areas include:-
   1. The shifting of emphasis by the authorities in the conduct of monetary policy, from control of interest rates to control of monetary aggregates.
   2. A change in the authorities' dealing tactics in the gilt-edged market.
   3. Large swings in the trade cycle together with high rates of inflation caused large interest rate movements.
   4. The financing of a persistently large public sector borrowing requirement which necessitated periodic increases in interest rates to facilitate sales of gilts.
   5. Hot-money movements.

Chapter 6

1. 1. The objectives are as listed in the 1959 Radcliffe Report.
   2. A discussion of policy conflicts is required. E.g. the maintenance of full employment and the control of inflation.

2. See section 6.3 - discount rate, open market operations, reserve requirements, moral suasion and controls. A discussion of each is required. The effectiveness of these techniques depends on the central bank's relationship with the commercial banks (see section 6.2.1).

3. 1. The role of central banks is summarised in section 2.5.1. The functions should be related to the Bank of England as banking systems in other countries is no longer included in the syllabus.
   2. The powers which a central bank (Bank of England) must have includes:
   (a) power to implement reserve requirements and to alter them;
   (b) have a monopoly of the note issue;
   (c) be the lender of last resort;
   (d) act as a banker to the government and the commercial banks.

4. The salient discussion areas include:-
   1. The need for a 'fulcrum' - i.e. a minimum reserve ratio(s), which banks must comply with.
   2. A well-developed and efficient market in government securities.

   If these two conditions obtain, then a central bank will be able to alter the reserve ratios of banks. However, problems may arise if there is no effective official control over the supply of reserve assets. The authorities may use open market operations for controlling interest rates rather than bank lending. In addition, the authorities' funding operations may entail the sale of new securities to cancel out cash being paid out on maturity of existing government securities.

In Britain there is:-

1. A well-developed market in government securities.
2. An effective reserve ratio.

However, two factors militate against the efficient conduct of open market operations:-

1. Funding policy.
2. A persistent government budget deficit.

5. 1. A discussion of the general techniques of monetary control is required - discount rate, open market operations, reserve requirements, moral suasion and controls.

2. As far as the effectiveness of each type of control is concerned, a discussion of the following points is required.

(a) The monetary authorities cannot control both price and quantity of money.

(b) The demand for bank advances is often fairly unresponsive to changes in interest rates in the short-run so that a rise in interest rates may have little effect, on the demand for bank advances in the short-run.

(c) Higher interest rates may attract money from other countries which may adversely affect the money supply.

(d) The use of reserve requirements may result in the formation of new markets which are outside the control of the monetary authorities, e.g. the euromarkets. Quantitative controls also have this effect, e.g. the supplementary special deposits scheme led to disintermediation. When the supplementary special deposits scheme was abolished, there was a very large increase in the monetary statistics.

Chapter 7

1. The answer to this question requires a discussion of all the items which are recorded in the balance of payments - current account (visibles/invisibles), capital account and official financing. The balance of payments always balances because it is based on the principles of double-entry book-keeping.

4.

	(millions of rurits) Dr.	Cr.	
Balance of VisibleTrade			
Exports of manufacturers		120	
Exports of raw materials/fuel		3,000	
Imports of manufactures	2,000		
Imports of raw materials/fuel	1,000	—	
	3,000	3,120	
			(surplus of 120m rurits)
Invisibles			
Banking	30		
Insurance	20		
Interest paid	1,400		
Interest received		30	
Shipping	80		
Tourism	—	100	
	1,530	130	
			(deficit of 1,400m rurits)

Balance of payments on current account:

= visibles + invisibles

= + 120 - 1,400

= - 1,280

The figures support the contention that Ruritania is a developing country.

Reasons:-

1. Exports of manufactures small whilst exports of raw materials/fuel large.
2. Earnings from tourism small and earnings from commercial services low.
3. Interest paid is substantial.
4. Net inflow of capital (i.e. borrowing on capital account) large.

5. Main points:

(a)

1. Explain balance of visible trade - imports and exports of goods.
2. Define terms of trade - ratio of changes in export prices to changes in import prices (see section 7.2).

(b) The effect of a change in a country's terms of trade on its balance of trade depends on elasticities of demand for and supply of goods being traded.

Chapter 8

1. Main points:
   1. Werner Plan.
   2. 'Snake' arrangements - its breakdown by 1974.
   3. EMS - description, also credit support facilities.
   4. Second stage of EMS - little progress made in recent years.
   5. Assessment of the operation of the EMS.

3. Main points:
   1. Description of purchasing power parity theory.
   2. Despite the theory's criticism it is valid during periods of inflation. High levels of inflation in one country relative to other countries means that its exports will become uncompetitive leading to balance of payments problems.
   3. The semi-fixed exchange rate regime of the EMS will come under pressure if member countries have widely divergent rates of inflation. The theory of purchasing power parity implies that there must be continual realignments.
   4. Indeed, when inflation rates and economic policies have been divergent, rather than restore price competitiveness through deflation which would add to unemployment, members have resorted to periodic realignments of currencies.

5. (a) If the central bank is formally committed to maintaining the exchange rate within narrow limits, then it must intervene if the exchange rate threatens to move beyond the limits set. If the rate is at the upper limit it should sell its own currency and buy others. If the rate is at the lower limit it must buy its own currency and sell others. Even if the rate is between the limits the central bank may find it expedient to intervene to check an undesirable trend.
   (b) If rates are floating then the central bank need not intervene. Mention should be made of 'dirty' floating.

Chapter 9

1. Main points;
   1. explain use of SDRs;
   2. not many SDRs in existence - more have been issued recently;
   3. IMF policy - phase out gold as an international monetary asset;
   4. development of SDR as a store of value;
   5. role of SDR as a unit of account;
   6. use of SDR as a means of exchange is limited.

5. Main points:
   1. Full definition of international liquidity is required.

2. The counterpart of surpluses of oil producers has been the deficits of oil importing countries. Problem of financing these deficits;
3. Role of eurocurrency markets in increasing liquidity;
4. Recycling;
5. However, countries have had problems in repaying debts - has led to rescheduling of debt and increased use of the IMF facilities.

6. Main points:
   1. demonetisation of gold;
   2. revaluation of central banks' holdings of gold;
   3. price explosion;
   4. calls for remonetisation of gold;
   5. role of gold within the EMS.

9. (a) Main points:
   1. Define international liquidity.
   2. 'Demonetisation' of gold.
   3. Role of U.S. dollar and movement to multiple currency reserve system.
   4. Role of SDR.
   5. IMF quotas.
   6. Role of Euromarkets.

   (b) In theory, floating exchange rates lessen the need for large reserves. However, 'dirty' floating has led to a need for reserves. Also large balance of payments imbalances have resulted from large increases in oil prices. The large balance of payments deficits resulted in a need to increase international liquidity.

INDEX